Imperial General

Imperial General

The Remarkable Career of Petellius Cerialis

Philip Matyszak

Pen & Sword
MILITARY

First published in Great Britain in 2011 by
Pen & Sword Military
an imprint of
Pen & Sword Books Ltd
47 Church Street
Barnsley
South Yorkshire
S70 2AS

Copyright © Philip Matyszak 2011

ISBN 978-1-84884-119-2

The right of Philip Matyszak to be identified as Author of this Work has been asserted by him in accordance with the Copyright, Designs and Patents Act 1988.

A CIP catalogue record for this book is available from the British Library.

All rights reserved. No part of this book may be reproduced or transmitted in any form or by any means, electronic or mechanical including photocopying, recording or by any information storage and retrieval system, without permission from the Publisher in writing.

Typeset in 11pt Ehrhardt by
Mac Style, Beverley, E. Yorkshire

Printed and bound in the UK by MPG

Pen & Sword Books Ltd incorporates the Imprints of Pen & Sword Aviation, Pen & Sword Family History, Pen & Sword Maritime, Pen & Sword Military, Pen & Sword Discovery, Wharncliffe Local History, Wharncliffe True Crime, Wharncliffe Transport, Pen & Sword Select, Pen & Sword Military Classics, Leo Cooper, The Praetorian Press, Remember When, Seaforth Publishing and Frontline Publishing.

For a complete list of Pen & Sword titles please contact
PEN & SWORD BOOKS LIMITED
47 Church Street, Barnsley, South Yorkshire, S70 2AS, England
E-mail: enquiries@pen-and-sword.co.uk
Website: www.pen-and-sword.co.uk

Contents

Acknowledgements vi
List of Plates vii
Maps viii
Introduction xiii

Part I: Of Roman Generals and Generalship 1

Chapter 1 Generals Before the Imperial Era 3

Chapter 2 The First Imperial Generals 20

Part II: Britain 37

Chapter 3 A Legate of the Ninth 39

Part III: Civil War 67

Chapter 4 The Wilderness Years 69

Chapter 5 Rebel With a Cause 100

Part IV: Petellius Cerialis Takes Charge 127

Chapter 6 Desperate and Dastardly Deeds Along the Rhine 129

Chapter 7 Aftermath: Return to Britannia and the World Restored .. 166

Notes 176
Bibliography 181
Index 182

Acknowledgements

As ever, there are numerous people who helped me to produce this book. I owe a particular debt to Professor Roger Wilson, Head of Classical, Near Eastern and Religious Studies at the University of British Columbia with whom I discussed the archaeology of Cerialis' exploits in Britain, and to the UBC as a whole, where I was generously allowed access to the library and accomodation on the premises when I needed access to particular documents. On the other side of the Atlantic Mike Haxell shared his practical experience as a re-enactor in Legio XIV Gemina Martia Victrix, a legion which appears frequently in these pages. Likewise the management of Lunt Roman fort helped me to understand the complexities of Roman fortifications. Adrian Goldsworthy helped shape many of the opinions which took final form in this book - but where there is error that is mine alone. Finally, I must thank my wife for tolerating a husband who has spent much more time in the first century AD than a reasonable person would stand for.

List of Plates

1. The tombstone of Marcus Favonius Facilis (Picture: courtesy of Adrian Goldsworthy)
2. Charred fragments of a clay pot, relics of Boudicca's sack of London. Now in the Museum of London (Picture: Malgosia Matyszak)
3. British swords dated AD 50–200. (Picture: Malgosia Matyszak)
4. Brigantia.
5. Gladiators Lupus and Medusa sparring in the arena. (Duel re-enacted by Svenja Grosser and Wolfgang Mueller of the Ludus Nemesis.)
6. The tomb of Classicanus, now in the British Museum. (Picture: Malgosia Matyszak)
7. The River Po near Ferrata, downstream from Cremona. (Picture: public domain)
8. The Roman forum. (Picture: Courtesy of Adrian Goldsworthy)
9. Vespasian. (Picture: Courtesy of Adrian Goldsworthy)
10. Domitian (Picture: Courtesy of Adrian Goldsworthy)
11. Legionaries of the Ermine Street Guard with a 'scorpion' bolt-thrower. (Picture: Courtesy of the Ermine Street Guard).
12. A legionary of Legio XIV Gemina Martia Victrix receives an. (Picture: used with thanks to Mike Haxell of the Roman Military Research Society)
13. Re-enactors of the Cohors Batavorum and Legio XV Gemina Martia Victrix. (Picture: used with thanks to Mike Haxell of the Roman Military Research Society)
14. A Roman legionary escorts a cart loaded with booty and barbarian slaves. From a bas-relief in the Vatican Museum (Picture: P. Matyszak)
15. A Roman general sits surrounded by barbarian prisoners. From a bas-relief in the Vatican Museum (Picture: P. Matyszak)

Maps

Map 1. Britannia, AD 43–80 ix
Map 2. North Italy x
Map 3. German frontier AD 69–70 xi

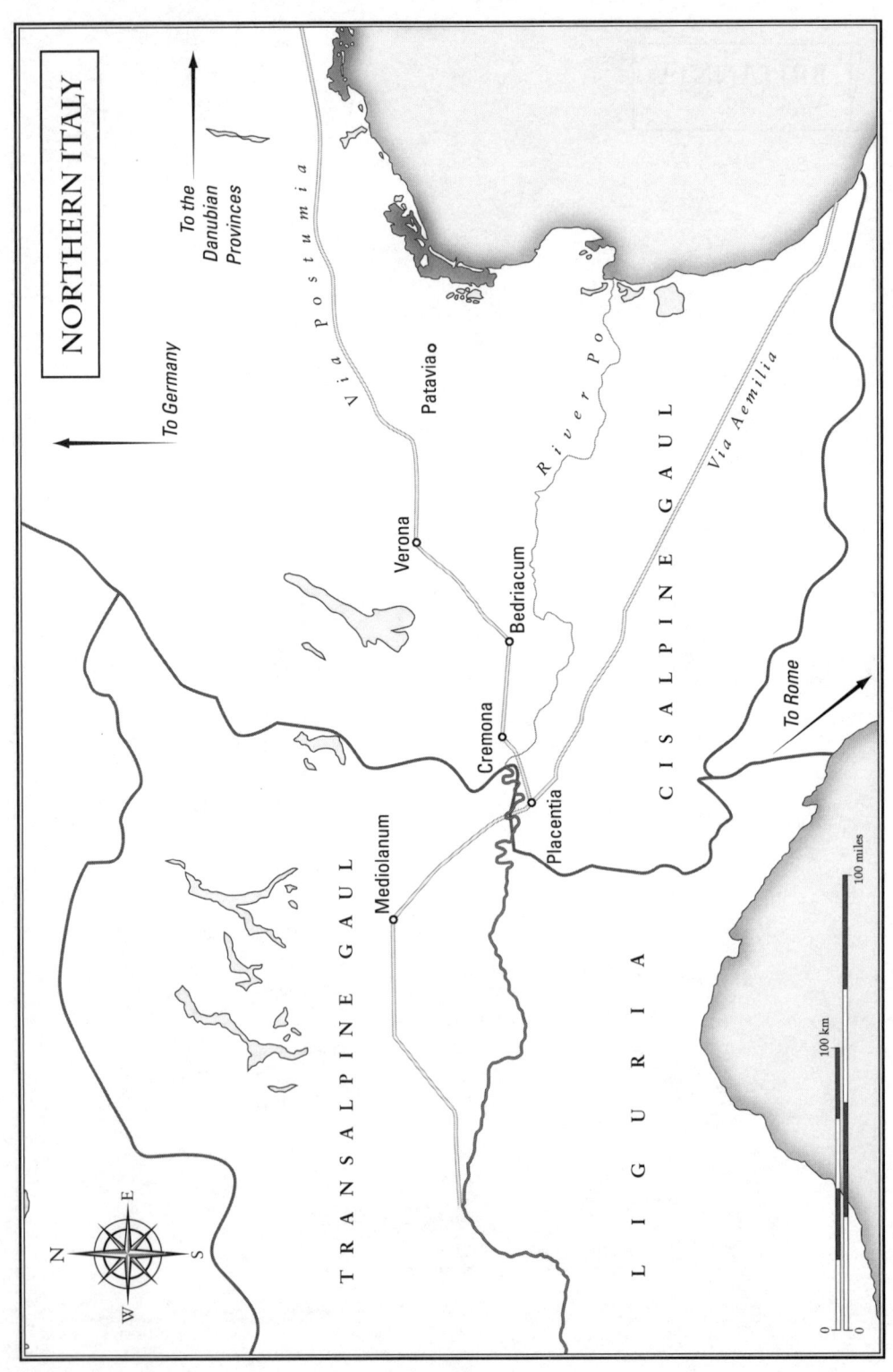

Introduction

If you are going to live in interesting times, it helps if you are an interesting person. The life and the times of Petellius Cerialis were seldom anything but interesting.

Rome packed more history into the years AD 60–74 than into the whole of the following century. Seven emperors held power and five of them died violently. There were three major provincial rebellions, a major foreign war, a few minor ones, and two full-scale civil wars in quick succession.

Petellius Cerialis was in the thick of the action. At low points in his career he was fleeing with a decimated force from British rebels, or lurking in disguise in the Italian countryside while on the run from the Roman government. At the high points he was on nodding terms with emperors and led Rome's legions into battle. The adjective most commonly used by ancient historians for Petellius Cerialis was *incautus* (reckless). He was ever the man to seize the moment, even when the moment repaid him in grief for doing so.

Through it all Petellius Cerialis proceeded with boundless optimism based on his own abilities and the beneficence of fortune. Even when the Roman world seemed to be collapsing around his ears he enthused about the benefits of Roman rule with an apparently unshakable faith in the system.

Nor did his optimism go unrewarded. He was on the winning side after his first provincial rebellion, again after his experience of civil war, and again after leading two major military campaigns. However hair-raising his path, it invariably led to victory, and Petellius himself came through unscathed. His is a remarkable story.

Telling the story of Petellius Cerialis means telling the story of the events in which he was a participant. The action moves from Britain to Italy and Rome, out to the Rhinelands and back to Britain again. Sometimes, especially in the early parts of the story, Petellius Cerialis is a minor figure on a large and dramatic canvas. On such occasions we abandon our hero to explore the wider picture, be it the conquest of Britain and the blood-soaked rebellion of

Boudicca, or the debauchery of a Neronian orgy and nefarious conspiracies in the Roman senate. There were army mutinies, senatorial suicides and old-fashioned governmental incompetence, all of which sooner or later affected the career of Cerialis. These are important to understand, both in terms of his career and for their own sake.

Putting Petellius Cerialis into his historical context means following the events of the two turbulent decades that encompass most of his career. When the turbulence subsides, so Cerialis too subsides from the historical record. Rome moved on from the violence of those civil wars to the age of the Antonines, a century of overall peace and prosperity that most historians consider to be Rome's golden age. It was a golden age which Cerialis did more than his share to bring about.

These two aspects of the book – the career of Cerialis and the era in which that career took place – are joined by a third, the aspect that gives this book its title. Cerialis was an imperial general, and a major function is to determine exactly what that term meant. We will study the generals of the republican era to see the historical context of what command of the Roman legions signified, and what was expected of the men who did so. By examining the careers of Cerialis' predecessors, both the dangers and complexity of a general's job are brought into focus, as is the fact that history had left a tension between the role of emperor and general that was never to be reconciled and which was in the long run to help bring down the Roman Empire.

Seeing Roman generals in action gives us a clear picture of the strengths of Rome's military machine. Yet the weaknesses are highlighted too, with poor leadership, shaky morale, violent indiscipline and mutiny, and commanders hoodwinked by ruthless and treacherous enemies. At times in this story, the Roman army appears to be its own worst enemy, defeated by internecine combat and a highly politicized rank and file. As an imperial general Cerialis saw the best and worst of Rome, and quite certainly the best and worst of its army.

Amid vacillation, uncertainty and dangers, Cerialis remained confident and forged ahead with the apparent belief that, no matter what befell along the way, it would all turn out right in the end. And it did – not least because he made it so. In the confusing and troubled years of the early twenty-first century we can do worse than look back to yet more-evil days and see how the ship of state was righted and helped into calmer waters.

Part I

Of Roman Generals and Generalship

Chapter 1

Generals Before the Imperial Era

Ancient Rome could not have become one of the largest empires the world has ever seen without being seriously good at warfare. Yet unlike the empires of the nineteenth century, the power of Rome's armies was not based on overwhelming technological superiority of the sort which pitted Victorian Maxim guns against Zulu spears. In fact, for much of its history the Roman republic fought against armies which were as numerous and well equipped as the Romans themselves.[1]

Yet the republic lost very few wars. The Romans won because they were ferocious fighters, well organized and led, and terribly persevering. From top to bottom Rome's society was organized for war, and generally the Romans would accept no other reason but victory for making peace. Any leader of such a people had to be, by definition, a war leader, and no one in the Roman republic was more honoured or revered than a successful general. This special place that generals had in the Roman psyche was exploited when republic changed to empire, and the men we call emperors styled themselves as *imperatores* – conquering generals.

Roman generals of the Imperial Era had to cope with the burden that cultural expectations had placed upon them: expectations which were sometimes strongly at variance with their current role in the imperial hierarchy. This issue was a major problem for Petellius Cerialis' immediate predecessors, so it is worth examining in detail how the role of Roman general evolved with the growth of Rome.

ROMULUS – FOUNDING FATHER
In the days before the *pax Romana*, an ancient state was expected to spend a lot of its time fighting, and Rome had a past that was more violent than most. In Roman tradition, when Romulus founded the city in 753 BC the very first thing he built was a defensive wall. This was a wise move. Whatever one thinks of the veracity of the legend of the foundation of Rome, the new city undoubtedly lay right across a pre-existing trade route and dominated the lowest crossing point of the Tiber.[2] This was not going to pass without

comment from the large and predatory Etruscan cities and mountain tribesmen of the region.

Romulus and Remus were allegedly the children of Mars, and within five months of Rome's foundation the god of battles was supervising the first clash between Rome and its neighbours. This was over the abduction of the neighbours' womenfolk to provide mothers for Rome's next generation. But even before the foundation of Rome, Romulus was already an experienced war leader – he had attacked Alba Longa in order to restore his maternal grandfather to power in that city.

It was Romulus who celebrated the first Roman triumph after defeating the Ceninensians (a Sabine tribe); Romulus who gained the first *spolia optima* (which is when a general wins a Roman triumph and the war by personally killing the enemy war leader in battle).[3] It was Romulus who led his army against the invading Camertines and slew six thousand of them, and he who defeated the Veientes, and the people of Fidenae. The biographer Plutarch says 'All men acknowledge that the success of the day [in battle] was due to Romulus who showed the highest degree of skill and courage.'[4]

Romulus, founder and king of Rome, was the very model of an ancient major general and an example and inspiration to those commanders who came after. He also established in Roman minds the idea that a Roman general commanded not merely Roman armies, but Rome itself. As will be seen in later chapters, this idea never completely went away.

CONSULS AND GENERALS

In archaic Italy a leader was a leader, whether he was leading political deliberations or the army into battle. Rome did not differentiate between a war leader and any other kind of leader. No one who held power in Rome could delegate fighting a war to subordinates. The price of power was paid on the battlefield. A Roman leader had to make the political case for war or peace, and in the event of war was expected to raise, organize, supply and motivate the troops. And in battle he was expected to do at least his fair share of the fighting.

When Tarquin the Proud, the last of Romulus' royal successors, was expelled and Rome became a republic, the role of political and military leader passed to the consuls. Lucius Brutus was republican Rome's first leader and he died in battle within months of taking office. Thereafter, in all the time of the Roman republic peace was only once officially declared.[5]

The consuls of republican Rome led a comprehensively militarized society in which politics and the army were inextricably combined. This is best seen in the principal assembly of the Roman people, the *Comitia Centuriata*, which, not co-incidentally, met outside Rome on the city's military training ground, the Campus Martius (the field of Mars).

The two major tasks of the Comitia were to vote on whether to make war and to select the consuls to lead them in that war. Given the military role of the assembly, the Romans considered it fair that voting was biased in favour of those who would actually be doing the fighting. A cavalryman's vote counted for more than a heavy infantryman's and an infantryman outvoted a skirmisher.

A further bias in the voting gave greater weight to the *seniores*, the older men. The different groups voted in order starting with the cavalry, and the vote of the majority in each block of voters counted as the vote of that entire block. Once a majority had been obtained voting was ended, so the lower orders often did not get to vote at all. This led to a very stable 'democracy', as the people whose votes counted most were the people with the weaponry and military experience to enforce their point of view.

Though it underwent numerous technical changes, the Comitia Centuriata was a major part of the Roman constitution. For soldiers in the early Roman Empire it was a reminder that, until just before their own generation, the army had selected its own leaders – and by Roman tradition, those who led the armies of Rome also led the state.

A REPUBLIC ORGANIZED FOR WAR

The leaders chosen by the Comitia were originally called *praetors* (which actually means 'leaders'), but in time this title was changed to consuls and praetors became the secondary magistrates of the republic. There were two consuls, partly because this put a check on executive power, as each consul was able to veto the other, but also because Rome frequently fought wars on two fronts and each army needed one consul apiece. (A consular army usually consisted of two legions.) If even more commanders were required, one of the praetors was given an army as well.

The senate allocated each consul his area of operations. This was his *provincia*, a name which originally comes from the Latin phrase *pro vincia*, 'vincia' being either from the verb '*vincere*', 'to conquer', or '*vincire*', 'to bind'. Either verb explicitly describes the primary function of the consul and his army. The mutation of the word to mean 'province' in the modern sense came later.

Legislation was a poor second to military command for early consuls. The constitution left voting on laws to meetings of the Roman people, though consuls, like tribunes, had the right to put forward proposals for consideration.

Since the main role of a consul was as a war leader, Romans of the republic tended to elect their consuls for their military ability – not least because those doing the voting would also be doing the fighting, and a bad general could get them killed much faster than a bad politician.

The consuls performed many of the functions of later imperial generals. They handled the administration and strategy of the army in the field, took the auguries that decided whether the gods were in favour of Rome offering battle on a given day, gave a hopefully inspirational speech to the troops immediately before combat, for which they had previously decided the order of battle on a field they should have personally inspected.

The major difference between republican and imperial generals was that republican generals had high political ambitions. (It often turned out that later imperial generals had similar ambitions, but in the republic these were encouraged, and the holder of the top job did not need to die before he was replaced.) The other difference between imperial and republican generals was that republican generals usually fought 'under their own auspices', which meant that they were in supreme command. An imperial general fought under the auspices of his emperor. This meant that, technically speaking, the overall military commander was the emperor rather than the man leading the army. By this device emperors maintained the fiction that Rome's rulers remained the war leaders of old.

Imperial generals tended to fade into obscurity when they laid down their command. But military success was the cornerstone of a republican Roman's political career. When we look at the roll-call of outstanding Roman leaders of the republic, there are few who did not distinguish themselves on the battlefield, and even with those few it was not for want of trying. Amongst the names known to every Roman schoolchild were:[6]

Cincinnatus c.536–430 BC, who was famously called from the plough to assume overall command of Rome's beleaguered armies, and who, having done that in a matter of weeks, and settled a political crisis in Rome while he was at it, returned to cultivating his fields.

Marcus Furius Camillus c.447–365 BC, who organized Rome's recovery from a Gallic invasion and sack, despite having been exiled from Rome when the crisis began.

Valerius Corvus c.386–285 BC, who was consul six times, and who gained the nickname 'Raven' from a bird that allegedly helped him to dispatch a gigantic Gaul in single combat.

Marcus Atilius Regulus c.310–250 BC, captured by the Carthaginians and sent to Rome to present their peace terms to the senate. He argued strongly against the terms and, as his parole demanded, returned to be killed by his indignant captors.

Quintus Fabius Maximus 275–203 BC, the general who took command after the Carthaginians had smashed Rome's armies in a series of battles, and whose success in holding off Hannibal gained him the nickname 'the Shield of Rome'.

Scipio Africanus 236–183 BC, who took the war to the Carthaginians in Africa, defeated Hannibal and went on to campaign successfully in Asia Minor

Aemilius Paulus 229–160 BC, who won the battle of Pydna and broke the power of Macedon.

Scipio Aemilianus 184–129 BC, conqueror of the Celtiberians in Spain and the man who finally reduced Carthage to rubble.

Caius Marius 157–86 BC, a populist who proved a surprisingly effective general. He defeated the troublesome Jugurtha in Africa and remodelled the Roman army to deal with a massive Germanic invasion of north Italy at the start of the first century BC. His long-running rivalry with Sulla (see below) caused immense harm to the Roman republic.

The list included others such as Decius Mus, Caius Flaminius and Claudius Marcellus, all of whom were generals who died leading their soldiers in combat – a reminder that those who wanted to lead Roman armies might pay dearly for the privilege. Despite a popular modern myth, neither in the republic nor later was a defeated general supposed to fall on his sword. He was supposed to fall on the swords of his enemies, and to take as many of them with him as was humanly possible.

THE DYNASTS 90–32 BC

Many of the themes of the terrible year of AD 69 were played out in the period 90–32 BC. Here too we see dissatisfied allies, misgovernment at the top, and above all the army asserting its right to choose the leaders of Rome.

Sulla and the Effects of the Social War

The Social War of 90 BC was anything but sociable. The name of the war comes from *socii*, which is the Latin for 'ally'. Ever since the mid-second century BC Rome's Italian allies had been increasingly resentful of their status as second-class citizens under the Roman hegemony. They were treated with increasing injustice and arbitrariness by Roman leaders interested in self-enrichment and short-sighted political ambitions.

Their rebellion is no less significant for being an obscure and confused affair. It is obscure not least because the Romans were so abashed about its causes that no historian gave the war a detailed treatment. Also, any historian who wrote such an account would have to admit that Rome only avoided defeat by giving her enemies what they were demanding.

What the Italians had been fighting was perhaps the only recorded case of the opposite of a war of independence. Apart from some die-hard Samnites who wanted Rome to be destroyed, most Italian communities were fighting to become Roman. Three consuls died in the first two years of the war before the Romans gave in. Once they agreed to give citizenship to anyone who would stop killing them to get it, the back of the Italian revolt was effectively broken. This capitulation had dramatic and far-reaching effects, which were to shape the course of Roman history.

Firstly, Rome acquired a massive number of new citizens. Many of these joined the army they had been fighting against only months before. These new 'Roman' soldiers had very little fondness for Rome. They had become citizens only to get the legal protection this afforded them from rapacious Roman officials. Many came from communities with only a rudimentary grasp of democracy. They stayed with the army, because in the previous generation the army had become more professional than a citizen militia. The development of soldiering as a career meant that soldiers could campaign for longer, as they did not have their own farms to maintain. But campaigns far from Rome also meant that many soldiers were no longer voters, and for the first time in Roman history the voters in the *Comitia Centuriata* were not the same as the men in the legions.

Thus towards the end of the Social War a significant percentage of the Roman army was neither pro-Roman nor personally invested in its democratic institutions. If ever there was a time when a republican aristocrat could use a 'Roman' army against his own city, it was in 88 BC.

The aristocrat who grasped this point was Lucius Cornelius Sulla, the first man openly to command a Roman army not as a servant of Rome, but very much in his own interest.[7] Not that Sulla's enemies were saintly constitutionalists wedded to the democratic ideal. They were every bit as bloody-minded and vicious as he. Nevertheless, in the following century it was Sulla's shadow that fell over the generals who fought to replace Nero.

Sulla was a Roman consul, but a consul whose wishes had been overturned by the popular vote. Rather than accept that vote, Sulla turned to the army. He announced – with considerable justification – that the vote had been perverted by demagoguery and mob violence. It was his job as leader of the state and leader of the army to restore order. So revolutionary was his march on Rome that all but one of Sulla's officers deserted him. However, the army wanted Sulla as its leader, and traditionally a Roman general led the Roman state – from the army's perspective this was a historic right which the partial separation of voters from soldiers had taken from them. The soldiers violently rebuffed heralds from the senate who ordered them to turn back and went on to restore Sulla to power.

Historically, the event set a precedent which was to be followed time and again. Over the centuries that followed, no one ever forgot that every Roman general was a potential ruler of Rome, provided only that enough of the army agreed. It was a lesson that the generation of Petellius Cerialis was to learn particularly well.

Pompey
Gnaeus Pompey was a powerful aristocrat from Picenum in northeast Italy. Pompey's father was an aristocrat who benefitted from the wars between Sulla and his opponents and had an army of three legions which was loyal to him personally.[8]

Pompey supported Sulla with such enthusiasm that he gained himself the nickname of 'the teenage butcher'. He secured Sicily for the Sullan cause, and went on to win victory in the Roman province of Africa against another Roman aristocrat, Domitius Ahenobarbus, and his ally the Numidian king.

Very significantly, although a general, Pompey was a *privatus* – a citizen with no official standing in the hierarchy of Roman magistrates. His authority came from the men whom he led. He was the first major Roman general to hold that position in his own right, and not as ancillary to a consulship or praetorship, or indeed any other office within the Roman government. Like many Roman generals in later years, his army itself gave him all the authority he needed.

Pompey demanded the right to celebrate a triumph for his African adventure. Properly speaking, triumphs were reserved for Roman magistrates, but Pompey got his. Later, an enemy of Sulla's called Quintus Sertorius seized control of Spain. Pompey demanded that he be allowed to fight Sertorius with *proconsular imperium*.

This proconsular imperium was the right of an ex-consul to keep control of his army if he had unfinished business with the enemy. The senate refused to give such unprecedented powers to Pompey on the very reasonable grounds that he had never been a consul, or any other kind of Roman magistrate. Pompey's ominous response was to refuse to disband his now unemployed army. The senate briefly considered the other uses to which Pompey might put this army – such as marching on Rome with it – and agreed that he could have his imperium after all.

After the defeat of Sertorius, Pompey once more showed a certain contempt for the constitution. He demanded the right to stand for election as consul. He was too young to be eligible to stand, had held none of the offices that qualified him, and anyway, he had put himself forward while outside Rome, which should have disqualified him.

At first there was only one reason why Pompey could get away with trampling Roman constitutional tradition (called the *mos maiorum*) in the way that he did. He was a general with a large and loyal veteran army. However, his remarkable career gave him credibility with the Roman people, who looked for success in their leaders. It also helped that Pompey was not above using his veteran soldiers to vote for him and to intimidate others into doing the same. He was elected.

The five years after his consulship were the high point of Pompey's extraordinary career. With pirates wreaking havoc on Roman trade, Pompey sought and gained a command with unprecedented powers to bring the threat under control. This command, known as *imperium maius*, later became one of the constitutional foundations of the office of Roman emperor. Essentially, a general with maius imperium outranked other generals, even in their own province.

Pompey did not disappoint those who had raised him to such extraordinary heights. It took him one summer to clear the entire Mediterranean of pirates, a task which had frustrated his less-capable peers for decades.

The end of his campaign left Pompey in Asia Minor in 66 BC, so he used his prestige from his success to take over command of a war being fought by Lucullus, the general who had virtually won it already. Though Lucullus might disagree, this was a blessing for the region, because Pompey used his near-imperial powers to enforce a political settlement which was so soundly based that it endured for centuries.

Yet this success too was not an unmixed blessing, for it taught the Roman public – including the Roman army – that the right general with exceptional power could achieve extraordinary things. And in later years soldiers who believed they had the right sort of commander became prepared to do whatever was necessary to put their general in power.

In 61 BC Pompey returned to Rome to a splendid triumph and signalled that he was now prepared to work within the existing political system by disbanding his armies. Henceforth he would base his power on his huge *auctoritas*, his personal authority. (Not to mention the influence that being the richest man in Rome gave him over cash-strapped senators.)

But by now the damage was done. It was evident to aspiring politicians and commanders that Pompey had become Pompey the Great (as he now styled himself) not by working the system, but by using personal command of his armies to flout the constitution altogether. The message for succeeding generations was that a general with an army could only be stopped from doing as he pleased by another general with an army. One who took this message to heart was an up-and-coming young politician called Julius Caesar.

Julius Caesar

The man whom Cato called 'The only sober person to want to overthrow the republic' was a scion of the Julii, a family of ancient renown and modest resources which had lately become resurgent in contemporary politics.

Caesar shared most of his characteristics with a typical Roman aristocrat of the late republic, but possessed those characteristics to a far greater degree. The average aristocrat was literate, articulate and urbane. Caesar was also stylish, decisive and breathtakingly self-confident. He wrote and spoke Latin of such force and clarity that his books have been standard texts for schoolchildren almost since they were written. Roman senators were ambitious and prepared to get into debt to further their political careers. Caesar was intensely, voraciously, determined to succeed, and the size of his debts became legend. Few generals of the late republic were gentle, compassionate characters, but Caesar was as outstandingly brutal to his foreign foes as he was forgiving to his Roman ones.

Add considerably higher-than-average intelligence to the mix, and it becomes plain why Caesar was among the outstanding leaders of his or any other era. He was a Roman, but more so than others.

Sulla had smashed the old certainties of the Roman constitution just as Caesar's generation was leaving childhood. These young men lived through the wrenching instability of civil war, and almost all had relatives who were killed by one side or the other. Caesar's family sided with Sulla's enemies and Caesar owed his life to the fact that his mother had enough family members on the other side to intercede successfully with Sulla for his life.

Perhaps due to his early misadventures in Rome, Caesar spent much of his early manhood in Asia Minor, where he became intimate with King Nicomedes of Bithynia (exactly how intimate he became was the topic of much gossip and scandal). He was captured by pirates and doubled his own ransom to something he believed to be more appropriate for his status. Freed, he hunted down and crucified his former captors. He took part in a siege of the Greek city of Miletos, and later, with typical self-confidence, took command in Asia Minor when war broke out, simply because no one else seemed willing to take charge.

Caesar's first official military command was as a praetor commanding an army in Spain. By then he had piled up such immense debts that his creditors prevented him from leaving town until someone stood surety for them. (The person who did so was Crassus, a multi-millionaire who saw Caesar as something of a protégé.) Once on campaign, Caesar became mildly notorious for concentrating his efforts on enemies of Rome with the most loot to plunder. In a few cases formerly inoffensive tribes became enemies of Rome precisely because Caesar had plundered them.

Though he spent little time on administration, the workaholic general was still able to leave a relatively tidy, though somewhat bruised and resentful, province behind when he returned to Rome to try for a triumph and the consulship. When his many enemies in the Roman senate refused to allow Caesar to stand for consul *in absentia*, Caesar decided to forego his triumph by returning to Rome for the elections.

As consul, Caesar forged an alliance with the two foremost men of his day, Crassus and Pompey, an alliance known to later generations as the first triumvirate. Pompey, the ex-Sullan, allied with Caesar, son of his enemies, because he needed land to give to his now-disbanded troops.

In the late republic, soldiers often campaigned for decades. After that, they looked to their general to persuade the state to make available land on which they could retire. This dependency of soldiers on their general was a major cause of political instability. Veterans needing land were prepared to support their commander against Rome if need be. And those veterans who had received land felt that they had obtained this as a personal favour from their general, to whom they were now indebted.

Caesar wanted a command in Gaul, and Crassus and Pompey used their combined political muscle to force the senate into granting this. Once he had secured Pompey's veterans their land, Caesar left to take up this command. He was to spend almost the rest of his life on campaign.

As a general, Caesar raised the bar for his successors. He was bold without being impetuous and decisive without being pigheaded. His tactical and strategic abilities were only equalled by the speed with which he put them to use. Less obviously, but equally importantly, he was a master of logistics and organization. He also demonstrated two of the prime requirements for a Roman general: the ability to get the best out of his subordinate commanders and to earn trust bordering upon devotion from his soldiers. However, like several of his successors, he failed totally at the final requirement: to reach a working accommodation with those in power in Rome.

With his army completely under his personal control, Caesar was able to go his own merry way while paying minimal attention to the senate. The senate and the Roman people were not consulted when Caesar launched his first war against the Helvetii, a tribe that wanted to cross Roman lands to invade Gaul. When the Gauls decided forcibly to eject the Romans from Gaul after Caesar had successfully defeated the Helvetii, Caesar joyously took up the challenge. He raised legions without official permission and paid them from the profits of his campaigns. (One of these legions was V Alaudae, 'the Larks', which played a major part in events to come.) Caesar crushed the Gauls and went on to defeat a German invasion and invade Britain. This last was again without senatorial permission, unsurprisingly, since by now most leading senators so loathed Caesar that they would on principle have denied him permission to do anything but commit suicide. While in Britain, Caesar allied Rome with some British tribes. It was allegedly in defence of these allies that Rome launched its conquest of Britain in AD 43.

When Caesar returned to Rome, he sought protection from his enemies. The senate could not do this because it was controlled by those very same enemies. However, Caesar's soldiers were ready, willing and able to support their commander. Like Sulla before him, and like many an imperial general after him, Caesar came to Rome a declared public enemy but with an army eager to forcibly adjust his status.

Pompey became the unlikely defender of the republic and the campaign the pair waged against each other in Greece was a masterclass demonstration of military genius in action. Pompey was on the brink of victory when his senatorial colleagues forced him to give battle at Pharsalus on 9 August 48 BC. Caesar leapt at the opportunity to fight his way out of trouble, and his veteran legions did a workmanlike job of demolishing the republican levies.

Caesar had extensive campaigning to do before his power was secure. He fought in Egypt, in Rome's province of Africa and in Spain before returning to Rome to celebrate a magnificent triumph. He appointed himself 'dictator for life' – a role which, despite his denials, was thoroughly monarchical. Ultimately, Caesar was assassinated in 44 BC.

For the historian, there are many points of interest in Caesar's career. Here, the main point to note was that Caesar came to dominate Rome not because he was a good politician, but because he was a brilliant general. A good politician does not get forced into staging a military coup to save his political (and possibly literal) skin, but a brilliant general can carry off such a coup. When he has power, a brilliant politician does not end up getting assassinated by his colleagues in the senate. Yet a brilliant general can command such loyalty in his army that they will carry his adopted son and heir to take over the state in his name. (As it happens Augustus, the adopted son, *was* a brilliant politician. He avoided Caesar's fate and established the imperial system.)

As a general Caesar achieved complete autonomy from the central government and he ultimately used that autonomy to bring down the central government. Caesar's imperial successors learned from this. Imperial generals in the field were supervised as closely as possible. Sometimes when it was impossible to move a general from his position, the emperors chose instead to replace any legions they felt were getting dangerously attached to their commander.

Mark Antony
Marcus Antonius, to use the name Mark Antony's mother gave him, was an aristocrat every bit as highly born as Caesar. Antony would have slightly bridled at the suggestion he was Caesar's subordinate. Admittedly, being younger, he was junior to Caesar, and being impecunious, he relied on subsidies from Caesar's massive war-chest of Gallic loot. However, he came from one of the foremost families in Rome, so Antony assumed that a place at the helm of the republic was his by right.

He had a somewhat scapegrace youth, much of which he spent outside Rome to avoid his creditors. While in the east he joined the competent but morally bankrupt general Aulus Gabinius. As a junior cavalry commander, he campaigned in Judea and in support of Ptolemy XII in Egypt. From there Antony went to Gaul in 54 BC and served Julius Caesar in a number of minor offices. His main value to Caesar was the political clout carried by his noble name. Antony had not seen a great deal of action before he returned to Rome four years later to be elected tribune. Such an action-packed early career was not unusual for a Roman aristocrat. Both then, and throughout the early imperial period, a military career often preceded a political one, and many imperial Roman politicians expected to serve with the legions for part of their career. Indeed, the early military career of Petellius Cerialis may not have been greatly dissimilar.

Antony was one of the few top-rank nobles who supported Caesar. Despite his (at best) patchy record in administration, the propaganda value of his name caused Caesar to make Antony his co-consul for 44 BC, the year he was murdered. To the consternation of his rivals, Antony proved that a drunken philanderer could also be an astute politician. He quickly elbowed Caesar's assassins aside and took command in Rome. Less easy to elbow aside was the veteran politician Cicero, who allied with Caesar's teenage heir, Octavian, and turned Rome against Antony.

While Antony was away from Rome trying to enforce his will on a recalcitrant governor in Gaul, Cicero had the consuls of 43 BC declare Antony a public enemy. The consuls then set out with an army against him, and with them was another commander, young Octavian, made a general of Rome by the official bestowal of imperium by the senate. This proved convenient for Octavian, because the consuls led from the front like good Roman generals. Though they defeated Antony in battle, both men were killed in the process.

Antony nursed the remnants of his army across the mountains into the interior of Gaul. There he allied with another of Caesar's old colleagues, Marcus Lepidus, and once more marched on Rome. The army of the republic stood in his way. But this army was loyal not to the senate but to Octavian, the heir and adopted son of Julius Caesar.

There followed one of the most spectacular double-crosses in history. Octavian abandoned the senate and allied with Antony and Lepidus to form a triumvirate. Legal, judicial and constitutional power was on the side of the senate. Antony, Lepidus and Octavian had the military power. It was no contest. Cicero and many others were killed in a bloody purge, and Octavian, Antony and Lepidus divided up the Roman world between themselves.

Caesar's assassins had escaped to the east of the empire. There, in the now time-honoured manner of rogue generals, they assembled an army with no authority whatsoever beyond that which their soldiery bestowed upon them.

Antony took the lead in crushing the assassins. He did this at Philippi in 42 BC with Octavian as his junior partner. Antony then took command of the eastern portion of Rome's growing empire. Campaigning against the Parthians had originally been Caesar's intention before he was assassinated. Now this campaign was Antony's first – and only – command against a foreign foe.

Antony attempted to reproduce Caesar's famous *celeritas* – speed of movement – by pushing swiftly ahead and leaving his siege train to follow. This was a bad idea when campaigning in open country against an enemy with superior mobility, as the Parthians swiftly demonstrated by destroying that siege train. Antony was unable to capture Parthian cities without artillery, and the Parthian cavalry limited his ability to supply his army by foraging. Antony was forced to retreat. His successful return to Roman territory with a substantial proportion of his army made the entire campaign a mitigated disaster. This promptly turned into an unmitigated disaster when Octavian promptly capitalized on Antony's diminished reputation to declare war against his former partner.

Marcus Vipsanius Agrippa

Octavian's new-found confidence in a military solution to Rome's dysfunctional government was partly based on the ability of Agrippa. The pair formed that most rare and powerful of combinations – an overall commander with a general whom he could absolutely trust.

Octavian was a poor commander in the field. His periodic bouts of ill-health often co-incided with important military campaigns. Even some of his own men considered him a physical coward. Yet if Octavian could not be a good general, he knew how to pick one, which was almost as good. Agrippa was one of Julius Caesar's junior officers, but the dictator evidently trusted him. He ensured that Agrippa was in Octavian's retinue. Thus, when Caesar was assassinated, Agrippa was in a good position to immediately organize the legions to support Caesar's heir. When Octavian and Antony gained control of Rome, Agrippa was rewarded with an appointment as tribune.

In 38 or 39 BC, while Antony was in the east and Octavian governed Italy, Agrippa became governor of Gallia Transalpina, that part of Gaul beyond the Italian Alps. He fought successfully against native tribes and Germans, but tactfully refused a triumph on his return. A triumph would have highlighted Octavian's failure to defeat Sextus Pompey.

Sextus was a son of Pompey the Great. This enterprising young man had control of Sicily and a fleet with which he threatened Rome's trade routes, especially the supply of grain to the capital itself. Octavian's attempts to defeat the menace had failed. In fact they failed so humiliatingly that Octavian at one point contemplated suicide. Now, with Agrippa by his side, Octavian returned to the fray in the mid-30s BC. Young Pompey was resoundingly defeated in a series of naval battles. This increased Octavian's strength to the point where he was able to force his fellow triumvir, Marcus Lepidus, from power.

Agrippa quite literally built up Octavian's popularity in Rome. As *aedile* (an office responsible for maintenance of public buildings), and later as consul, he oversaw the construction of baths, porticos and aqueducts and the building or restoration of numerous temples. Indeed the Pantheon in Rome today still sports on its architrave the legend M. AGRIPPA ... FECIT ('Marcus Agrippa made this'). Yet most of what Agrippa did, he did in Octavian's name, and it was Octavian who reaped the propaganda benefits.

When the crunch came with Mark Antony there was no question but that Agrippa would be Octavian's senior commander. Agrippa was instrumental in winning the decisive battle of Actium.[9] (Antony claimed that Octavian spent the battle prostrate on the deck of his flagship, overwhelmed by cowardice or seasickness.)

With Antony's defeat and suicide Octavian became master of Rome and, perhaps to distance himself from his blood-stained past, took the name of Augustus Caesar. Agrippa was joined to what was now the imperial family by marriage. His children Lucius and Gaius became imperial heirs (though neither lived long enough to succeed to the title). A later descendant, Gaius Caligula, did become emperor, albeit not a good one. Caligula's sister, Agrippina, was a contemporary of the young Petellius Cerialis and the mother of Nero, Petellius Cerialis' first commander-in-chief.

Given the less-than-stellar record of his descendants in power, Agrippa himself was a remarkably good governor. He served in Asia Minor and Gaul (again) and in each case caused the locals to bless the death of the republic. (Even Marcus Brutus, 'the liberator' who killed Caesar to free Rome from tyrants, had been remarkably tyrannical when governing the east).

Agrippa also fought a number of further campaigns in regions as diverse as Spain (19 BC) and Pannonia (13 BC). Shortly after this latter campaign he died at the age of 51.

The important aspect of Agrippa's career was not the political offices he held, nor even his military commands. It was that in both civilian and military office, Agrippa acted not to further his own career but that of another. To republican generals the long-term objective of all their actions was to place themselves at the head of the state. The idea of remaining a permanent subordinate to another – and to yield to that man the credit for everything one achieved – would have been intolerable to any Roman aristocrat capable of imagining it.

Incomprehensible as the career of Agrippa might have been to the illustrious line of republican generals who came before him, it made perfect sense to those who came afterward. Marcus Agrippa was the first of a new breed: the Imperial General.

SUMMARY
The long history of the republic had entrenched certain ideas in the Roman imagination and these proved hard to extinguish in the early days of the Empire. One was that the leader of the state should be a general. Another was that a general of particular ability should lead not just his army, but all of Rome. In politically troubled times this opinion was held with particular vehemence by the soldiers of the general concerned. Furthermore, the army had always chosen Rome's leaders, firstly in the *Comitia Centuriata*, and later simply imposing its will by brute force.

This problem became entrenched in the dying days of the republic. The 'dying' of those days was often all too literal and was largely due to the unhealthy attachment of soldiers to their commander. The violent change from republic to empire, and the constitutional fudges by which Augustus tried to pretend that the transition had never happened, made it impossible to properly resolve the fundamental problems between emperor and general.

Throughout the imperial era, the emperor constantly had to struggle with the troublesome belief of Roman soldiers that their particular general could do a better job of running the state than the current incumbent. This made things hair-raisingly dangerous both for imperial generals and for the emperors they served. Over the four hundred or so years that the Roman Empire lasted in the west, emperors and generals killed each other off at an average rate of just under two per year.[10] During the lifetime of Petellius Cerialis at least a dozen provincial commanders were executed by the emperor. Yet of the nine emperors of whom Cerialis was a subject, six (or seven if Claudius was deliberately poisoned) died of unnatural causes, five of them because of mutinous soldiery.

For an emperor to be secure in his position, he needed to show that he was a capable and pro-active commander of the army. As will be seen, the Julio-Claudian emperors up to Nero made extraordinary efforts to do this. By various strategies they ensured that victories reflected credit on themselves rather than on the generals who won them. This was not egoism, but essential for the emperor's survival and the wellbeing of the state. The only emperor to neglect this duty was Nero. This neglect helped to bring about his death and plunged Rome into chaos.

Chapter 2

The First Imperial Generals

Emperors were well aware that armies tended to develop a dangerous attachment to their generals. Therefore to prevent a repeat of Julius Caesar's example, they tried in various ways to keep their generals loyal to themselves.

In the early years of the empire, the principate was still a collective family enterprise of the Julian and Claudian clans. Therefore, emperors considered it safe to give high command to close family members, or relatives by marriage. For example, Augustus was prepared to place a substantial proportion of the empire's military might in the hands of his stepson Tiberius.

By the time of Nero, trust within the Julio-Claudian family had deteriorated to the point where emperors routinely executed their nearest and dearest for treasonable behaviour, either potential or imagined. Giving high command to close family members became unthinkable, not least because, once these family members had their own armies, executing them became very much harder. Under the Flavians, family members once again commanded armies, but thereafter emperors tried to command for themselves. However, an emperor could not be everywhere, and once the bond of family trust was broken, no other fully satisfactory means of securing a general's loyalty was ever found.

DRUSUS, FAMILY GENERAL

Background

Drusus, or Decimus Drusus Claudius Nero to give this general his full name, was the youngest son of Livia Drusilla and Tiberius Claudius Nero. Tiberius Nero fathered Drusus in 38 BC and was Livia's husband until Augustus decided that he wanted that position and informed Tiberius Nero of his impending divorce.

Both Drusus and his older brother Tiberius remained in the household of Tiberius Claudius Nero until their father's death. There was a strong bond between the brothers, who both served as generals under Augustus.

In a failed attempt to bond the triumvirs, Augustus had wed his sister to Mark Antony, and Antonia was the offspring of that union. With his usual deft touch, Augustus married Drusus to Antonia and so ensured that Antony's daughter did not become a focus of resistance to his regime.

Drusus himself seems to have been a very likeable individual. Antonia became devoted to him, and the couple had three children who survived to adulthood.

Early Commands
Both Drusus and Tiberius were entrusted with important military commands at an early age. Drusus had barely turned twenty-one when he and Tiberius campaigned against the Helvetian tribes of what is now Switzerland (a campaign that saw that country's only naval battle, fought on Lake Geneva).

Thereafter, Drusus was sent to Gaul, presumably to cut his administrative teeth with command of what was now a peaceful province. Things did not turn out that way. An invasion by German tribes gave Drusus his first experience of the people whom he was to spend the rest of his life fighting. Drusus gave the German invaders a sound thrashing and followed this up with an invasion of his own. Under his command Roman legions penetrated deep into German territory.

After a brief spell as praetor in Rome, Drusus returned to the frontier to build on his earlier success. In 11 BC he was back on German soil, and his various victories had caused Augustus to award him triumphal ornaments.

The giving of triumphal ornaments was an experiment by the Augustan regime. The emperor had decided that a full-blown Roman triumph generated more favourable publicity and public goodwill than was safe for anyone but the emperor to enjoy. Therefore, a deserving general was given the awards and ornaments a republican general would have received after a triumph, but without the 'inconvenience' of actually having to celebrate the event.

Germany
In 9 BC Drusus was made consul of Rome. Augustus was very capably handling the legislative and administrative aspects of this office. Therefore Drusus the consul adopted the once-traditional role of consul as war leader. He campaigned against the Chatti and Marcomanni tribes and did much to lay the foundations for what appeared to be the inevitable subjugation of Germany.

However, what German warriors were unable to achieve, Drusus' horse accomplished. A fall from the beast left Drusus with a compound leg fracture, which effectively brought his campaign of conquest to an end. Unsurprisingly, in an age innocent of antibiotics, the injury became infected. Drusus lingered on whilst his distraught brother Tiberius rushed from Italy to be at his deathbed. Tiberius personally escorted the remains of Drusus to Rome. There, his stepfather Augustus ordered the ashes to be placed in the Augustan family tomb. German tribes aside, the passing of Drusus was universally lamented. He was a hero of the Roman populace and loved by his soldiers, who raised a memorial to him in Germany. He was awarded the honorific title of Germanicus, a name which passed to his descendants, together with a high standard for other imperial generals to follow.

The career of Drusus showed the crucial strategic importance of the Rhine frontier. Italy and Rome were most exposed to the threat of barbarian invasion from that quarter (as the career of Varus was to show). However, picking the right general to command on the Rhine was crucial for the emperor. Imperial Rome was in danger not only from the barbarians over the Rhine, but also from the general and soldiers keeping the Germans out.

II. PUBLIUS QUINCTILIUS VARUS

Background

Varus was one of those unflattering nicknames with which many Roman aristocrats found themselves afflicted (other examples include Strabo, 'squinty', and Verrucosus, 'warty'). Varus means the opposite of Valgus, or 'bandy-legged', and suggests that the bearer of the appellation habitually had his knees turned in toward each other.

The name was certainly ancient. A Quinctilius (the name is sometimes spelled as Quintilius) Varus was consul of Rome in 453 BC until he died of the plague. Another was dictator in 331 BC, and a father-and-son team both called Quinctilius Varus fought with distinction in the second Punic war against Mago, the brother of Hannibal.

Our Quinctilius Varus may have been less disturbed about being named after an unfortunate physical characteristic than by a distressing tendency of his immediate predecessors to kill themselves. We know from a passing reference from the historian Velleius Paterculus that his grandfather ran himself through with a sword.[1] His father, Sextus Quinctilius Varus, was quaestor in 49 BC and was as determined to oppose Julius Caesar as Caesar was to forgive him for doing so. This Varus was captured by Caesar at

Corfinium on the outbreak of the civil war and was promptly released. He fled to Africa and joined another Varus in the campaign against Caesar's subordinate general, Curio.[2] He was again captured by Caesar, and was again forgiven. Determined not to be pardoned a third time, Varus joined the senators who assassinated Caesar. When the ringleaders of the assassination were driven from Rome, Varus joined them in the east. After the republican cause died at the Battle of Philippi, Varus decided to do so as well and asked one of his followers to stab him with a sword.

Early Career

Publius Varus was probably born in 46 BC and came to adulthood in the early years of the Augustan principate. Fortunately for him, Augustus was more concerned with earning the trust and support of the Roman nobility than he was in Varus senior's feud with the new regime. Indeed Varus seems to have been personally acquainted with Augustus, and accompanied him on a tour of the eastern provinces early in his reign.

'Varus Quinctilius, descended from a famous rather than a high-born family, was a man of mild character and of a quiet disposition, somewhat slow in mind as he was in body, and more accustomed to the leisure of the camp than to actual service in war' (according to Velleius Paterculus).[3] Evidently the emperor Augustus found the character of Varus congenial, and in 13 BC Varus was given the signal honour of sharing a consulship with Augustus' stepson (and eventual successor) Tiberius. The pair also shared a family connection, for, like Tiberius, Varus was at the time married to a daughter of another Augustan general, Agrippa (p.00). Later Varus went on to marry Claudia Pulchra, another member of the imperial clan, a great niece of Augustus and a relative of the future emperor Claudius.[4] While in the process of insinuating himself into the imperial family, Varus was also able to arrange influential marriages for his sisters.[5]

From this it appears that Varus had been quick to learn that in the new era advancement depended a great deal more on imperial great nieces than it did on the opinion of the Roman senate, and certainly much more than the now virtually meaningless votes of the Roman people.

Commands

Syria: Having the ear of the emperor helped Varus to a quaestorship, probably in 21 BC. He moved smoothly through the offices of aedile and praetor. During the imperial period, command of a legion was often the next step after a praetorship, and Varus probably became legate of Legio XIX, the same unit he was later to lead to disaster in Germany.

Varus' first provincial command was in Africa. It is not known when he started, but he completed his term in office in 6 BC. ('Africa' to the Romans signified not the entire continent, but the province which comprised most of the domains of Carthage, Rome's defeated enemy.) By all accounts Varus was a solid administrator. He also seems to have done a reasonably good job of implementing the various reforms Augustus decreed for the province. The most significant part of this posting is what we are not told about it, for given Varus' later record, any misdemeanours or derelictions would have been brought to light as harbingers of what was to come.

We have a more complete account of Varus' next command, as in 2 BC he succeeded Saturninus as governor of Syria. (This is the Saturninus whom the Bible tells us was governor when 'Caesar Augustus decreed that all the world should be taxed.') The highly complex state of affairs in Judea at the time of the birth of Jesus has been chronicled by the historian Josephus in his *Jewish Antiquities*.[6] While Judea was a special case, there is little doubt that other areas of Varus' provincial command were almost as politically sensitive. Syria, in short, was both one of the most tricky and rewarding offices a governor could hold during the early principate. Having command here suggests that Varus had acquitted himself well militarily in Africa, for the governor of Syria had four legions under his control.

At this time Judea was held for Rome under King Herod.[7] Varus enters the historical record there by presiding over the trial by Herod of one of his sons (who was sentenced to death). Herod died three years later and Judea had one of its periodic lurches from instability into chaos. The kingdom was divided amongst Herod's three sons, and Varus led three legions into Galilee to quell a flourishing little civil war. This he did efficiently but brutally. The towns of Sepphoris and Emmaus were flattened by the legionaries who went on to crucify some 2,000 individuals as a salutary lesson in civil obedience. It appears that in this rebellion Varus enriched himself from plunder and selling rebels as slaves. He may also have taken bribes elsewhere, as Velleius Paterculus remarks that 'he entered a rich province as a [relatively] poor man, and left a poor province as a rich man'.[8]

After his Syrian command Varus returned to Rome, and there he remained. This was perfectly normal, as Augustus had a large number of supporters whom he needed to reward with a limited stock of provincial commands. Varus had already done well with his consulship and governorships in Africa and Syria.

However, there may have been some coolness with Augustus at this time, for Varus had hitched his star firmly to that of Tiberius, who was currently out of imperial favour, in exile, with some actively advocating his execution. As a matter of simple caution it would not be wise for Augustus to put a supporter of Tiberius in command of Roman legions at a time when something drastic might have to be done about Tiberius himself. This pause in Varus' career was a reminder that no imperial general could concern himself purely with the enemy before him.

What was happening back in Rome was at least as important, and sometimes even more dangerous.

Germany: It is probably no co-incidence that Varus was given his next command as governor of Germany in AD 6, soon after Tiberius was restored to favour and returned to Rome. With command of the Rhinelands Varus took control of three legions, Legiones XVII, XVIII and his old command, Legio XIX. It is probable that Varus was intended to hold the legions in readiness for a further push to the Elbe once Tiberius had dealt with a troublesome rebellion in Pannonia. However, the delay caused by the Pannonian revolt had given the German tribal leaders time to prepare for the coming Roman attack. They were led by Arminius, a young aristocrat of the Cherusci, one of the leading German tribes. Arminius had considerable experience of how the legions operated. He had been associated with them in many of their campaigns, and was counted by the Romans as a man of equestrian rank. Arminius quickly decided that the way to stop Rome from conquering the rest of Germany was to stop the legions before they got started.

That his legions might be in danger before they advanced into unconquered territory appears not to have occurred to Varus. The historian Cassius Dio remarks that Varus behaved as though he was administering a settled province instead of occupying hostile territory. Varus spent his time collecting taxes and organizing the peoples under his rule. He readily acceded to Arminius-inspired requests to weaken the legions by dispatching soldiers to protect merchant convoys and to garrison towns allegedly at risk from bandit attacks.

Towards the end of the summer of AD 9 Varus and his legions were in the northeast of the province. False reports came of a minor rebellion to the west, apparently of the sort Varus had sorted out with minimal effort in Judea. Accordingly, the general decided to deal with the matter while leading his troops to their winter quarters (probably at Castra Vetera), which lay in the same direction. Segestes, the father-in-law of Arminius, smelled a kangaroo-sized rat in the way that developments were unfolding, but was unable to shake Varus' faith in the treacherous Arminius.

Unsurprisingly, Arminius found an excuse to absent himself from the Roman marching camp just before the legions entered the gloomy depths of the Teutoberg Forest. The weather was wet and vile with continuous storms and rolling thunder. The legions plodded along their route, further slowed by wagonloads of civilians who were accompanying the Romans to their winter camp.

The German ambush was set at a point where the road narrowed to a strip with marsh on one side and forest on the other. The recent discovery of the exact site of the battle, at Kalkriese near modern Osnabruck, has allowed archaeologists to reconstruct roughly what happened (and to rather smugly point out that the nineteenth-century memorial to Arminius is over 50 miles southeast of the actual site of his victory). It appears that the Germans mustered behind a series of low hills and literally fenced the Romans into the killing ground using woven wattle barriers of the kind used to contain herds of cattle. It was a battle that no Roman who served afterward on the Rhine frontier would ever forget.

As was to be expected of Roman soldiers, the legions went down fighting. There was a series of running battles over the course of three days. At some point in the proceedings Varus decided that the situation was hopeless and followed the family tradition of suicide. He would certainly have known that he faced capture and torture at the hands of the Germans. Even if he survived that, he would afterward have had to explain to Augustus that he had lost three Roman legions.

With the utter destruction of the Rhine armies all that stood between Rome and the German hordes was the Alps. And the only thing that prevented the Germans from a march on Rome was their inability to co-ordinate such an invasion before the winter. Before the following spring the Romans had moved troops from Gaul and Pannonia to plug the gap in their lines.

Augustus famously mourned the defeat in Germany by banging his head against the doors of his palace and lamenting 'Quinctilius Varus, give me back my legions!'[9] This is probably propaganda in Augustus' usual masterly style. In presenting the public with a dramatic image of a distressed, head-banging emperor, the fact that he blamed not Arminius but Varus for the loss of his legions was all the more convincing for being incidental. The implication was that the blame lay with the incompetence of Varus rather than the superiority of German arms, which was somewhat reassuring to the panicked peoples of Italy.

Thus was set another precedent. No imperial general could ever win, for victory belonged to the soldiers and the emperor. But imperial generals had a personal monopoly on failure.

III. GERMANICUS

The Varian disaster required prompt action on the political front by Augustus. On the military front Tiberius had by now established himself as the empire's premier troubleshooter. He raised new legions and moved others freed by the ending of the Pannonian revolt into place along the Rhine frontier. (The numbers of the lost legions XVII, XVIII and XIX were never used again.) But Tiberius the general was something of a stop-gap. Augustus was now elderly and failing, and urgently needed Tiberius the apprentice emperor to prepare to inherit rule of Rome. The command of the Rhinelands passed to a young general carefully groomed for the job – Tiberius Julius Caesar Germanicus.

'Germanicus' was a reminder to the Roman people that Drusus, the lad's father, had campaigned against the Germans with distinction. In picking up where his father had left off, Germanicus was following a tradition already established by the generals of the republic. The 'military families' of the Scipiones, the Fabii and indeed the Neronian Claudii all had pedigrees as generals who had fought and (usually) won in the name of Rome. So in sending the son of Drusus to do battle with the Germans, Augustus was, as ever, applying republican principles with his own imperial twist.

The twist was that, given the early deaths of Agrippa and his sons Gaius and Lucius, Tiberius was heir to the empire, on the understanding that inheritance was to pass on through the line of Germanicus. The Roman people were not particularly fond of the stolid and uncharismatic Tiberius, but Drusus had been widely popular and his son had inherited and built upon this stock of goodwill.

Germanicus was very much a product of the imperium. He was born in 15 BC, when Augustus was looking forward to completing his second decade in power. His first official position came with the early quaestorship at the age of twenty. The usual minimum age for this magistracy was twenty-five, but no one was going to argue with Augustus, especially as Germanicus was now married to Agrippina, granddaughter of both Augustus and Agrippa.

Germanicus received his early military training with his uncle Tiberius in Pannonia and Dalmatia. In AD 10 he was awarded triumphal ornaments.

These triumphal ornaments were given as a way of boosting the young man's *auctoritas* (personal authority). With the award he was entitled to the standing of a praetor in the senate. Germanicus was already being groomed for his future role.

Germany

Thus in AD 12 Germanicus replaced Tiberius as general in Germany with command of eight legions. Though pleased with the appointment of Germanicus, the legions were far from happy with their lot. It had been essential to get the army of the empire up to strength after the Varian disaster. Furthermore, Roman pride insisted that the Germans be given a salutary series of defeats as soon as possible. Consequently, veteran soldiers who had been expecting and were entitled to a discharge after the Pannonian wars were forced to remain under the eagles, fighting a grim and profitless war of attrition.

Personal loyalty and fear of the formidable personality of Augustus kept disaffection in the legions in check. But with the emperor's death in AD 14 military operations ground to a halt. The Rhineland legions began something between a mutiny and a general strike. Such indiscipline by the legions had been almost unheard of during the glory days of the republic. However, since the time of Sulla, legions had been much less restrained about expressing dissatisfaction with pay or conditions. One army had mutinied and killed its commander (Valerius Flaccus in 86 BC), and even Caesar had to deal with violent disaffection among his soldiers. Keeping the troops happy was now a preoccupation shared by both emperor and general, and both were aware that their lives might depend on their success in doing so.

Germanicus hastened to confront the mutinous troops. He was relying on his personal popularity to restore order, and with hindsight the result was predictable. The legions offered to march on Rome and make Germanicus emperor. Germanicus refused with horror. If the troops insisted on such folly, Germanicus told the men, he would kill himself.

In later years, and certainly under Caligula or Nero, a general in such circumstances would not need to kill himself because the emperor would assuredly do it for him. Even the relatively benign Tiberius probably did not greatly appreciate this indication of his relative's popularity with the army. Germanicus may have been his nephew, but Germanicus had failed in one of his most important duties as a general – to keep to the fine line between motivating the troops and becoming dangerously popular.

Germanicus was eventually able to restore order in his mutinous army. He offered concessions (later retracted) and relied heavily on his family charisma. At one point he displayed his son to the men. This boy was something of a mascot to the army, who called him Caligula, or 'little boots'. By such means Germanicus scraped through this dangerous period, though at some cost to his reputation and dignity.

To help everyone forget the recent unpleasantness, Germanicus quickly led the army on a massive excursion across the Rhine. On this and later excursions the Romans mercilessly massacred men, women and children alike. Exception was made for a certain Thusnelda, who was spared because she was pregnant with the son of the renegade Arminius, who had to live the rest of his life knowing that his son was a Roman captive.

Germanicus devised a technique for outflanking the Rhineland tribes by moving the legions by ship from Gaul to the German coast and striking inland from there. He returned to the Teutoberg in AD 15 and finally laid to rest the unburied bones of the legionaries slain in the Varian disaster.

Arminius and Germanicus duelled with their armies into the following year. Emboldened by a series of minor successes, Arminius challenged the legions to a head-on battle at Idistavistus, from which he barely escaped with his life (many of his men were less fortunate). Germanicus fought bareheaded at this battle, the more easily to be seen and encourage the troops.

Germanicus felt that his mastery of the sea gave him the perfect means of outflanking the Germans. Yet transporting armies by sea was always a gamble in antiquity, and every gamble inevitably fails in the long run. A storm hit the legions as they returned from their German triumph, and Germanicus easily paid in drowned legionaries the price that Arminius had paid in slain warriors on the battlefield.

Tiberius probably already wanted to recall Germanicus. His intended successor needed experience in the east of the empire. But Germanicus could hardly finish his German campaign on a low note, so he was allocated another season on the Rhine. Germanicus retrieved one of the legion eagles lost in the Varian disaster, and with this success ceded command to his brother Drusus and returned to Rome.

The German adventure had been spectacular. Germanicus had restored respect for Roman arms along the frontier. But the repeated forays over the Rhine were essentially huge punishment raids that ultimately did nothing for the Roman conquest of Germany. The most significant result of Germanicus' tenure was that command of the legions along the Rhine was split between the governors of Upper and Lower Germania. Germanicus had resisted the temptation to lead his legions against the emperor, but another general might not.

Later years were to demonstrate both the wisdom of splitting command of the German legions and that even this precaution was inadequate. The legions on the Rhine guarded the Roman Empire against the Germanic threat – but what guarded the Roman emperor against the legions on the Rhine was the precarious loyalty of his generals.

Germanicus Goes East
Tiberius allowed his nephew to celebrate a spectacular triumph in AD 17: the last triumph in Rome not celebrated by a reigning emperor.[10] Germanicus then went on to share a consulship with Tiberius before travelling east.

The trip was partly so that the eastern provinces could get a look at their future emperor. But it was also so that Germanicus could sort out the ever-disputed issue of the kingship of Armenia. This small kingdom lay between the Roman and Parthian empires, and each empire preferred to have its own client king in power. The Parthians had recently ejected the Roman claimant and it was Germanicus' job to put him back. For this task, and as a reflection of his status, Germanicus was given *maius imperium*, which meant that he technically outranked the governors of the eastern provinces.

Tiberius probably intended Germanicus to travel as a general, albeit a very senior one. In the event, the journey east turned into a truly imperial procession. Germanicus was celebrated wherever he went. After establishing the popular king Artaxias on the Armenian throne, he went on to meet with the Parthian king Artabanus. Many assumed that Germanicus' diplomatic inexperience and headstrong character would provoke war with Parthia. Instead, Roman prince and Parthian monarch agreed a settlement that would leave the frontier stable for almost a generation.

Regrettably, Germanicus did not stop there. He interfered in the affairs of the East from Cappadocia and Commagene through Palmyra and on to Egypt. Roman senators were forbidden even to enter the country, but Germanicus breezily assumed that his *maius imperium* gave him not simply the right to enter Egypt but also to intervene in Egyptian affairs. Tiberius commented on this sniffily in the Senate, but soon a larger and more dangerous contretemps overshadowed this indiscretion.

The governor of Syria, one Calpurnius Piso, took it on himself to reverse some of the decisions Germanicus had made in his province. There was a dispute about who had overall command of the legions in the area. Piso made a clumsy and blatant attempt to prejudice his troops against Germanicus, which led to Germanicus officially withdrawing his friendship and ordering Piso out of his province.

Germanicus' wife, Agrippina, loathed Plancina, the wife of Piso. Plancina (a close confidante of Tiberius' mother, Livia) hated Agrippina right back. The mutual antagonism of two powerful wives provided an unhelpful backdrop to the turf war between two of the empire's senior commanders.

Before Tiberius could intervene between his squabbling generals, Germanicus died. His mortal illness was sudden and of causes unknown. On his deathbed Germanicus accused Piso of poisoning him. Piso did not help his case by attempting to retake command of Syria by force once Germanicus was dead.

The death of the hugely popular Germanicus in AD 19 caused a mini crisis in Rome. Amid unprecedented scenes of public mourning, Piso was brought to trial and condemned to death, not for poisoning, which was a dubious charge at best, but for treason. Piso had not respected *maius imperium* and had meddled with the loyalty of his army. Tiberius ordered an official account to the trial and its conclusions to be sent to every legionary base in the empire.[11] It was that important to tell the troops exactly what had happened and what the emperor had done about it.

Later generations noted from the career of Germanicus the danger a charismatic general posed to his emperor. True, Germanicus was no threat to the rule of Tiberius. He was young, his succession was assured, and he could afford to turn down the offer by the army to depose Tiberius. Reasonably enough, though, Tiberius and his successors felt that the decision of whether a general should succeed them should be theirs, not their general's. No general, even if an imperial heir, was ever again given such powers as Germanicus had wielded.

Emperors and Generals
Tension between emperors and generals continued after the death of Germanicus. Tiberius allegedly suspected Lentulus Gaetulicus, commander in Germany, of disloyalty. The general was recalled to Rome, but he did not come. Gaetulicus disingenuously insisted that he was needed right where he was to keep the legions loyal to Tiberius. This was an unmistakeable warning. If Gaetulicus did come to Rome, his legions were coming with him. Tiberius backed down. Gaetulicus kept his command and remained in Germany.

Elsewhere, Tiberius took the opportunity of rotating command rapidly amongst a number of Rome's traditional military families. In Africa the renegade Tacfarinas led the Musulamii people in a guerrilla war against

Rome. The great old name of Furius Camillus was again associated with a Roman victory, and even a Cornelius Scipio was given the chance to shine where Scipio Africanus had distinguished himself.

The east was under the command of Vitellius, scion of a family long associated with the imperial regime. In AD 35 Vitellius competently managed a mini crisis with Parthia. The Parthians attempted to re-open the question of the Armenian succession and were assured by defeat in a brisk war that Rome's position on the matter was unchanged.

Caligula succeeded Tiberius. Since Caligula attempted to centralize power on himself, he had a difficult relationship with his generals. The young emperor quickly and decisively dealt with the ambiguous issue of Gaetulicus in Germany. He arrived in the province unannounced, and promptly had the general executed for treason. Command went to the strict disciplinarian and rising star of the old aristocracy, Servilius Galba. Galba's career was later to get still more interesting but for now change between the easy-going appeasement of Gaetulicus and the severity of Galba became proverbial. 'This is Galba, not Gaetulicus' became a catchphrase for any Roman who had to adjust to new and harsher circumstances.

After the execution of Gaetulicus, Caligula accused the governor of Pannonia of subverting the loyalty of the troops by allowing them 'improper relations' with his wife. Husband and wife were executed on their return to Rome. It was a dangerous time to be an imperial general. Aulus Flaccus was removed from office in Egypt and executed. Publius Petronius, governor of Syria, had constantly to risk either execution for not carrying out Caligula's orders or an immediate revolt by the Jews if he did obey them (for example, the order to put a statue of Caligula within the temple in Jerusalem was never carried out due to Petronius' masterly procrastination).

Another commander in the east was Cassius Longinus, proconsul in Asia in AD 40. He was recalled to Rome in chains, apparently for no other reason than his relative of the same name had been among the leading assassins of Caesar. Caligula was rapidly accumulating enemies among Rome ruling class and was in no mood to risk Cassius following the example of his famous namesake.

That the legions remained loyal to the descendant of Drusus and Germanicus was Caligula's only safeguard against a provincial revolt. Even so, it is probable that Caligula would eventually have faced a challenge from a general who was not prepared to go quietly to his fate. In the event, the far-from-unexpected assassination of Caligula took place in AD 41, just six years into his reign. The accession of the amiable Claudius was greeted with near universal relief by the commanders of the imperial legions.

IV. GNAEUS DOMITIUS CORBULO

Corbulo reached the praetorship during the reign of Tiberius, but his later rise to power began when he became intimate with the imperial family through his sister Caesonia, who was Caligula's wife. Corbulo received a consulship in AD 39. He was sidelined in the early years of Claudius' reign, possibly because of an old scandal which dated back to his appointment as curator of the roads of Italy. He had renovated the roads of the Italian peninsula as his brief had required, but had treated his workers brutally. He used the same brutal streak to extort money for the roadworks from local municipalities, which sent a flood of complaints to Rome.

In AD 47 Corbulo applied his distinguishing characteristics of severity combined with exceptional organizational ability to his next command: the Rhineland legions. Finding that Galba's term in office had left him with a well-organized and disciplined army, he promptly invaded Germany. Corbulo was well on the way to conquering the Chauci when messages arrived from Rome. An aggrieved emperor Claudius pointed out that imperial permission was required before the conquest of neighbouring territories, so Corbulo was to pull the army back immediately. The order was obeyed reluctantly, but not before Corbulo made his famous comment that only the generals of the republic had truly known what it meant to command.

Denied military glory, Corbulo returned to his roots in civil engineering and set the legions to constructing a canal almost twenty miles long between the river Meuse and the Rhine. This dramatically reduced the risk of flooding across the entire region and added a defensive feature to the frontier. Corbulo's dictum was that victory was won not with the sword, but with the *dolabra*, the legionary shovel. It soon became proverbial within the army.

From this point onwards, Corbulo was a contemporary of Petellius Cerialis, though a much more senior figure. Cerialis' commander, Suetonius Paulinus, was a general of the same rank as Corbulo, and a rival for his stature.

Syria

At first Paulinus' star rose faster, for Claudius had little further use for the recalcitrant Corbulo. However, in AD 54 Nero considered Corbulo's uncompromising severity exactly what was required to get the eastern legions back into shape. These legions had been enervated by years of inactivity and good living. Tacitus claims that many units consisted of 'sleek, citified businessmen, who had never stood a night watch and to whom camps and ramparts were strange novelties'. To such men, Corbulo came as a dramatic shock. Once he received his command he immediately hauled the army from its traditional bases near the cities and took it on a training march to the Armenian highlands in mid-winter. So bitter was the cold that it was reported that when one soldier dropped his bundle of firewood, his hands dropped off with it. These exercises did their job of toughening the army, and just in time. It had to fight the following summer, when Rome and Parthia once again fell out over the Armenian kingship.

The Parthian king was preoccupied with a civil war at home and unprepared for the threat Corbulo's renascent army presented. The kingship was settled in Rome's favour and high-ranking Parthian hostages were sent to Rome as guarantors of Parthia's good behaviour.

War with Parthia

This good conduct lasted until AD 58, when the Parthians, yet again, supported a usurper to the Armenian throne. This time, they were prepared to fight for the usurper's claim. Meanwhile Corbulo had spent four years fashioning the Syrian legions into a highly trained killing machine. The war was an unqualified success for Rome. The two major cities of Armenia were Artaxata and Tigranocerta. Corbulo captured both, for when he stormed and flattened Artaxata, Tigranocerta promptly surrendered. Corbulo then installed Rome's preferred candidate on the throne with the battered Parthians unable to prevent his doing so.

This set the pattern for several years in which the Romans forcibly installed Armenian kings whom the Parthians ejected soon afterwards. The campaign of AD 58 was repeated in AD 63. By this time, Boudicca had rebelled, and both Paulinus and Petellius Cerialis had seen hard fighting on their side of the empire.

On this latest occasion, Corbulo did not take direct command of his war. He remained to protect Syria while the actual campaign in Armenia was bungled by a subordinate. As a result of his ham-fisted generalship, the Parthians installed their own preferred candidate. Only then did Corbulo once more take the well-worn route into Armenia to sort things out. Eventually a compromise was agreed, by which the Romans accepted the Parthian candidate – provided that the candidate went to Rome to receive his crown from Nero personally.

It is of note that Corbulo refrained from taking direct command of military operations until he had to. When he sent Tiridates to Rome, he also sent his own son-in-law to assure the emperor of his loyalty. This lower profile was necessary, for Nero was becoming increasingly erratic and tyrannical. He may have noted the affection Syrian legions were beginning to develop for their commander. Though a martinet, Corbulo made sure that his legions went to war well trained, well organized and well supplied. And soldiers throughout the ages have preferred their generals to win with minimal casualties on their side.

Almost beyond doubt, Corbulo received highly discreet messages from the beleaguered Senate in Rome. These would have hinted that Corbulo might use his highly trained veterans to either restore the Roman republic or at least replace Nero with himself. If he did receive such overtures, Corbulo rejected them and remained unwaveringly loyal.

Retirement with Extreme Prejudice
When Nero took himself on a tour of Greece in AD 67, his rule was already looking shaky. Yet Corbulo unhesitatingly followed orders to join the imperial retinue. He was by now the most famous and respected general of his age. He had served Rome well, if brutally, in civil administration and in the German wars. In the east he had turned a slovenly and undisciplined army into a fighting force respected by the Parthians and which had brought peace to the eastern frontier. By any reckoning, he had done his duty by Rome and his emperor. Even separated from his legions, his loyalty and his reputation should protect him.

Unknown to Corbulo, a treacherous officer had secretly laid charges against him. This man wanted either revenge – Corbulo was not gentle with subordinates – or imperial favour. He got both. Nero immediately promoted the informer to chief centurion and ordered Corbulo's death.

Typically, Corbulo did not entrust his execution to anyone else, but undertook the task himself. His final words before he drove his sword into his own chest were 'I deserved this!' Perhaps he referred to an invitation to treason that he had received, but not reported to Nero. More probably Corbulo was expressing regret that he had not taken up that invitation and acted on it.

Nero had disposed of Corbulo. But he apparently did not consider the effect this would have on his other commanders. Rebellion became much more attractive when remaining loyal meant dicing with death. The next commanders whom Nero suspected of disloyalty promptly decided to prove him right.

Part II
Britain

Chapter 3

A Legate of the Ninth

AFRICA AND BRITAIN IN THE 40s AD
The Euphrates and the Rhine were not the only borders of the empire that saw conflict during the Julio-Claudian principate. At this time the Roman Empire was still expanding, albeit at a more measured pace than in the last century of the republic. A young man in search of military glory had much of the world to choose from. During the years of Petellius Cerialis' boyhood Roman generals distinguished themselves in two major areas of operation.

AFRICA
Africa had been unexpectedly active. Under Tiberius, the Mauri people had been organized into a Roman client kingdom – technically independent, but subordinate to Rome.[1] Later, the emperor Claudius converted the kingdom into the provinces of Mauretania Caesariensis and Mauretania Tingitania.[2] The two new provinces shared a smouldering resentment at losing their independence and a determination to take this out on Rome. It did not help that the Romans had reorganized the neighbouring province of Africa for large-scale grain production, and in the process dispossessed the native Berbers into the Aurès mountains, thus contributing to general instability in the area.

When the Mauretanians rebelled, Corbulo's rival, Suetonius Paulinus, was sent to suppress the rebellion. The legion of which Paulinus was legate, III Augusta, had considerable experience at fighting in Africa. This experience, combined with the competence of Paulinus himself, resulted in the rebels promptly being defeated and driven into the Atlas mountains. Rather to the rebels' surprise, Paulinus followed them, leading the first Romans ever to venture into this wilderness. Paulinus later wrote a description of the area, which Pliny the Elder incorporated into his epic *Natural History*.[3]

Paulinus reported the desert beyond the mountains was uninhabitable Saharan *reg* of bare rock and gravel. He retreated with his men complaining of heat and thirst. A subordinate, one Hosidius Geta, ventured even deeper into the desert in what proved an all-too-literal hot pursuit of a Mauri leader. He and his men might have perished if not for a providential shower of rain.

This campaign brought Suetonius Paulinus to fame. A passing comment by Tacitus implies that Paulinus was rewarded with a consulship, and over the coming decades his would remain a name to be reckoned with.

BRITAIN

Local difficulties with the climate notwithstanding, Mauretania was under Roman control within two or three years. This easy pacification was not mirrored in the recalcitrant lands in the northwest corner of the empire. The Romans invaded Britain in AD 43, as the rebellion in Mauretania came to an end. Had the Romans known the amount of time, blood and money it would take to turn Britain into a productive province, they might not have bothered. To understand affairs in Britain in the first century AD requires a good working knowledge of events as they unfolded, and every Roman general in the province needed to master a brief rather like the one given below.

Early Contact With Rome

Early indications that Britain might prove a tough nut to crack dated back to the time of Julius Caesar, who conducted two substantial excursions to the island in 55 and 54 BC. These expeditions were something between reconnaissance in force and large-scale raiding. They highlighted two major problems for a future conqueror: the intractably independent British character and the equally unreasonable weather.

Both factors made themselves apparent within hours of Caesar's arrival in Britain. The landing of the legionaries was bitterly contested, and when Caesar finally established a beachhead he was unable to follow up the retreating Britons because his cavalry transports had been driven back to Gaul by seasonal gales. While Caesar was digesting this bit of bad news, the Britons ambushed Legio VII. (This legion was the ancestor of Legio VII Claudia, alongside which Cerialis later fought.) Casualties were few, but this chain of events set the tone for Roman campaigns in Britain thereafter.

Caesar was opposed by Casiavellaunus, a British chieftain who rapidly discovered the futility of taking on the legions head on. Thereafter he concentrated on hitting the Roman military support infrastructure, such as bases and supply lines. Casiavellaunus did this with such success that Caesar withdrew from Britain at the end of the campaigning season and was thereafter distracted by events elsewhere. The Romans did not return for almost a century.

A Short History of the Conquest

Phase I: The military operation In AD 43 Claudius mustered four legions for the conquest of Britain. Since these legions are in themselves important actors in the story that follows, a brief introduction is in order.

II Augusta was a legion born in the civil wars. Its soldiers had defeated Mark Antony before Octavian's infamous double-cross of the republic and had thereafter loyally backed Octavian all the way to becoming emperor. This was one of the legions used to plug the Rhine frontier after the Varian disaster and took part in punitive invasions by Germanicus that followed.

IX Hispana had fought with Caesar in Gaul and after the civil wars the legion moved to Spain. The readjustments following the Varian disaster saw the legion transferred to service along the Danube, and it is highly probable that some sub-units of the legion fought under the command of Suetonius Paulinus in Mauretania, and that these were the men led dangerously deep into the desert by Hosidius Geta.

XIV Gemina was formed from the fourteenth legions that fought on either side of the civil war. Once merged, the legion took the 'Gemina' (twin) appellation. XIV Gemina campaigned in Germany alongside a number of legions that later take a prominent place in later events.[4]

XX Valeria was one of the legions that fought alongside XIV Gemina in Germany. Earlier, the legion had experience of working with IX Hispana during the Spanish wars of Augustus. The legion distinguished itself in wars on the Danubian frontier. It is unlikely that any of its officers or men were aware that after the invasion XX Valeria would never leave Britain again.

As it was, these legions were, to put it mildly, less than enthusiastic about returning to the island to which Julius Caesar's men had paid such an unproductive visit. More precisely, they flatly refused the order of their general, Aulus Plautius, to board the transports taking them there. It turned out that the time it took to coax the soldiery off the docks in Boulogne worked in the Romans' favour. Gallic sympathizers had kept the Britons well informed of events on the other side of the channel and a large army had been impatiently waiting there to repel boarders from the island's shores. As the days dragged by without any sign of the Romans, the British, who lacked a supply system to keep their warriors encamped for a long period, simply drifted back to their homes. Many believed that the Romans were not coming at all. Consequently when Aulus Plautius eventually made his landfall (probably near Richborough in Kent) there was no one waiting to meet him.

Rome's invasion strategy was one that had been refined through centuries of warfare with the peoples of the Mediterranean. In modern terms it would be defined as political high-intensity warfare. The Romans were not interested in seizing strategic areas of real estate such as vital passes, or in cutting lines of communication. Instead they headed directly for the enemy's seat of government by the shortest possible route. The intention was to destroy the enemy's will to resist by capturing the capital and preferably by destroying en route whatever armies tried to stop them. After this, the leaders of the defeated nation would negotiate terms and Roman civilian administrators would move in.

Landing in Kent, south of the Thames estuary, was not ideal for this strategic vision. But the landing site was a legacy of the career of Germanicus. After he had drowned an army, Roman generals preferred to keep their soldiers at sea for as short a time as possible. In this case a short Channel crossing meant that the army had a long march westwards to where the Thames could be comfortably crossed. While the army was marching there, the Britons made their first serious stand at the River Medway, near Rochester. Rome was victorious, but the struggle took two days. It has been suggested with some plausibility that the early beachhead on the hostile bank of the Medway was made by Batavian auxiliaries, a unit famous for their skill at aquatic operations.[5] As with many auxiliary units, the Batavians were led by their own tribal nobility. One of these noblemen was a young cohort commander called Julius Civilis, of whom the Romans were to hear much more in later years.

At the Medway the Britons came close to capturing the legate of IX Hispana, who rashly led his legion prematurely across the river. This was Hosidius Geta, whom we last saw struggling with a water shortage in Mauretania. As in Africa, Geta and IX Hispana overcame this temporary setback. They turned the tide of battle so successfully that Geta was awarded triumphal ornaments for his achievement. Another of note at this battle was Flavius Sabinus Vespasian, legate of II Augusta, a distant relative of the Sabinus who was in command in Pannonia until Caligula took a lethal interest in his case. Vespasian, working with his brother (also called Sabinus), contributed to the Roman victory by taking his men across the Medway and consolidating the Batavian bridgehead.

The legions drove north to the Thames, destroying British opposition as they marched. Somewhere near modern Tilbury they crossed, again with the help of the Batavian auxiliaries.

Meanwhile Vespasian took II Augusta west to conquer the Durotriges tribe in a series of assaults on their hill forts. He took the hill fort known as Maiden

Castle (where a skeleton has been unearthed with the bolt from a Roman siege weapon still embedded in its spine). It is reported that Vespasian fought 'thirty battles' and crushed two warlike tribes. He captured the Isle of Wight, and at Weymouth secured the invading army an alternative supply route from the continent.

Now, with the Roman army ready for its final push, Plautius paused. One reason for the invasion of Britain had been for the Emperor Claudius to burnish his military reputation. Augustus had been a general and his successor Tiberius an even better one. Caligula, though no general himself, was the son of Germanicus the iconic commander, beloved of the Roman people. Claudius had no military credentials to offer, and it was important for his credibility with people and army that he obtained some. As someone who had been put in power by the Praetorian Guard, Claudius fully appreciated the role of the army in keeping him there. Therefore he intended personally to lead the legions at the taking of the enemy capital.

Claudius arrived, bringing reinforcements and the first elephants seen on British soil since the woolly mammoth. Plautius had already broken the back of the British resistance so Claudius' march north was something of a triumphal parade. His biographer Suetonius says that 'he fought no battles and suffered no casualties'.[6] On an arch erected to mark the occasion Claudius proudly recorded that he received the submission of eleven kings. The highlight of the imperial visitation was the taking of Camulodunum. Claudius personally led the army and thereafter formally announced that the mission to conquer Britain was accomplished. With the fraught political situation in Rome requiring his personal attention, Claudius hurried back, returning to the city within six months of his departure. Roman coins proclaimed '*Britannia capta*', though a generation would pass before this claim became reality.

Phase II: The political dimension To be fair, the Romans never for a moment considered the 'enemy' to be a monolithic political entity, just as they never considered Camulodunum 'the capital' rather than 'a capital'. The British opposing the invaders were a not a single army but a tribal confederation, and at that a confederation in which relationships between the different tribes were edgy at best.

Casiavellaunus, the leader who caused Julius Caesar such difficulty, is generally assumed to be of the Catuvellauni tribe. This tribe was of an expansionist character, and had recently been expanding from their ancient capital of Verulamium (St Albans in modern Cambridgeshire). This caused considerable friction with the Trinovantes, who had previously considered themselves top dogs in the region. Certainly this had been the case when Caesar had been there almost a century before, and this is one reason why the Trinovantan capital of Camulodunum was the initial target for the Roman legions. (Another reason was because the Catuvellauni had recently taken control of the place.)

Not all Britons opposed the invaders. The Atrebates had been allies of Rome since Julius Caesar's installation of Commius as a client king. Perhaps unsurprisingly, the Atrebates were not fondly regarded by their neighbours, and soon fell under the heel of the Catuvellauni. It was this mistreatment of a Roman ally that gave Claudius his excuse to invade.

Just north of the Trinovantes was the Iceni tribe, who had been getting the worst of the recent ructions. Consequently the Iceni were sympathetic to the Roman invasion, which focused hostile tribal activity elsewhere.

Military leadership of the Britons not surprisingly fell to the Catuvellauni, more particularly to a pair of sons of the recently deceased Cunobelinus, and therefore possibly descendants of Casiavellaunus.[7] One of this pair, Caractacus, had been the force behind the recent expansion of his tribe. As this had not endeared him to other members of the British confederation, it was Caractacus' brother Togodumnus who commanded operations against the Romans.[8] By some accounts, Togodumnus was killed in the fighting that followed the Roman crossing of the Medway and, certainly by the time that Claudius marched on Camulodunum, Caractacus was unambiguously in charge.

The arrival of Rome into what had previously been a hotbed of violent tribal politicking and warfare had the effect of dampening fierce rivalries in the face of a common enemy. But these divisions certainly did not go away, and understanding their nature became essential for any senior Roman with command in the area.

Tribal relations were to play an important part in the life of Petellius Cerialis, both immediately on his arrival in Britain and later. This is because, though the Romans had by AD 45 established a solid base in southeast England, much of the island remained unconquered. Nor was Caractacus a spent force. He was determined not only that the rest of Britain should remain unconquered, but the Romans should also be pushed out of the lands they currently held. This was no futile hope, for the Britons were well aware of the example of Varus in Germany and the Teutoberg massacre of AD 9.

Plautius went to a well-deserved *ovation* in Rome (a form of minor triumph) in AD 47. Hosidius Geta followed and became consul in AD 49.[9]

Plautius' most successful subordinate, Vespasian, followed in AD 51 to be rewarded by Claudius with both a consulship and triumphal honours.

Phase III: The second wave   The first post-invasion commander was one Ostorius Scapula. Ostorius intended to defeat the Silures in the west of Britain, in the area that is now Wales. With the army engaged in offensive warfare, the occupation force became dangerously stretched.

Ostorius was aware of the peril and took the precaution of ordering the tribes within Rome's area of influence to disarm. This measure provoked exactly the revolt that Ostorius was attempting to forestall. Ostorius had included the Iceni in his unilateral disarmament decree, and up to that point the Iceni had fondly believed that they were an allied but independent nation. It took a short, sharp campaign to convince the tribe otherwise. Once conquered, the Iceni bitterly resented what they saw as a Roman betrayal of their early friendship. Roman diplomacy of later years only partly succeeded in soothing away that resentment.

Ostorius also intervened in northern Britain when the Brigante tribe rebelled against their pro-Roman ruler. It was essential for Rome to keep the Brigante friendly, for they occupied most of the territory north of the Roman area of occupation. So important was this that Ostorius interrupted his drive west to ensure that the Brigante queen, Cartimandua, retained her throne.

This distraction allowed the pugnacious Caractacus to rally the Silures against the Roman threat. The Iceni and Brigante had already tied up Roman resources, so Ostorius had little choice but to bring another legion into play against Caractacus. This was XX Valeria, which had been garrisoning the captured capital of Camulodunum. To ensure that the city remained under Roman control, Ostorius obtained imperial permission to establish there the Roman military colony of Colchester, which he populated with discharged legionaries.

Thus in AD 49 the first Roman colony in Britain was founded – a grim reminder to the native population that Rome intended to make Britain her own. Because thereafter the Britons kept fighting for far longer than the Romans considered reasonable, XX Valeria was never available to return to garrison Colchester, so the new colony remained constantly vulnerable.

Caractacus was now the *de facto* leader of all who feared assimilation by Rome. However, unlike Casiavellaunus, he did not take to heart the lesson that it was unwise to tackle the legions head on. His attempt to do so saw the British cause crushed on the banks of the Severn. With his army destroyed, Caractacus was forced to seek shelter amongst the Brigante, the only tribe in the region still independent of Rome. Thanks to Ostorius' early intervention, the Brigante – or at least the leadership – remained pro-Roman. When she discovered Caractacus in her kingdom, Cartimandua promptly handed him over to Ostorius (who sent him on to Rome). Cartimandua saw little reason to abandon her alliance with the Romans for a cause already faltering and, indeed, her consistent loyalty paid dividends for her people over the following decades.[10]

If Cartimandua and the Brigante demonstrated the benefits of accepting the Roman presence, Ostorius seems to have deliberately used the recalcitrant Silures as an example to those who resisted. His apparent determination to extirpate their people drove the Silures to stubborn resistance. Ostorius was but the first of many generations of commanders over the following millennia to discover just how fruitless and frustrating campaigning on the Welsh marches could be. Several years later, with the Silures still stubbornly unconquered, the Roman general perished in harness, worn down by constant campaigning – and the uncongenial British climate.

His replacement was Didius Gallus, a man accustomed to tricky tribal politicking. He had freshly returned from managing the turbulent client kingdoms of Rome at the other side of the empire on the Black Sea. His experience proved useful in AD 57 when Queen Cartimandua of the Brigante had a distinctly unfriendly separation from her husband and expelled him from the kingdom. The husband, Venutius, was seen as the best potential leader of the Britons since Caractacus. Therefore anti-Roman Britons gave the disaffected Venutius their full support when he attempted to re-enter his wife's domains by force. In the end a legion (probably IX Hispana) forcibly intervened to quieten down the domestic disturbance. Venutius was forced into a grudging reconciliation and Cartimandua was secure on her throne once again.

While successful in diplomacy, Didius Gallus achieved little militarily. This may have been because midway through his governorship Claudius died and was replaced by Nero. Nero was distinctly ambivalent about the cost and effort that had been sunk into the conquest of Britain. At one point (either on his accession or later) he considered pulling out from the island altogether. Rome had just received a setback in Armenia and the veteran Roman legionaries could be deployed to great effect elsewhere. (It did not help that shortly before Gallus' arrival the Silures had given XX Valeria a nasty mauling in circumstances now obscure.)

Therefore the politically sensitive Gallus held the legions in check while he waited to hear from Rome. A false move on the political front – such as committing his soldiers to an extensive campaign – might prove more dangerous to the general than to the soldiers sent to do the actual fighting.

Nero eventually concluded that a withdrawal from Britain would reflect badly on Claudius, and therefore on himself, since Claudius was his adoptive father. In AD 57 he replaced Didius Gallus with a general who had earned his laurels campaigning against hostile tribes in the mountains of Asia Minor: one Quintus Veranius. This was a clear indication that Nero had decided to resume military operations. Britain was to be pacified with due dispatch. However, before Veranius could make much of an impression he too was on his death bed, the second general to die in Britain of causes unknown.

Fortunately for Nero, the extensive frontiers of the empire gave him a ready supply of generals with suitable qualifications and experience to replace Veranius. He selected a man with the confirmed ability to fight hostile tribes in rough terrain. This was Suetonius Paulinus, whom we last saw in action amid the mountains of Mauretania.

INTRODUCING PETELLIUS CERIALIS

The legate of IX Hispana who stood down at that time bore the name Caesius Nasica. This is of considerable interest, as the family name of the man who subsequently took over the legion was Quintus Petellius Cerialis Caesius Rufus. This strongly suggests that Caesius Nasica was the brother of Petellius Cerialis.

The Petellii were a relatively old clan of uncertain origins – the first Petellius to make consul was Quintus Petellius Spurinus in 176 BC. That particular Petellius died after making a rash move on the battlefield, which Tacitus uses to suggest that recklessness was something of a family tradition. The family was plebeian, and two of its members as tribunes were instrumental in engineering the overthrow of Scipio Africanus, the great general who defeated Hannibal.

Our Quintus Cerialis was probably adopted into the Petellian clan. Adoption was very common among aristocratic families in the empire. In fact, Nero himself was the biological son of Domitius Ahenobarbus, and had been adopted by the emperor Claudius.[11] Imperial adoptions aside, for poorer aristocrats such as the Caesi, putting a child through the various offices of state was an expensive business. Many families could not afford to do this for more than one child. So it was not uncommon for a family to farm out a second or third son to a well-connected family with no offspring to perpetuate the family name. If this happened to our Petellius Cerialis, the Rufus Petellius who adopted him must have had close links with the Caesius family. In turn the Caesius clan was linked with the currently middle-to-low-ranking senatorial Flavian family of which Vespasian was a member.

The link between the families became even closer when Petellius Cerialis married Vespasian's daughter Flavia Domitilla. Though Flavia died at some time in the 60s, she left her husband with a daughter, and probably also a son, and through these children Petellius maintained close ties with the Flavian family.

Such a close web of family connections was very common amongst the Roman aristocracy of the day. The bond of marriage and family helped with the exchange of services and favours, which was not simply how the Roman elite functioned, but which also underpinned the working of the entire bureaucracy of the empire.

In fact, 'bureaucracy' is a misnomer, for it refers to a system of government that was only invented centuries later. In ancient Rome, one rose to high office entirely through back-scratching, patronage, bribery and nepotism. This was not considered corruption, as that would imply that there was some other system to be corrupted. Nepotism and favouritism *was* the system. So, just as the legate of Legio XX (Vespasian) had received his command by influencing Claudius' freedman Narcissus, Vespasian probably pulled strings to ensure that command of IX Hispana went to his relative Caesius Nasica. It is equally likely that Caesius Nasica arranged to be replaced by his brother when he stood down.

That brother, Petellius Cerialis, was a man in his early to mid-thirties. Since a legionary legate had usually held a praetorship in Rome, it is assumed that Petellius had advanced that far in his civilian career. Whether he had any previous military experience is unknown, but it is highly likely that he had served somewhere as a *tribunus laticlavus*. These young tribunes were appointed as understudies to the legion commander, ready to assume nominal command of the legion should the legate die (whether at the hands of barbarian tribesmen or executioners from Rome). The word 'nominal' in the previous sentence is because a newly promoted legionary legate could call on the services of the camp prefect and *primus pilus* (senior centurion), who between them were perfectly capable of handling the administrative and tactical functions of the legion. In so far as a legate was required, it was to tell the legion what to do. How to do it could be left to highly competent and, in the case of the British legions, highly experienced subordinates. In fact, later events in Italy were to show that mutinous legions still had a high degree of functionality even after they had killed or were simply ignoring their senior officers.

The Anglesey Campaign

The state of Britain: Petellius Cerialis' senior commander, Suetonius Paulinus, was a highly competent general. His ability in the field was beyond doubt. His initial years in Britain saw two highly successful campaigns that drove Roman suzerainty ever further westward. There was, however, some question about Paulinus as a civil administrator. The defeat of Varus in Germany had not been entirely due to incompetence as a commander. Much of his culpability came from his inability to judge the temper of the people he was governing. It soon became evident that Paulinus was guilty of the same lapse.

The Britain where Petellius Cerialis arrived to take up his new command was not a happy place. The British had been subjugated for less than a generation and the impositions of Roman rule (such as the ban on weapons) were keenly resented as a restriction on liberty and tradition. Nor had the benefits of Romanization yet been given enough time to make themselves felt. In fact, where the amenities of Roman culture were being constructed, the locals in the area had to pay for them and the amenities were themselves another source of resentment. Such benefits as currently existed fell largely to Roman colonists. Many of these had made themselves at home at Lyn Dunn, 'the fort by the lake', which marked the head of navigation on the Thames – the point at which seagoing ships could proceed no further upriver. The small trading town was renamed Londinium in AD 50 and was fast growing into the merchant capital of Britain. It formed the hub of the province's ever-expanding road network and was the site where supplies for the legions were offloaded, and such assets as Britain produced – tin, hunting dogs and slaves – were shipped back to the empire.

Other new towns were springing up in the conquered areas, but most settlers had made themselves at home in the lands around the new colony of Colchester. Here a temple to the Roman goddess Victoria now supplanted the shrines to the war-god Camul, after whom the city was formerly named. Many of the colonists were ex-soldiers who had little affection or respect for the people whom they had been fighting for decades. Tacitus (whom we can regard as a particularly reliable source for Britain as his father-in-law was later governor of the province) says that the ex-legionaries acted with brutal disregard for even those rights that the Britons were theoretically allowed.

The original lands on which the colonists were settled were the confiscated estates of the former king. But new settlers simply dispossessed local tribesmen from their farms and homes (sometimes enslaving the original occupants in the process). They were aided and abetted by serving soldiers who hoped for similar licence when their time came to retire.

To add to Britain's problems, the officials who should have been watching over the mood of the native people and the conduct of the settlers were themselves incompetent and venal. The problem stretched all the way back to Rome.

The emperor Nero was not only uninterested in provincial governance, he was also spectacularly bad at it. His utter inability to manage the finances of the empire had put the state into the red. Attempts to balance the budget took the triple form of debasing the coinage, squeezing more from the upper classes and increasing taxes in the provinces. Rome was waging war at either side of the empire, with difficult and expensive campaigns being fought simultaneously by Corbulo in Armenia and Paulinus in Britain. Despite this, Nero's subordinates mimicked his lavish extravagance, his disregard for subject peoples and his equal disregard of the need to balance the books. Nero's misgovernment was felt throughout the empire, but particularly in the west, as the hellenophile emperor gave some largesse to the Greeks of Achaea and Asia Minor. In Britain the problem was particularly acute as the local aristocracies were generally neither pro-Roman in inclination nor outlook and deeply unwilling to give Rome the benefit of the doubt.

A major part of Romanizing the empire lay in capturing the hearts and minds of the local elites. It was these whom the Romans tried to convert from tribal leaders to local magistrates by showing how Roman rule could benefit them personally. Kings and chiefs were courted with offices and titles, which reassured them that their position was secure within the new world order. Some Britons, such as King Prasutagus of the Iceni, readily understood this and adapted to the new situation, but by and large Britain's local leaders remained unconvinced.

Neither Nero's imperial procurator, based in London and intent only on maximizing revenue from the province, nor Paulinus, who remained focused on the military situation in the west, made any attempt to remedy this. Rome did have officials of ability and goodwill in the province. Certainly, if we are to judge from his later conduct, Petellius Cerialis would have attempted good relations with the local population (and very intimate relations with the female portion). But at this time he and those like him were both too junior and too few to alter the course of events.

Then, at the end of AD 59, while the political situation in Britain trembled in the balance, Paulinus withdrew a large part of the army of occupation out of the conquered lands to reinforce his campaign in the west.

Mona One theory explaining this highly injudicious move is that Paulinus was eager for military glory. He saw himself as a rival to Corbulo, who was distinguishing himself in the wars against Parthia. Paulinus wanted a decisive and therefore glorious campaign. A decisive campaign needed more troops. Another possibility is that Nero had ordered his general in no uncertain terms to get on with the British campaign and wrap up the conquest as soon as possible. Indeed, a combination of both these factors may have been at work. In any case, Roman Britain was left with auxiliary troops in local garrisons, supplemented by detachments of Roman legionaries. Many of these legionary detachments were from IX Hispana. Thus the soldiers of Petellius Cerialis were dispersed in bases across the north and east of Roman Britannia. Effectively, Rome no longer had a legion in the eastern part of the island, but relied upon scattered garrisons.

Paulinus had concentrated XX Valeria and XIV Gemina on a particular objective – the island of Mona (known today as Anglesey). This island was separated from the mainland by a shallow channel. It served the Britons as a place of refuge where tribesmen displaced by the advancing legions rallied, rested and resumed the fight. The isle was also the centre of Britain's Druidic cult, and this alone made it worthy of attack in the eyes of the Romans, who vigorously extirpated this religion wherever they found it. This was an exception to the usually tolerant Roman approach to religion, but the Romans believed that Druids sacrificed captured soldiers and divined the future in their entrails.[12]

With their customary industriousness the legionaries built themselves a fleet of flat-bottomed boats and prepared to cross the strait between Mona and the mainland. It is probable that the Batavian auxiliaries were present, as some cavalry forded the straits Batavian style, swimming by the sides of their horses. Tacitus has painted a dramatic picture of the Britons waiting to meet the attackers. 'A mass of men and weapons, among whom moved women in robes of deathly black, like the Furies with wild hair, brandishing their torches, while druids stood in a circle, lifting their hands upwards to call down curses on our men, who were dumbstruck by the extraordinary spectacle.'[13]

But it proved impossible to keep the hard-headed legionaries overawed for long. In due course they took the island with their usual dispatch and rapidly brought the few survivors of their initial onslaught to terms. But even as the Romans set about the task of lopping down the sacred Druidic groves, word reached them that the imprecations of the Druids had not been in vain. A storm had broken in the east that threatened to sweep the Romans from Britain altogether.

Boudicca

Rebellion breaks out   The storm that broke in AD 60 had been gathering for some time.[14] That it was finally unleashed by the insensitive arrogance of Roman officials was no surprise. However, few Romans expected that an uprising would begin with the Iceni.

Apart from the short contretemps when the Romans forcibly removed their weapons, the Iceni had been a model tribe for the Romanization process. Prasutagus and his wife Boudicca had gone a long way towards adopting Roman ways. Relations with the Romans were polite, if not friendly. If the site found at Thetford in 1981 is, as supposed, the royal residence, then King Prasutagus was already building along Roman lines.

When Prasutagus died, his will made Nero co-inheritor of his estate, along with Prasutagus' two daughters. This was not an unusual arrangement. Probably the king intended to give the Roman authorities a financial incentive to accept his will and succession plans. However, there can be no doubt that Nero was intended to inherit a share of the king's personal estate and not the kingdom itself.

Matters relating to imperial estates and the emperor's personal financial affairs in each Roman province were dealt with by the imperial procurator stationed there. In Britain this was a man called Decianus Catus. He and his retainers came to the Iceni to collect the emperor's share of Prasutagus' estate. They arrived at the capital of a tribe of cautiously friendly allies. They departed leaving behind a ravening horde of murderously hostile enemies.

This transformation was achieved by a combination of greed, depravity and plain stupidity unequalled in the history of civil administration. Rome was militarily at full stretch in Britain. The majority of the army was engaged in fighting far away to the west. The last thing the Romans needed was trouble in the east. Yet Decianus proceeded to loot and plunder the home and possessions of the late Prasutagus as though Nero had inherited the lot. Then, with no legal justification at all, he and his retainers went on to pillage the houses and lands of other Iceni noblemen. It was as if the legions had just conquered the tribe. Certainly Decianus and friends acted as though the entire army was still around to enforce peace afterward.

In fact, even the legions would have found it hard to control the Iceni once Decianus was through. At some point in looting the royal palace, the Romans decided to rape the king's young daughters. This was more than even sexual violation, because it rendered the girls unmarriageable. Either unthinkingly or with malice aforethought, Decianus had destroyed the royal line. When Boudicca forcibly objected to this treatment of her home and family she was tied up and flogged.

The conduct and attitude of Paulinus and signals he had received from officials at Nero's imperial court may have encouraged Decianus to believe that he could get away with his outrageous behaviour. But why he thought that the Iceni would take it lying down is forever a mystery. It is possible that Decianus had underestimated the role of the formidable Boudicca in the government of the Iceni. Modern scholars have noted the similarity of her name with that of the Celtic goddess Boudiga. It is very probable that Boudicca was a priestess of high standing. It is even possible that the Romans got her name wrong, and Boudicca was actually the priestess's formal title. It is also possible that Decianus acted as he did with the intention of breaking the spirit of the tribal leadership. After his visit, the Iceni armed themselves to the teeth with such speed that it is clear that at best the rule on not having weapons had been allowed to lapse. At worst the rapid rearmament suggests that a rebellion was already contemplated and, knowing this, Decianus imagined that his show of force would subdue the Iceni.

In either case Decianus made a misjudgement of epic proportions. The Iceni were far from cowed. Nor had the death of Prasutagus left them leaderless. Boudicca was ready, very willing, and extremely able to take over. She immediately mustered the Iceni into an army. As word of the atrocity at the palace spread, outraged tribesmen promptly massacred every Roman or pro-Roman living on their lands. Then they turned south towards Colchester.

Colchester Mere decades ago the tribesmen of the Trinovantes in the area would have met an invading Iceni army with one of their own. That was before their experience of Roman rule. Now the impromptu army with the Trinovantes met the Iceni, welcomed the invaders with open arms and enthusiastically joined them in butchering every Roman they could find. The settlers paid the price of their arrogance and greed, for few Britons were prepared to defend, shelter or even warn them of the approaching onslaught.

By some reports the situation in Britain was made even worse by one of Nero's closest advisors, the philosopher Seneca. It would appear that Seneca had been practising a form of extortion common among senators in the last days of the Roman republic. He would force provincial dignitaries to accept a loan. Then he would not accept repayment until he had extracted compound interest at exorbitant rates, which vastly increased the original sum. This was what Boudicca probably meant when she said 'It would almost have been better if they had enslaved us immediately, instead of forcing us to ransom ourselves from slavery every year.'[15]

Seneca, like many of Nero's other courtiers, was feeling the pinch of subsidizing his master's extravagant lifestyle. He needed his loans (plus interest) repaid in full, no matter what the cost to the tribesmen who had to foot the bill. If these exactions by Seneca did help to provoke the British revolt, this may be one reason why relations between Nero and his senior advisor cooled rapidly after news of the uprising reached Rome.

In Britain, Nemesis descended upon Colchester. The settlers reacted with very un-Roman fear, uncertainty and doubt. No attempt was made to evacuate non-combatants. Perhaps this was because all the information that the settlers had to go on were the contradictory and (deliberately) misleading reports of the local tribesmen. These same tribesmen probably arranged the series of foreboding 'omens' that afflicted the colony, such as the unexpected collapse of the Roman statue of Victory.

The town had ramparts from before the Roman occupation. These had been torn down in AD 49, but settlers with legionary training could have at least partly restored them within days – had they the will. As it was, their desultory attempts to construct fortifications were sabotaged by the native people.

Messengers asked Decianus for information and assistance. In response the procurator sent back 200 lightly armed men. Given the size of the army Boudicca had now mustered, such a force did not even qualify as pathetic. When the massive wave of tens of thousands of British tribesmen hit the city, these 'reinforcements' simply did not count at all.

Some ex-legionaries made a stand in the Temple of Claudius. This temple was the centre of the imperial cult in Britain, the most hated symbol of Roman overlordship in a city the Britons heartily loathed anyway. The Romans in Britain had habitually appointed local tribal aristocrats as priests of the imperial cult and forced these conscripts to spend their fortunes performing their duties. Because of the funds unwillingly lavished upon it, the temple was a solidly constructed building. There the survivors tried to hold out until help arrived, and from there they had to watch the Britons massacre their friends, neighbours and families.

The Britons systematically flattened Colchester. They burned whatever would catch fire and demolished the rest to the foundations. Even the tombstones in the graveyard were knocked flat. (One tombstone that appears to have received this treatment was that of Marcus Favonius Facilis, a centurion of XX Valeria. Ironically, because it was pushed flat, the stone was protected by the earth. Thus the attempt to destroy his memorial resulted in it surviving through the centuries intact to the present day.)

Petellius Cerialis to the 'rescue' With a huge uprising in progress and Paulinus so far away that he had barely received the news, command of the military situation fell to the most senior man on the spot. That was the commander of IX Hispana, Petellius Cerialis. If the beleaguered defenders of the temple in Colchester could be saved, Cerialis was the only man who could do it. His IX Hispana was the last organized military force in the east of the province. Yet even this legion was so thinly spread that it would take days to bring it all together. And the situation was deteriorating by the hour.

Petellius Cerialis did what he could. He mustered a scratch force of legionaries, supplemented with whatever auxiliaries he could lay hands on. His ad hoc little army had probably somewhat more cavalry than normal, because horsemen could be gathered from a larger catchment area.

With hindsight, one knows that the defenders of Colchester were already doomed. The most sensible thing Cerialis could have done would be to head post-haste for London. There, he would have to hope that II Augusta had already received word of the disaster and was marching from its base near Exeter in the west. With his scratch force from IX Hispana, and with reinforcements from II Augusta and the rest of IX Hispana as they arrived, perhaps Cerialis could defend London until Paulinus got there. This sensible plan was never put into operation. Instead Cerialis decided to confront Boudicca's army head-on.

Cerialis could not have known he was too late to save Colchester. The last defenders in the temple had already been overwhelmed and slaughtered after a desperate defence lasting two days. Instead of meeting the Iceni near the colony, Cerialis and his scratch force ran into a very large British army somewhere on the way to London.

It should not be thought that these Britons were an inchoate mass of unorganized peasantry. As Plautius had discovered twenty years previously at the Medway, the Britons were more sophisticated than that. They were well able to organize large numbers of tribesmen into a force disciplined enough to give legionaries problems in a stand-up fight. Theirs was a warrior culture. Every adult male was expected to fight for the tribe, and training for warfare was a routine part of adolescence. Even with the wrenching social changes under Roman occupation it is as unlikely that military training was dropped from the curriculum as it was that all weaponry had been meekly handed over to the Romans (rather than being stashed under eaves and in barns for exactly an eventuality such as this).

We are explicitly told that the British rebels mustered a substantial corps of their traditional war chariots.[16] If these could escape confiscation by the Romans, personal weaponry and armour certainly could as well. That the British army retained its cohesion instead of scattering over the countryside was itself enough to tell Cerialis that this was no random mob. His opponents were well armed, well trained and well organized. Thanks to the loot from their rampage to date, the Britons were currently well supplied too. It goes without saying that they were very highly motivated.

The numbers on either side in the fight that ensued are sketchy to say the least. At the best estimate Petellius Cerialis had between 2,500 and 4,000 men. There were probably well over 50,000 Britons. This British army was huge because it comprised the full fighting strength of the Iceni and the Trinovantes (and several opportunistic minor tribes who were along for the pillage). Also, Boudicca forcibly conscripted any Britons her army met en route. Those who refused were cut down on the spot. In normal warfare some farmers stayed behind to tend the fields so that the warriors had food for the coming winter. This year the grain warehouses in London and the legion supplies would have to tide the British over the winter. Boudicca was literally committing her people to live free or die of starvation.

Massively outnumbered, the Romans under Cerialis never stood a chance. The young legate saw his troops collapse under the sheer weight of the enemy. The only military decision to make was whether the commander should die with his infantry, or retreat with his surviving cavalry. Cerialis fled.

He made his way around the British army and through rebel-held territory to his camp at Longthorpe near modern Peterborough. Here archaeologists have found signs of hasty attempts to strengthen the fortifications. The camp was designed to hold 2,400 men. Now, fresh defences were hastily built to allow the fort to be held by a much smaller number.[17] Tacitus tells us that Cerialis was 'saved' by these fortifications. This suggests that the Britons tested them, but we do not know how severely.

Being knocked to the sidelines did not mean that Cerialis had no further part to play. Cartimandua of the Brigante was under severe pressure to join Boudicca's revolt. Cerialis and his diminished garrison needed to prove that

Rome was still diplomatically and militarily active on her borders. Cerialis had still the remaining infantry of IX Hispana, which, being based elsewhere (mostly at Lincoln), had not joined in his Canute-like attempt to stem the British tide. Cerialis had also saved much of his cavalry and would have had some auxiliaries and whatever recruits he could force into armour. His was a small force, but a significant one.

London Paulinus arrived in London after a series of forced marches through unfriendly countryside. He had with him XIV Gemina and some local auxiliaries. He probably expected to find II Augusta already there, waiting along with much of Cerialis' IX Hispana. Instead he discovered that IX Hispana had been defeated and the well-mauled remnants were now holed up near Peterborough. Even worse, II Augusta was nowhere to be found. The legion was under the command of the Prefect of the Camp, a man called Poenus Postumus. Since the camp prefect was in charge, something nasty must have happened to the legate. Perhaps in consequence Postumus was afraid to venture from his base into what was now thoroughly hostile terrain. Thus while Cerialis had engaged the enemy precipitately, Postumus had not budged from barracks at all.

(One of the officers of II Augusta was Gnaeus Julius Agricola, future father-in-law of the historian Tacitus. He was currently serving on Paulinus' staff as a military tribune. As a result, he escaped the disgrace that fell on his legion and went on to play a considerable part in the story to follow.)

It is difficult to divine what Postumus was thinking. He may have imagined that II Augusta was doing the best service possible holding down the west while the east was in flames. If so, he was wrong. Given the massive scale of the rebellion, most of the island was lost. If Boudicca triumphed in the east, the later defeat of a single legion in the west was inevitable. As Paulinus well knew, the Romans had to form a single army to basically attempt the reconquest of everything north and west of Kent.

Without the support of II Augusta and IX Hispana, Paulinus could not even hold London. He made the painful decision that the city must be abandoned to its fate. XIV Gemina withdrew from London to meet with Legio XX Valeria, which was hurrying east to join it. Paulinus took as many able-bodied men as could keep up with the Roman column of march. The women and children, the aged, the ill and those who refused to abandon home and family were left to the mercy of Boudicca. And Boudicca was feeling far from merciful. As Tacitus remarked, her army 'were set on retribution with scaffolds, fire and crucifixions'.[18]

London suffered the same fate as Colchester. The Britons flattened everything they could and then burned it. So intense was the fire that even today there remains under the modern city a stratum of clay baked solid by that heat. The population was disposed of along with the buildings, but with sadistic inventiveness.

> Those who were taken captive by the Britons were subjected to every known form of outrage. The worst and most bestial atrocity committed by their captors was the following. They hung up naked the noblest and most distinguished women and then cut off their breasts and sewed them to their mouths, in order to make the victims appear to be eating them; afterward they impaled the women on sharp skewers run lengthwise through the entire body. All this they did to the accompaniment of sacrifices, banquets, and wanton behaviour, not only in all their other sacred places, but particularly in the grove of Andate. This was their name for Victory, and they regarded her with most exceptional reverence.[19]

As Tacitus remarks, this was not 'the usual commerce of war'. The intense hatred of the Britons testifies to a fundamental failure of government. Paulinus and his predecessors had concentrated so completely on the military situation that they had totally ignored the people already under their power. The people of London and eastern Britain paid the price. An estimated 70,000 Romans and their supporters lost their lives and the Romanization of the province was set back a generation. In terms of money and manpower the cost was immense. Little wonder that Catus Decianus did not stay to observe the havoc he had wrought. He jumped ship for the continent as soon as he was able. From there he has been forgotten by history. No doubt Nero's minions were not so remiss and gave Decianus their full attention for the (undoubtedly brief) remainder of his life.

For Petellius Cerialis, the important question was what Boudicca intended to do next. Apart from those elements of IX Hispana he had managed to concentrate at his base at Longthorpe, some remained cut off in isolated garrisons. Others were probably massacred before they even knew that the Iceni were in revolt. Cartimandua of the Brigante had come under pressure from her nobles. With little alternative in the matter, she had reluctantly allied herself with the rebel cause. Therefore a retreat to Brigantine territory was out of the question. If Boudicca turned north, Cerialis and the remnants of IX Hispana were doomed.

Instead of attacking IX Hispana or following up the retreat of Paulinus, Boudicca turned her attention to the city of Verulamium (modern St Albans). Boudicca was apparently intent on destroying not just the Roman military presence but all signs of Roman occupation on the island. So Verulamium was obliterated as London and Colchester had been. In human terms this was a ghastly tragedy. From a purely military perspective it was something of a relief. With Boudicca and her Britons busy elsewhere, Paulinus had time to consolidate his forces. Auxiliary and detached units rejoined the main army. Gaps in the ranks were filled with whatever discharged soldiers were able to locate the Roman standards.

By the time Boudicca's forces left the smoking remains of their latest conquest, Paulinus was ready ... or at least as ready as he ever would be, given that the wretched II Augusta remained unmoving in its camp, obdurately unresponsive to what one imagines were by now incandescently furious instructions from its general.

Showdown The Romans estimated that they were facing some 230,000 rebels. This number seems implausibly high, even with women and other non-combatants included. But even assuming that the figure was exaggerated by fifty percent, the Britons had sufficient men under arms to comfortably outnumber the eleven thousand or so men of the Roman force by at least ten to one.

The Britons had slaked their immediate desire for vengeance on the unfortunate towns in their path. Now they turned their attention on the Roman army. Paulinus too was ready for a decisive confrontation. Given his acute mismanagement of the civil situation, he needed a resounding victory before his tenure as governor in Britain could be regarded as less than disastrous. And if Boudicca was not stopped soon, he would have only deserted fields and smoking wreckage to govern in any case.

Britain had long been a centre of religion for what has been loosely known as the 'Celtic' people. The influence of British druids had been felt as far afield as Gaul and north Italy, which was one reason why the Romans had invaded Britain in the first place, and why Paulinus had been attacking Anglesey when the revolt broke out. So now, in the absence of anything resembling a British capital at which to aim his army, it appears that Paulinus headed for British religious sites in the Midlands (possibly in the area of Mancetter, or Towcester on Watling Street). By threatening these sites, Paulinus wanted to provoke Boudicca into giving battle.

Boudicca needed little encouragement. Britain would not be liberated until the Roman army of occupation was removed, so Paulinus was probably next on the warrior queen's agenda in any case. She would have been intent on wiping out his army (and feeding her men on the army's stores for the winter) before the arrival of Roman reinforcements from the continent in spring. With both sides intent on a decisive battle, events moved rapidly to a climax.

Paulinus selected his battle ground with care. The fact that he was able to choose where to make his stand shows that far from forcing the Britons to give battle, he was confident that once provoked by his arrival near their sacred sites, the Britons would come to him. For the legions this was very definitely a victory-or-death scenario. Paulinus positioned his men in three divisions with their backs to a densely wooded forest. That way he could not be surrounded – and if defeated his men had nowhere to run to anyway. The actual battleground was a wide, grassy meadow sloping up towards the woods. The meadow could only be approached through a relatively narrow defile. This meant that it would be hard also for the Britons to escape if they lost the battle. Paulinus knew that the legions would have to soak up at least one British charge. His chosen battlefield therefore allowed the legions to be deployed in depth across a narrow frontage.

The thinking behind this was based on a fundamental principle of warfare that the Romans had first established in battles with the Gauls. Basically it was that the Romans had local superiority no matter what numbers opposed them. The legionaries fought shoulder to shoulder with swords held underarm and used for primarily for stabbing. British swordsmen were accustomed to slash at their opponents (indeed some Gallic blades have been recovered which did not even have a point). A Briton needed five feet of the battle line to himself or he risked decapitation from the warrior fighting beside him. The Romans could get by with three feet.

Thus every fifteen feet of the line of battle saw three Britons fighting five Romans. The surplus British warriors would normally flow around the flanks of the Roman force. Paulinus' choice of a battleground made this impossible. The other option for those Britons who were not fighting was simply to wait their turn. But even here, the well-drilled Romans had the advantage. Given the slightest lull in the fighting a tired or wounded legionary could turn and drop out of the fighting line to be replaced by someone from the rear ranks. The British equivalent was based on stepping over the corpse of a newly slain front-rank warrior, and fighting to the death. Paulinus' choice of battlefield meant that, despite their considerable advantage in manpower, the Britons were now effectively outnumbered.

The battle   Cassius Dio and Tacitus have each supplied different versions of Paulinus' pre-battle speech. Cassius Dio says that Paulinus gave a different address to each of his three divisions. In essence his opening comments were that favourite old chestnut of outnumbered commanders. Victory would be all the more glorious for being won by so few. There was a disparaging series of remarks along the lines of 'they are just Britons': the carrot – licence to plunder; the stick – a graphic description of the consequences of failure at the hands of Boudicca's ungentle warriors.

> You've heard about the atrocities these accursed race have inflicted on our people – in fact some of you have even seen them for yourselves. It's up to you whether you let the same thing happen to you, and let Rome be driven completely out of Britain … we'd do better to die fighting bravely than be captured and impaled, to see our own intestines being cut from our bodies, be skewered on red-hot spits, or die in boiling water. We have to conquer or die right where we stand.[20]

The British army arrived slowly, gradually filling up the lower portion of the meadow. Boudicca's forces were arrayed mostly in tribal groups. Each shouted their own war cries or sang their particular battle songs. Boudicca herself rode in a chariot. As depicted in the famous modern statue that stands beside the Thames, Boudicca was armed with a spear and accompanied by her two daughters.[21] She was a tall woman with long, tawny hair and the traditional torque of a tribal leader about her neck. As might be expected, she roused her men with a list of Roman injustices and abuse. In an earlier speech Dio also has her fearing for future generations of her people as slaves of the oppressor:

> To be frank, we have brought this on ourselves. We let them establish a foothold on our island and did not throw them off at once as our forefathers did with their famous Julius Caesar … so now everything we have is despised and trampled underfoot by men who care for nothing but profits. Even at this late stage we can do what we should have done before, and remember to do our duty for freedom. We are all peoples of this island, and call ourselves by a common name. We should consider ourselves as family, and remember that we are fighting for our children. If we, who were born and raised as free people, forget what we are fighting for, what will our children remember when they are born as slaves? I don't need to make you hate things as they are now. You hate

them already. I don't need to make you fear the future, you fear it already ... But you don't need to fear the Romans. They are neither as numerous or as brave as we.[22]

Dio then launches into a lively description of the battle. From this and the account of Tacitus, a rough idea of events can be reconstructed. The initial engagements were with the British chariots, which Paulinus kept away with archers. He had some success, since the charioteers were unarmoured, though these repaid their suffering in kind when they got in among the archers. The Romans supported their missile troops with auxiliaries and cavalry, which the Britons countered with foot and horse of their own. The fighting grew steadily more intense as the mass of the British army moved uphill. The Roman legions remained silent until the Britons made their charge. Only when their opponents were mere yards away did they unleash their pila and give their own battle cry. The pilum (plural: pila) was a heavy spear with the tip on a long, thin iron shank. This gave the weapon tremendous penetrative power, which mowed down the British front ranks.

Tacitus tells us that the Romans then counter-charged in wedge formation – a risky tactic that increased the likelihood that the legionaries would be enveloped on their flanks. The intent was clearly to break the momentum of the British attack and get their army moving backwards. Paulinus had seen that the British had parked wagons containing their possessions and families at the bottom of the slope. This solid wall of stationary traffic meant that the British army could not give way at the rear. So the men were forced against the wagons, and from there they had nowhere to go. Warriors who needed five feet of frontage to wield their swords were jammed shoulder to shoulder so that they could hardly move at all. And all the while the armoured mass of legionaries moved inexorably forward, making deadly use of their short stabbing swords.

Attempts by the Britons to break out and find some fighting room were swiftly contained by auxiliaries and cavalry, detailed for that express purpose. As the battle wore on, all that stopped the British from breaking was that it was physically impossible to run. Boudicca's army was trapped and the battle became a massacre. An estimated 80,000 Britons died on the battlefield. Not all were warriors, for the Romans had civilian casualties to avenge. The legions did not stop when they cut down the warriors and reached the wagons. They killed the women, the children, and even the oxen. Paulinus suffered 400 dead, and the same again in wounded. Boudicca's rebels were destroyed as a fighting force.

Aftermath Suetonius Paulinus in Britain had starkly revealed one of the major challenges that faced a Roman with a provincial command. He had not only to be a general, but also a governor. Quinctilius Varus was an adequate governor but a failure as a general. Paulinus was an excellent general. He responded quickly and decisively to the crisis of the rebellion. When he discovered that II Augusta and IX Hispana were not coming to reinforce him, he did not flinch from the painful decision to abandon London to its fate.

However, Suetonius Paulinus the governor was a disaster. It is true that he probably had orders from Nero to finish the war in the west as speedily as possible, and Nero was not tolerant of failure. Yet even his contemporaries suspected that Paulinus was driven as much by rivalry as obedience to his orders. Domitius Corbulo had beaten the Parthians in Armenia, so Paulinus became intent on conquering the remainder of Britain. That a substantial portion of the island had already been conquered and required governing was ignored.

It is no co-incidence that the rebellion occurred just as the vast majority of Rome's military force was on the other side of the island. The scale and promptness of the revolt suggests some preparation on the part of the Iceni. But even if Decianus Catus had precipitated a storm already brewing, this does not let Paulinus off the hook.

Was Paulinus unaware of the dangerous level of festering discontent among his subject peoples? If so, then he was incompetent. If he was aware of the problem yet still stripped the east of troops (and then led them as far from the potential hotspot as was humanly possible for him to go) then he was negligent. If he had a strong suspicion of what would happen whilst he was away and wanted the glory of crushing a revolt, then he is despicable. None of these possibilities allow that Paulinus had any understanding of, or sympathy for, the peoples he was supposed to govern.

If this was the case before the rebellion, the general's lack of empathy becomes even clearer in the aftermath. It proved impossible to bring the remnants of Boudicca's force to battle once more, so the vindictive legions concentrated on wiping the Iceni from the face of the earth. The Romans did not withdraw to winter quarters but remained '*sub-pellibus*' – under canvas – in the field.

In spring, as soon as was practical, reinforcements arrived from Rome. Two thousand legionaries, eight cohorts of auxiliaries and a thousand cavalry arrived, mostly destined to refill the ranks of IX Hispana. Presumably the same ships brought a replacement legate for II Augusta. This legion also needed a new Prefect of the Camp. The dilatory Postumus had promptly fallen on his sword at the news that Paulinus had triumphed and was about to deliver on his earlier threats.

Through the summer Paulinus continued to persecute with 'fire and sword' any tribes he considered hostile. His campaign of vengeance was not just against the Iceni, but reached as far afield as Somerset. Destroyed buildings and skeletons once believed to be the work of Vespasian are now tentatively believed to be partly the work of Vespasian's son Titus, now an officer under the command of Paulinus.[23] Boudicca was long gone from the scene, having poisoned herself (by one account) or died from illness (according to another). The Iceni made sure that the Romans never found her body.

Replacement The scorched-earth policy of Paulinus brought him into direct conflict with the imperial procurator who had replaced the unlamented Decianus Catus. This man probably felt little sympathy for the people who had killed tens of thousands of Romans. But as procurator, it was his job to ensure that Britain became, if not profitable, at least not a massive drain on the finances of an empire already strained by Nero's extravagances and the war in the east. And Britain could not generate much income whilst the benighted peoples of the island fought a guerrilla war from the forests against Romans who demolished whatever buildings and crops they could find. It will be remembered that the Britons had gone so enthusiastically to war that none remained to do the spring sowing, so the east was devastated as comprehensively by famine as by the legions.

Civil government had to be restored if for no other reason than civilians paid taxes and Rome needed the money. Yet Paulinus would offer no concessions to his defeated enemy. He ignored the pleas of the new procurator and the argument that peace would return to the province if he would only take his boot from the neck of a conquered foe. When his appeal to Paulinus failed, the procurator appealed to Rome.

Nero sent his freedman Polyclitus, an emissary from his own household. Polyclitus had not only to mediate between squabbling officials but also to bring the Britons to terms. This proved difficult. The Britons could no more believe that Paulinus' fate could be decided by an ex-slave than they could accept that they were supposed to treat such a man as their superior. In keeping with the luxury and expense of the imperial court, Polyclitus had arrived with a huge train of retainers. His sybaritic lifestyle earned him scorn rather than respect.

Neither procurator nor governor would budge. Reconciliation was impossible. Therefore, as soon as the loss of some ships off the British coast gave a pretext for Rome to demand the resignation of Paulinus, the general was ordered to yield command to Petronius Turpilianus, an ex-consul ordered to Britain for just that purpose.

The determinedly non-aggressive approach of the latter – he neither disturbed the enemy nor was challenged by them – was proof that Paulinus may have won the war, but he had been comprehensively defeated on the diplomatic front. The replacement procurator and governor were gradually successful in restoring peace to their battered province. The practice of forcing British nobles to pay for their own Romanization was scaled back and replaced by a charm offensive. Though the literary sources are silent (as is their wont in periods of peace and tranquillity), the archaeological evidence shows reconstruction and renewal underway in the cities and the countryside.

Paulinus returned to Rome. His success in keeping Britain a Roman province was considered to have outweighed his failures in other departments. In AD 66 he was awarded a consulship for his achievement. There was glory too for the legions that had won Paulinus his decisive battle. XX Valeria gained for itself the epithet 'Victrix' and XIV Gemina was henceforth to be called by the added accolade of 'Martia Victrix'. Undoubtedly the wretched II Augusta also acquired a few choice epithets, though neither formal nor complimentary.

It is probable that around this time the legate of IX Hispana also returned to Rome. Official propaganda needed heroes whose glory could partly mask what had been an expensive and unnecessary debacle. It also needed scapegoats, and the two obvious choices were unavailable. Postumus of II Augusta was dead. If Decianus Catus was not, he probably wished he were. This left Petellius Cerialis.

Given the confusion and the paucity of information available, Petellius Cerialis could argue that he had acted for the best. While the fate of Colchester was unknown, attempting to save any survivors was imperative. Prompt intervention might have nipped the rebellion in the bud, and Cerialis had no way of knowing how far things had deteriorated. He misjudged, yet he could hardly have done otherwise. Had he not tried to relieve Colchester, it might have turned out that his inaction had allowed a feeble rebel force a huge boost at the expense of a plundered Roman colony. Given the information at his disposal, Cerialis had chosen to take a risk and act decisively and offensively.

Arguably, he was more culpable in the hours immediately before the engagement. Scouting to discover the size and temperament of an enemy force was now standard practice. Either Cerialis had not done this properly, or he had failed to react appropriately to the information. (Or once he knew what he faced, Cerialis had simply been unable to get his small army out of the way in time.)

In his initial decision to take the army towards Colchester instead of London, Cerialis had to gamble that he had made the right choice, and in that he was unlucky. But unlucky generals were no more popular than incompetent ones. Rome was unforgiving in demanding success, and only success, from its commanders. Failure, even for very good reason, was hardly tolerated. As Augustus had demonstrated with Varus, a failed commander was on his own. Petellius Cerialis had been senior officer in an area where a major rebellion had broken out. He had failed to contain that rebellion. The defeat and decimation of his men had taken a whole legion out of play just when the defence of London needed every soldier it could get. Excuses, even good excuses, were irrelevant.

For much of the remainder of the decade, the career of Petellius Cerialis was under a shadow. He became an obscure figure who received neither civilian office nor military rank. Under other circumstances, Cerialis might have cursed his fate. In fact, fortune had been kind to him. In the years immediately preceding AD 68 few things were more valuable or healthier for an aristocratic Roman than a very low profile.

Part III

Civil War

Chapter 4

The Wilderness Years

The generation of generals between Agrippa and Petellius Cerialis was unusual in many ways, and one of these was that the commanders of this era were spared the unpleasant experience of fighting fellow Romans. This was certainly not the case in the last years of the republic, when Licinius Crassus was practically the only general of any standing who did not go to war with his fellow citizens. His contemporaries Sertorius and Pompey certainly did, as, notoriously, did Julius Caesar, and after him Mark Antony and Octavian.

Through all of the chaos of civil war, Rome's generals spent at least some time fighting foreign foes, but it was only after the restoration of law and order under Augustus that they were able to resume doing this on a full-time basis. Though the ructions of AD 68/69 were to be followed by almost a century of civic peace, thereafter until the end of the empire imperial generals were likely to spend at least part of their career either suppressing rebellious Romans or leading them.

Certainly in the years immediately before Nero's overthrow, the question was not whether his subjects would rebel against his increasingly erratic and tyrannical rule, but when that rebellion would occur. Petellius Cerialis had returned to Rome after seeing a major revolt in his own province. One wonders what he made of the febrile atmosphere during the last years of Nero's Rome.

NERO – A THOROUGHLY BAD EMPEROR

> Large wooden empty wine vats were lowered into the middle of the lake. Planks were laid across these, and taverns and [prostitutes'] booths were built around the edge. Nero, Tigellinus and their fellow-banqueters occupied the centre. They feasted lying on purple rugs and soft cushions, while the celebrations went on in the taverns. They would also enter the booths and have uninhibited sex with the women there. These included the most beautiful and distinguished women in the city ... not

just commoners, but girls and women of the very noblest families. Every man could help himself to whomever he wanted, for the women were not allowed to refuse anyone ... here a slave would debauch his mistress in front of his master or a gladiator would take a girl of noble family while her father watched ... Many men died in the pushing, drunken brawling and general uproar, and many women, too, as some were suffocated and others were carried off.[1]

The modern idea is that the Romans were enthusiastic orgiasts (an image largely based on graphic descriptions of the misdeeds of Nero such as that above). But in fact the Romans were generally strait-laced about sex to the point of prudishness.[2] Therefore the debaucheries of Nero were as shocking to contemporary Romans as such reports would be today of similar misconduct by a modern head of state.

There was, however, method in Nero's madness. The emperor well knew that much of the Roman senatorial class loathed him with a passion. He was also well aware that if it came to a rebellion against his rule, this rebellion would be led by a senator.

Nero's problem was that the Roman Empire could not function without its senatorial class. It provided the generals, administrators, governors and legislators which the state absolutely needed. So Nero could not do without his senators, although he would greatly prefer that they did not lead rebellions against him. So he took every chance to humiliate them, destroy their credibility and diminish the respect with which they were regarded by the people and the army. This was partly what events such as the orgy by the lake were intended to do. Partly, though, these orgies were simply because Nero was a narcissistic degenerate who put his own love of debauchery above common sense and decency.

Nero was secure against rebellion by a member of the imperial family, basically because he had killed the lot. Even among the crowd of perverts and occasional lunatics who disgraced the imperial purple over the centuries, Nero stands out as the man who ordered the killing of his own mother, his step-brother and one of his wives. (He allegedly kicked another wife to death while she was pregnant.) Other relatives, however distant, were also extirpated, so that when Nero died, the Julio-Claudian line died with him.[3]

Nero was determined to extinguish his own clan because its members shared his only claim to rule the empire. This claim was based on the fact that Nero was a descendant of Rome's first emperor, Augustus, and even that claim was mainly through the maternal line. Nero was adopted as Claudius' son and historians have long been divided as to whether conspiracy to kill his adopted father should be added to Nero's crimes. Claudius undoubtedly died at a convenient time for Nero to take power. But it remains uncertain whether the mushrooms which killed him were poisoned or naturally poisonous.

The early years of Nero's reign were rather promising. Yet even in those early years, Nero displayed an inappropriate love of rowdy behaviour. His pastimes such as acting and chariot-racing were unbecoming of the dignity of an emperor. When his politically astute mother Agrippina attempted to control her wayward son, she became estranged from Nero, who ordered her execution.[4]

Even before Boudicca's revolt Nero had begun his feud with Rome's senate. Knowing that any senior senator was a potential future emperor, he 'feared men of high repute' (says Plutarch). Consequently, he eliminated anyone that he saw as a threat, ignoring Seneca's earlier advice that 'no matter how many you kill, you can't kill your successor'.

The Gathering Storm
While Nero was tireless in his efforts to destroy the dignity of Rome's senatorial class, he either did not know or did not care about the effect this was having on his own public image. The general public may have sneered at senators as they performed in imperial orgies or as gladiators in the arena, but they felt equal or greater contempt for the man who organized the demeaning spectacles. Even worse, Nero's conduct alienated the army on which his security ultimately depended.

In AD 64, soon after Petellius Cerialis returned home, the modicum of public support which Nero enjoyed among the wider public suffered a major setback. A great fire enveloped and destroyed much of Rome. Nero was away in the city of Antium when the fire broke out, and he hurried back and played an active part in bringing the massive blaze under control. So far so good, but afterwards Nero was carried away by a vision of a new Rome rising from the ashes of the old. He embarked on unrealistic and ruinously expensive building projects. Despite massive public resentment, a considerable percentage of the city's area became a magnificent imperial palace called the 'Golden House'. It also became a byword for imperial profligacy – it was not as if Nero did not already have magnificent imperial properties which occupied almost the entire Palatine hill.

Taxes went up to pay for this and other building projects. As Tacitus (with some hyperbole) remarked, 'Italy was thoroughly exhausted by contributions of money, the provinces were ruined, as also the allied nations and the free states, as they were called. Even the gods fell victims to the plunder; for the temples in Rome were despoiled and the gold carried off.' Increased taxes were resented particularly bitterly in the province of Judea, where agricultural decline and guerrilla activity were already driving down the economy.

Nero's enemies propagated with relish a rumour that Nero had deliberately arranged the fire as a drastic form of urban clearance and thereafter used the conflagration as a backdrop whilst he declaimed epic verse on the fall of Troy. So pernicious was this allegation that even today the image of Nero 'fiddling whilst Rome burned' is firmly fixed in the public imagination.

Like all good character assassinations, a modicum of truth underlay the invention. Nero was very fond of giving public artistic performances, for all that he was a terrible singer; so bad, in fact, that some of those compelled to attend his performances allegedly faked their own deaths to get out of the theatre.

Vespasian was now in Nero's entourage. After his heroics in Britain, Vespasian's career had suffered from the enmity of Nero's mother Agrippina. (This was nothing personal – Agrippina disliked all favourites of Claudius' former freedman Narcissus.) Once Agrippina had been executed, Vespasian enjoyed a modestly successful governorship of the Roman province of Africa. Thereafter he had the privilege of accompanying Nero on that tour of Greece which featured the execution of Corbulo among its lowlights. Vespasian came perilously close to joining Corbulo in Hades when one of the emperor's stage performances sent him into a deep and dangerous sleep.

As it was, Vespasian suffered only expulsion from the imperial court, which was itself no bad thing, but it also left his career, and indeed his very survival, perilously in the balance. Some idea of how real was the danger threatening Vespasian after his failure to be enraptured by Nero's performance is shown by the execution of the philosopher Thrasea Paetus. He died after he ostentatiously failed to join other senators in praising the wonder that was the emperor's voice.

Danger to Vespasian translated into some degree of risk for his brother Sabinus and other members of his circle, including Petellius Cerialis. Just before his Greek expedition the emperor had shown this very clearly. Some senators were discovered plotting to kill Nero and replace him with one of their own. Naturally, the conspirators were killed. So were their friends. Relatives and dependants were hauled before courts (sometimes presided over by Nero himself) and generally sentenced to death. Nero's former advisor Seneca was among the victims, and his fall took with it the philosopher's nephew, the poet Lucan. A conspiracy in AD 66 led by a relative of Corbulo may have sealed the general's fate.

For Corbulo, however, the problem was not simply that he had a treasonous relative. Corbulo was a successful general, and that alone was dangerous. Nero had been appalled by the plotters' assumption that the army would be happy to see him dead. Indeed, one of the conspirators was a centurion. Nero personally asked this man why he had wanted to kill his emperor. The centurion curtly replied that this would be the best thing he could have done for Rome in all his long career.

Augustus and Tiberius had been generals. Tiberius had been a particularly good one. Caius Caligula had gone to Germany with the apparent intention of taking legions from there to invade Britain with himself at their head (he was foiled by bad weather). Claudius had made a particular effort to join the troops in Britain, however briefly. But Nero was a resolutely civilian emperor who made no attempt to help his soldiers identify with him. In fact, his hobby of singing and acting on stage was even more likely to disgust the military than the general population.

Nero's deep (and completely justified) suspicion that he was losing the loyalty of the army led directly to the execution of Corbulo. Corbulo had been a general with the authority and the soldiers to usurp an emperor rapidly running out of friends. But which generals could be trusted? Nero became murderously uneasy about anyone who commanded an army. Rufus and Proculus, commanders in Upper and Lower Germany respectively, were summoned to the imperial court and killed on their arrival.

But Nero had painted himself into a corner. If he could not trust his generals, who was to lead his armies? A capable general was a threat. An incapable general was likely to suffer defeat, which would further tarnish Nero's increasingly poor reputation.

Then Judea burst into violent rebellion. The Roman garrison in Jerusalem was massacred. Cestius Gallus hastened from Syria with a legion to restore order. Instead, Gallus lost his legion and almost his life in a Jewish attack in the pass of Beth-horon. Thereafter the rest of Judea joined the rebellion. Before Gallus could even begin the task of restoring Roman rule, he died. Perhaps this was a result of the stress of the previous year, atop the stress of wondering how Nero would take his disastrous defeat at Beth Huron.

Nero put Licinius Mucianus Crassus in command of Syria, but decided to give Judea to another general. He chose with care. He needed a man of undoubted military experience; competent, but incapable of generating a following in the senate. Someone, perhaps, of a provincial family whom the snobby senators despised because poverty had once forced him into trade as a dealer in second-hand mules. Someone 'of energy and enterprise who could without risk be entrusted with great power, because he was an obscure nobody', says the biographer Suetonius.[5] Someone, in fact, precisely like Flavius Vespasian. Vespasian was then living quietly in a small, out-of-the way Italian town, and undoubtedly thought that the arrival of imperial messengers meant that he was about to stop living altogether. Instead of a death sentence, the messages gave Vespasian command of an army and as much of the province of Judea as he could conquer.

Exit Nero, to No Applause
By now Nero had few supporters among the people, fewer in the army and almost none in the senate. Rome was rife with rumours of Nero's latest atrocities and of plots to dispose of him. After a long stay in Greece (Nero only returned in AD 68) the people of Rome were alienated from their emperor. There was a corn shortage in the capital, and Nero got the blame for that as well.

The people of Rome were riotously discontented. Yet the long-expected rebellion started not in Rome but in faraway Gaul. The instigator was Gaius Julius Vindex, a Roman senator from Aquitaine. There is nothing to suggest that Nero had done anything personal to Vindex. It was just that, like much of the Roman Empire, Vindex had simply had all the Nero he could take. Gaul was suffering from the same levels of taxation that had inflamed the Jewish revolt, but while the leaders of the Judean revolt had other grievances to work with, Vindex based his uprising purely on the financial suffering of the Gallic people – and the fact that Nero was a rotten emperor. The historian Cassius Dio puts these words in his mouth:

> He has pillaged the empire and murdered the cream of the senate. He despoiled and murdered his own mother. He does not even try to pretend that he is a worthy emperor. Others, it is true, also have committed murder, extortion and pillage, but words fail me when I try to describe what else he [Nero] has done. Believe me, my comrades and allies, I have personally seen this man – if 'man' is the right term for someone who gave his body in 'marriage' to [the imperial favourite] Sporus ... I've seen him singing, acting on stage as a mythological character ... should I call him Imperator, or Caesar, or Augustus? Never! Claudius and Augustus himself bore those titles which he abuses. This man is

Thyestes, or Oedipus, Alcmeon or Orestes or whatever character he is playing on stage at the moment, and he has surrendered his titles for these names. It's time that we stood up against him and saved ourselves, saved the Romans and freed the entire world![6]

Nero was not particularly disturbed by the attempted rebellion of an obscure senator, for all that many disaffected Gauls rallied to the man. The principal city in the area, Lugdunum, remained loyal, and the revolt might well have spluttered out. Nero's real problems began when Lucius Verginius Rufus, the current governor of Germany, arrived to deal with the situation.

Rufus met Vindex's Gauls near the town of Vesontio. The two leaders met in a conference. Talks failed, but the fact that Rufus felt there was anything to discuss is in itself interesting. In the event, Rufus' legionaries took matters into their own hands and opted for an impromptu military solution. They easily overpowered the rag-tag force of provincial rebels and killed them in large numbers. Vindex committed suicide. Thus it appeared that Nero's confident dismissal of the threat had been vindicated. At least it seemed so until considerably less reassuring tidings followed on the heels of this first report.

After crushing Vindex, the Rhineland soldiery of Rufus' legions repudiated Nero as emperor. They destroyed their images of Nero and proclaimed Rufus their *imperator*. As the army had habitually once done in the Comitia Centuriata in years gone by, the soldiers were exercising their 'right' to choose Rome's leader.

The now-deceased Vindex had been no general and had known that the army would never support him as emperor. His intention had been to get the ball rolling. Before his death he wrote to every nearby provincial governor urging one of them to lead the rebellion. It may have been this that Vindex proposed in initial talks with Rufus. If so, Rufus turned down Vindex then, and now was appalled that his army had nominated him anyway. He tried hard to reverse the army's decision, and in the end got his mutinous troops to agree that whoever ruled Rome should be appointed by senate and people, in true republican style. This was still a repudiation of Nero. But then, once his army had rejected their emperor, Rufus was committed to rebellion. If he had stayed loyal and his army did not kill him for it, an ungrateful Nero certainly would.

Though it had cost him his life, Vindex had indeed started something. Sulpicius Galba, the governor of Hispania Tarraconensis, began to issue pronouncements as 'legate of the people and senate of Rome'. This was not quite rebellion, but it was an explicit disavowal of Nero's authority. There is a credible report that Galba had recently intercepted messages from Nero ordering his death. Therefore his lack of enthusiasm for the imperial cause was understandable. Galba's fellow governor in Hispania, Salvius Otho (a former favourite of Nero), joined the rebels. So did Clodius Macer, governor of the province of Africa. This rebellion was no longer something Nero could laugh off. Belatedly, he responded.

Nero declared himself sole consul for the year. He raised a legion – I Adiutrix – from sailors in the imperial fleet. Troops were summoned from Illyria and Dalmatia and mustered in north Italy. If Nero was unaware of the depth of his unpopularity, he received another hint when his new army defected to the rebels.

Had Nero been merely incompetent, matters would never have become so desperate. He started well. He once had good advisors, popular support, an acquiescent senate and a loyal army. When he came to power the only cloud on the horizon was that the cost of supporting the army was increasing faster than the tax revenues to pay for it. The only military challenge was the Parthians, and these were more of an opportunity for military glory than a serious menace.

In fourteen years Nero swept away all these advantages with what – had he intended the result– would have been masterly skill. He took the financial situation from worrying to dire, yet still his taxmen helped to spark major rebellions in Britain and Judea. He ignored or executed his advisors and alienated those allies he did not murder. He surrounded himself with a clique of hangers-on who demonstrated their worth by abandoning him as soon as his cause looked lost. One such man was the commander of the Praetorian Guard, who now tried to secure his position with Nero's successor by bribing his men to support Galba's revolt.

As he reaped the rewards of his misgovernment, Nero became ruler in name alone. When he found his property being looted by his servants, he had not even the power to stop them. The senate declared him a public enemy and an outlaw, and no one disagreed. In the end, Nero's empire shrank to a small villa outside Rome, and his subjects numbered just four freedmen. And none of these would obey Nero's last command: that one of them should kill him. When the sound of horsemen was heard outside, Nero finally summoned the courage to stab himself. He died while giving instructions as to how his tomb should be decorated. Perhaps entranced by the brilliance of the design he had envisaged, he uttered the famous last words '*Qualis artifex pereo*' – 'I die, such an artist!' Nero had indeed been an artist – of his own downfall. There were lessons to be learned from his fate, and the question was whether his successors would take these lessons to heart.

INTERLUDE – PETELLIUS CERIALIS AND THE FLAVIANS
During the last years of Nero's reign Petellius Cerialis kept so low a profile that he was effectively invisible. He had not, as he might once have expected, advanced to the consulship after his return to Rome.

Having failed in this, as a legionary legate with military experience, he could have sought a further command, or perhaps a provincial governorship. However, while Nero's decimation of senate and generals left plenty of job opportunities, it also left little incentive for anyone sane to apply for them. Nor did Cerialis have the necessary viciousness to be an imperial favourite, or the servility to grovel to those who did.

Cerialis was still living down his role in the partial destruction of IX Hispana in Boudicca's revolt. But on top of this, as Vespasian's relative, Cerialis shared in the disgrace and danger resulting from his father-in-law's nap during one of Nero's performances. This incident may also have caused a cooling in family relations. When Vespasian was appointed to command in Judea, there is no record that Cerialis was considered for a place in the army of reconquest.

It may be that Cerialis now shifted his allegiance to the brother of Vespasian, Flavius Sabinus. With Vespasian commanding a substantial portion of Rome's total military power, Nero wanted his general's older brother under his eye in Rome. No one was so indelicate as to use the word 'hostage'. Nevertheless, Nero let Vespasian know that his emperor was taking a close interest in his family. Since Vespasian's loyalty was important, Nero's interest was currently benevolent. Thus among the doomed emperor's last acts was the nomination of a Flavius Sabinus as a consul for AD 69. This was probably Vespasian's nephew rather than the brother himself, but it was still a sign of imperial favour.

Unfortunately, the main source – and sometimes the only source – for detailed information of this period comes from Tacitus, and the great historian was distinctly ambivalent about both Cerialis and the Petellian clan. Therefore we know less about some details at the end of Nero's reign than we would like. However, it is clear that while Vespasian's oldest son, Titus, was on campaign with his father, the other son, Domitian, remained in Rome along with Vespasian's brother, Flavius Sabinus, and Petellius Cerialis, the father of Vespasian's grandson.

It is hard to believe the assertion of Domitian's biographer, Suetonius, that as a youth Domitian was so hard up for cash that he tried to prostitute himself to a wealthy senator.[7] In later life Domitian was an elegant rhetorician and writer, so he must have received the standard (and expensive) education of a young aristocrat. Domitian was a solitary youth. His mother Domitilla died while he was young, and he hardly knew his father. Vespasian had gone from his governorship in Africa to Nero's court in Greece to internal exile in Italy and then on to Judea while Domitian was in Rome. A gloomy introvert, Domitian lacked the charisma of his older brother, and had no coterie of friends.

Apart from the noble Flavians, there was a shadowy figure in the background. This was the freedwoman Caenis, ex-slave of Antonia Augusta, the former matriarch of the Julio-Claudian clan. Acting for her mistress, Caenis had played an active part in the intrigues of the previous generation. It was she, for example, who brought word to Tiberius that his henchman Sejanus was plotting to overthrow him. Even now Caenis had close and friendly relations with the great families of the Roman aristocracy. With Antonia Augusta now dead, Caenis was free and quietly wealthy, and a mistress in her own right – albeit the mistress of Vespasian, for whom she worked diplomatically behind the scenes.

These, then, were the Flavians in Rome – a political group with considerable clout. That the absent Vespasian was commanding a major campaign reflected lustre on the rest of the clan, as did the favour shown by Nero. Sabinus had his own political connections, and so did Antonia Caenis. So too did the Petellii, the adoptive family of Cerialis. Thus, as the year AD 68 came to a chaotic climax, the Flavians were well positioned within the Roman elite. They were not so closely identified with Nero's regime as to be dragged down with his fall, and yet they had sufficient influence that none wanted to offend them. Certainly it was not in the interest of any would-be emperor to fall out with Vespasian; a man with three legions at his back, which were getting more battle-hardened by the day.

Galba – 'He would have been thought a capable emperor had he not actually been one'[8]

Tacitus tells us that the rise to power of Servius Sulpicius Galba 'revealed a secret of empire – that emperors could be made other than in Rome'.[9] That Galba was brought to power by the army ripped off the fig-leaf of constitutional pretence Augustus and his successors had contrived to hide the fact that leadership was, as it had been in the early republic, bestowed by the army. If the year AD 69 was to prove anything, it was the lasting truth of what Augustus had himself proven in 31 BC. No one could command the Roman Empire who could not command its legions.

Galba himself recognized this fact and diplomatically identified himself as a 'military man'. The term *vir militaris* meant an aristocrat whose talent for war was at the service of people and state. And this is how Galba saw himself. His family, the *gens Sulpicia*, had given Rome a consul in 500 BC, just nine years after the birth of the Roman republic. (The Sulpicians were to continue this tradition until 650 years later when the last of the line, Sextus Sulpicius Tertullus, was consul in AD 158.) Sulpicians had led Roman soldiers throughout the history of the republic. A Servius Sulpicius Galba fought in the first Macedonian war as consul in 211 BC. Others campaigned in Spain and another in the third Macedonian war a generation later. The Servius Sulpicius Galba who was great grandfather to the emperor of AD 69 served under Caesar in the Gallic wars. His grandson, also a Servius Sulpicius Galba, was consul in AD 22. On his mother's side the Galba of AD 69 was the grandson of Lucius Mummius, the Roman general who destroyed Corinth in 146 BC and ended the Achaean war. In short, like the Julian and Claudian families, the Sulpicians were a top-ranking family with an outstanding military record. And thanks to Nero, there were no rival Julians or Claudians left.

At the time of the extraordinary events in AD 68 Galba was already near the end of a long and illustrious career. He was a stocky man of medium height with blue eyes, a bald head and a hooked nose. He so suffered from gout that his walk was lopsided and he could hardly open a scroll with his crippled hands. He had an austere character and an imposing personality which was justified by an impressive curriculum vitae. This included a praetorship and a subsequent spell as governor of Aquitania, where he had been succeeded in office by Salvius Otho, a man he counted as a friend.

After a consulship in AD 33, Galba led the Rhineland armies on a successful campaign against the Germans. Then he went on to govern Africa, where Vespasian was later to hold the same office. In Africa, too, Galba was a successful commander, for he quashed a minor native rebellion. His final post was as imperial legate governing Hispania Tarraconensis, a job which he performed with his usual dedication and honesty. He was now sixty-four years of age. Galba must have thought that this would be his last command before a peaceful retirement in Rome.

Instead, Galba left his province as a rebel leader with the newly raised legion VII Galbiana behind him. Despite mottos such as 'The restoration of liberty' and 'The salvation of mankind', there was no doubt of Galba's intentions. He had unilaterally adopted himself into the imperial house by calling himself 'Caesar', so Rome was to have a new emperor – himself.

Rome unquestionably needed firm government. Since Nero's death the city had been a lively place. The senate was ineffectually attempting to rule as if the republic had returned, while those with a firmer grip on reality were locked in a deadly game for power. Nymphidius Sabinus, the praetorian prefect who had bribed the Praetorian Guard over to Galba, had since decided that he might do better as emperor himself. He was killed by those who disagreed. The Roman mob had rioted enthusiastically at the fall of Nero and were ready, willing and able to do it again at a moment's notice. The city was packed with soldiers from whatever parts of the empire Nero had been able to summon them. These thronged the capital, uncertain whom they should now follow.

The populace was diverted by contradictory rumours about the character of their new ruler. On the one hand he was said to be honest and incorruptible, a Roman of the old school and a stickler for tradition. However, like many republican senators, Galba was avaricious and severe to the point of brutality. In Spain he had sentenced a man to death by crucifixion. His victim protested that he was a Roman citizen and citizens were not supposed to be crucified. All he got for his objection was a higher and better-quality cross than the others.

The Rhine armies well knew Galba's severity. Galba had taken over when the easy-going Gaetulicus was executed by Caligula and had rigidly enforced discipline. To add to the negative impression Galba had left on the German legions of a past generation, the present Rhineland army still felt slighted that their Verginius Rufus had not become emperor. When the popular governor of Lower Germany, Fonteius Capito, gave voice to their discontent, Galba promptly had him executed. This did not greatly add to the enthusiasm and loyalty of the Rhine legions.[10]

Lest Verginius Rufus repent of his nobility in not seizing the empire for himself, Galba summoned him from Germany to Rome. Instead of commanding an army, Rufus now had the 'honour' of joining the emperor's personal entourage. (Rufus went on to live a long life. This, as he would cheerfully and frequently point out, was among the benefits of not being emperor.) His replacement in Upper Germany was Hordonius Flaccus, an aged, ineffectual and gouty nonentity. Lower Germany was placed in the charge of Aulus Vitellius, a good-natured, overweight man of noble lineage and remarkable laziness whose preferred challenge was a huge meal. The legions well knew that these human dynamos had been foisted on them specifically because they were unlikely to cause trouble to Galba, the Germans or anyone else, and their opinion of their new emperor fell yet further.

The Praetorians had sent an honour guard to escort their new emperor to Rome. They were somewhat disquieted by what they found. Even before he arrived in the capital, Galba had executed his fellow rebel, Clodius Macer. It became clear that even as emperor Galba had no intention of abandoning his former severity. The Praetorians were in for a further shock. In the past they had received a generous cash payment whenever there was a change of emperor. Not with Galba. The generous bribe Tigellinus had promised the Guard for switching its allegiance was repudiated with the lofty words 'I choose my soldiers, I do not buy them.' As pithy phrases go, this one was a death sentence. The Praetorians never forgave Galba for this broken promise.

Things Fall Apart
The new emperor had to hold the line on two separate fronts. Gaining the loyalty of the Rhine legions was a huge, perhaps impossible, task. Yet Galba also had to get himself, if not loved, then at least accepted in Rome. Thanks to Nero's building programme and general extravagance, Galba had inherited an empire and a city on the verge of bankruptcy. Bribing the people with bread and circuses was impossible for the cash-strapped Galba, even if he had been the type of man to try it. Instead, Galba set about restoring the imperial finances with brutal disregard for anyone who did not share his taste for austerity.

Painful taxes were imposed on wealthy Romans and on provincial cities. Those who had received extravagant gifts from Nero were obliged to repay them, whether or not they still had the means. The military odds and ends floating around Rome were brusquely informed that the new emperor had no use for them. They were either discharged or sent packing back to their units. Some soldiers did not go quietly and the subsequent riot added further unease to a city already on edge. A mutinous remnant of Nero's recruits remained quartered near the Portica Vipsania about a mile from the city centre while the authorities worked out what to do with them.

Galba's brief career as emperor demonstrates yet again how remarkably deft Augustus had been and what an impossible job he left to his successors.[11] When he came to power Augustus faced a situation just as potentially lethal. By a mixture of personal charm, ruthless politics and shrewd calculation, Augustus defused every problem and made ruling Rome look easy.

Not so Galba. Though a capable governor and general, he was utterly out of his depth. Any compromise to political reality he considered a moral failing. He alienated allies, misjudged the mood of the people and army, and marched to disaster in the pig-headed yet typically Roman belief that being in the right was all that mattered. Consequently he was resented by the people who now rather missed Nero's shows and parties. He was disliked by the upper classes who resented his financial impositions and by the senate, which begrudged his authority. And the only military force in the capital, the Praetorian Guard, was quietly seething with fury at his tight-fistedness.

Galba lasted as long as he did because of his advanced age. What the Romans would not have tolerated in an emperor twenty years younger, they endured from Galba. It was generally assumed that once the aged Galba had passed on, his successor would be the genial Salvius Otho, son of Galba's old friend of the same name. When Nero fell, Otho had been governor of Lusitania. He had been among the first to throw in his lot with Galba and had accompanied him to Rome. Otho was once a favourite of Nero, so the people hoped that as emperor he would combine the best qualities of the past and present regimes. They gritted their teeth under Galba and assured themselves that things could only get better.

In January of AD 69 it became apparent that the Rhineland legions were not going to be as patient. The legions based at Moguntiacum (Mainz) were IV Macedonica and XXII Primigenia. These refused to take the annual oath of allegiance. Their act of rebellion had certainly not been instigated by Vitellius, governor of Lower Germany. At the time he was enjoying a sumptuous New Year's banquet blissfully unaware of what the troops in Upper Germany were up to. The spark for rebellion came from a subordinate who used the discontent of the legions to extricate himself from a tricky situation.

The commander of IV Macedonica, Aulus Caecina, had been *quaestor* (the magistrate in charge of financial matters) in Spain at the time of Galba's rebellion. Caecina had speedily and enthusiastically endorsed Galba for emperor at a moment when the latter's candidature had briefly faltered. His reward was command of IV Macedonica in Germany. Then Caecina's replacement in Spain came across puzzling discrepancies in the accounts and rapidly established that this was because Caecina had cooked the books in Spain to cover large-scale embezzlement.

It was not the sort of thing that the strait-laced Galba would tolerate. He immediately ordered that Caecina be prosecuted with the full force of the law, but – due to the Saturnalia holiday – charges of theft and misappropriation of public funds had not yet been formally laid. Now Caecina was prepared to put armies into motion and overthrow an empire to make sure that they never would be.

Yet Caecina lacked the authority to lead the army in rebellion. There was only one candidate whom the Rhineland legions would accept as emperor,

The tombstone of Marcus Favonius Facilis, centurion of Legio XX Valeria Victrix. This was violently thrown down by Boudicca's rebels soon after it was erected, and preserved intact in the soil for almost two millennia. (Picture: courtesy of Adrian Goldsworthy)

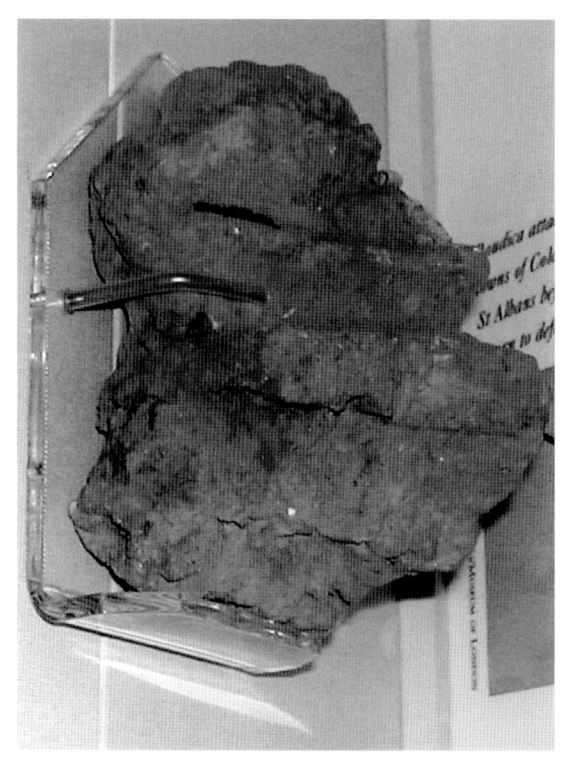

Remnants of Boudicca's literal burned-earth strategy. These charred fragments of a clay pot are almost certainly relics of Boudicca's sack of London. They are now preserved in the Museum of London, not far from their original resting place. (Picture: Malgosia Matyszak)

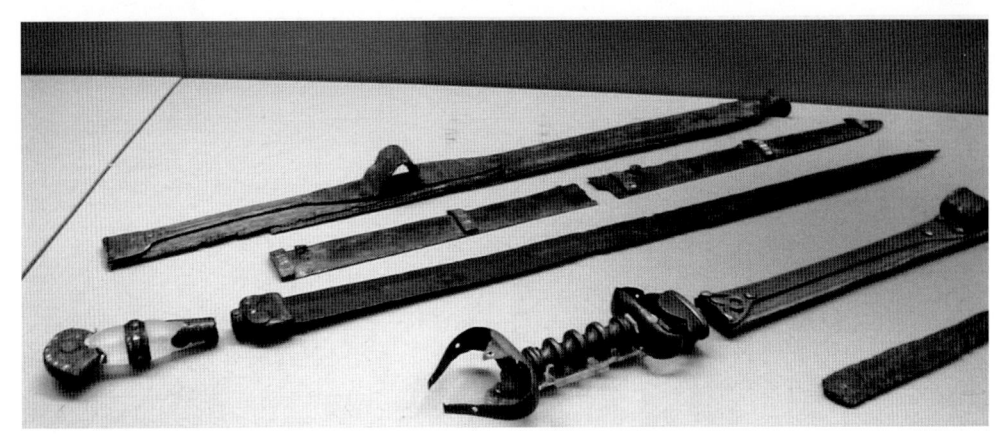

British swords dated AD 50–200. Both swords are of iron with brass fittings. Such swords were used by wealthy, aristocratic members of a warrior band. The right-hand sword is from Cotterdale in North Yorkshire and might have seen action in Cerialis' Brigantian campaign. (Picture: Malgosia Matyszak)

Brigantia as the Romans saw it – boggy, expensive to invade and without mineral or agricultural assets. It was kept as a buffer state on the northern border of Roman Britain for as long as was practically possible.

The tomb of Classicanus, now in the British Museum. Classicanus, whom Cerialis may well have met before his departure from Britain after AD 61, was a moderate governor who set the tone for Cerialis' own civil administration. (Picture: Malgosia Matyszak)

Gladiators Lupus and Medusa sparring in the arena. Though Otho conscripted these fighters at short notice, they made a valuable contribution to his campaign in AD 69. (Duel re-enacted by Svenja Grosser and Wolfgang Mueller of the Ludus Nemesis.)

The River Po near Ferrata, downstream from Cremona. This illustrates why Otho was hopeful that he could keep the Vitellians penned on the north bank of the river until his army was reinforced by the Danubian legions. (Picture: public domain)

The Roman forum today as seen through the Arch of Titus. Somewhere in this area, in AD 69 the Emperor Galba was killed and both Vitellius and Flavius Sabinus met their deaths. (Picture: Courtesy of Adrian Goldsworthy)

The fortunes of Cerialis rose and fell with those of his father-in-law Vespasian (left). When Vespasian was in disgrace, Cerialis was also, and when Vespasian was a rebel, Cerialis had to run for his life. But when Vespasian was emperor, Cerialis was the empire's top general. (Picture: Courtesy of Adrian Goldsworthy)

Domitian as the imperial general he wanted to be. Young Domitian's attempts to find military glory were frustrated by senior members of the imperial establishment. In later life, however, Domitian proved a competent campaigner. (Picture: Courtesy of Adrian Goldsworthy)

Legionaries of the Ermine Street Guard with a 'scorpion' bolt-thrower. These portable artillery pieces were used with devastating effect on Germans who camped too close to Castra Vetera on the Rhine Frontier. (Picture: Courtesy of the Ermine Street Guard).

A legionary of Legio XIV Gemina Martia Victrix receives an award in a presentation re-enacted by the Roman Military Research Society in the United Kingdom. (Picture: used with thanks to Mike Haxell of the Roman Military Research Society)

Re-enactors of the Cohors Batavorum on the march, accompanied by colleagues from Legio XV Gemina Martia Victrix. In the past, relations between the two units were often less than cordial. (Picture: used with thanks to Mike Haxell of the Roman Military Research Society)

A Roman legionary escorts a cart loaded with booty and barbarian slaves. From a bas-relief in the Vatican Museum (Picture: P. Matyszak)

Rome Victorious. A Roman general sits surrounded by barbarian prisoners, whilst Victory bears a palm leaf and crowns him with laurel. A victory trophy occupies the right-hand part of the scene. From a bas-relief in the Vatican Museum (Picture: P. Matyszak)

and Caecina had decided to inform Vitellius that he was it. No one else in the region possessed the necessary rank or had a sufficiently noble family. Vitellius might not make a particularly inspiring emperor, but as Caecina told IV Macedonica, at least he would be their emperor. Caecina took it for granted that his immediate superior, the ineffectual Hordonius Flaccus, could do nothing to stop him. So whether or not Caecina had a future now depended on how the legions in Lower Germany under Vitellius' direct command would react to their general's *de facto* promotion.

Vitellius was informed by courier of events in Upper Germany. His response was hardly that of a man eager to take events by the scruff of the neck. He politely informed his army in Lower Germany that the legions on the upper Rhine were in revolt and it was their duty to go to war against them. This, after all, was what they had vowed to do in their recent oath of allegiance. (Unlike the upper Rhineland legions, those under Vitellius' command had indeed taken the oath, albeit grudgingly. In fact some malcontents had stoned the emperor's statue beforehand, making the oath-taking less than a ringing endorsement.) Furthermore, Vitellius disingenuously pointed out, if the legions refused to fight for Galba they would have to find an alternative emperor.

Since he had arrived at the frontier Vitellius had been a genial and easygoing commander. He had put aside his habitual sloth to give his new command a thorough inspection, in the course of which he had given the troops the impression that they could, after all, have done much worse. Therefore, at the urging of their impetuous legate Fabius Valens, I Germanica declared for Vitellius. The remaining legions, V Alaudae and XXI Rapax, followed this example.

News of the turbulence on the frontier reached Rome. The extent of the rebellion was as yet uncertain, but it was manifestly clear to Galba that the troops were not mutinying in favour of anyone else: they were mutinying against him. Since sentiment in Rome was somewhat similar, he decided to placate the anyone-but-Galba majority by publicly announcing his successor. This gave him an escape route. If the pressure to step down became overwhelming Galba could at least hand over power to a prepared successor. Knowing there was a replacement waiting in the wings might calm both the fractious city populace and the mutinous legions.

However, while it was known that Galba was planning to announce his successor, the actual announcement was a shock. Galba anointed not Otho, as was generally expected, but Calpurnius Piso. Piso was a man after Galba's own heart, an old-school aristocrat, austere, rigid and humourless. He was perhaps a worthy successor, but to most, including the appalled Praetorians, merely a younger and more durable Galba. When Piso was presented to the Praetorian Guard only the front ranks managed a cheer. The rest remained silent, waiting for some mention of a cash donation. When it became apparent that the customary bribe was not coming, the expected cheers became sullen mutters. The senate was only slightly more amenable, but duly went through the motions of endorsing Piso as Caesar to Galba's Augustus.

The question none dared to ask was 'What of Otho?' Piso was no fool and must have known that Otho would have been a more popular successor to Galba. In fact Otho had been acting as though he was already Galba's heir. He had warm relations with the Praetorians and had cultivated senior senators with flattery, gifts and favours. 'Otho for emperor' had abundant support among soldiers, senate and people.

Otho was an intolerably popular rival to Piso. Therefore, the reality of Roman dynastic politics demanded that Galba's death be followed by Otho's before the imperial corpse had gone cold. Tacitus is firmly against Otho for his foppishness, his 'decadent' lifestyle and past support of Nero. Yet even he admits that in choosing Piso as his heir, Galba had effectively handed a death sentence to his most loyal supporter. To a very large degree, what Otho did next was self-defence.

Coup d'état

Otho had to act fast. His carefully cultivated support was already withering away. His proposed replacement seemed such an upstanding citizen that there was a risk people would actually support him. It was time for Otho to demonstrate some of the qualities necessary in an aspiring imperial candidate. Ruthlessness naturally, but the ideal candidate also needed the ability to plan ahead, and to adapt those plans at a moment's notice. However Machiavellian, no conspirator is capable of conceiving and executing a coup d'état on just four days' notice. Yet Otho smoothly pulled off exactly such a feat. This suggests that even when he assumed he was emperor-in-waiting, Otho had not relied on luck and Galba's goodwill. Not only contingency planning but a great deal of the preliminary spadework for a coup must have already been in place.

The disaffection of the Praetorians was hardly a secret. Otho had bribed two of the Praetorians to work on their fellow-soldiers. Further bribes were dispensed where they would do most good. A rumour had spread through the ranks that Galba was preparing to transfer to the legions many of the Praetorians whom he distrusted. Right on cue Galba duly transferred a number of soldiers whose only fault was that they had seemed partial towards Otho or had received favours from Nero.[12] The Praetorians were getting their rumours from a well-placed source.

Such was the mood of the troops that they actually contemplated a spontaneous coup on the evening of 14 January, when a golden opportunity presented itself. Galba was returning from a dinner outside the palace, and it would have been a simple matter for his treacherous bodyguard to do away with him en route. Cooler heads among the plotters prevailed, and everyone agreed to wait until the next day, for which plans were already in place. That morning, while Galba was performing a ritual sacrifice, Otho made an excuse to leave the imperial entourage. He hurried to the Praetorian camp and was escorted within by a small group of loyal supporters. Apparently the group was much smaller than Otho hoped, but he put a brave face on it. His bluff worked on the tribune on duty at the camp. The unfortunate officer was unaware of the plot, or how well it was supported by the men, and stood aside to let events take their course.

In fact, such was the mood of the majority. 'Few were prepared to actively undertake so atrocious an act of treason, but most were in favour of the idea, and were more than ready to let it be done.'[13] Otho worked hard at persuading the waverers. He made it loudly and repeatedly clear that the old habit of cash donations would once more follow a change of ruler – and very generously at that. With this promise Otho secured the Praetorian barracks, and with it most of the available weaponry in the city.

When informed of the crisis, Galba reacted sensibly. He turned down the idea of confronting the Praetorians in their barracks, preferring to first sound out the feelings of the Praetorian cohort currently on guard at the palace. Young Piso was sent to rally the troops, presumably because he was more popular than Galba himself. Tacitus gives Piso a pretty speech for the occasion, but it was the words 'we will pay you a lot of money' that temporarily won the day. An attempt to recruit the leftovers of Nero's muster at the Vipsanian portico met with little success. The eastern legions had always had a soft spot for Nero and were delighted that his former favourite was taking charge. The men sent to bring over the Illyrians departed hastily amid a shower of javelins. However, Galba had treated kindly a troop of German auxiliaries when they were taken ill, so they decided to support the emperor. They set out for the palace but, being unfamiliar with the big city, got lost along the way and only turned up after it was all over.

Rumour and counter-rumour swept Rome. Galba's supporters flocked to the Palatine demanding Otho's head. This inspired Galba to try to repeat

Piso's earlier success. The imperial heir was dispatched to Praetorian barracks on the Viminal hill to bring the rest of the Guard back to their senses. Encouraged by a rumour that Otho had been slain, Galba himself left the Palatine with Piso and accompanied him to the forum.

This was a misjudgement. In the forum Galba's escort encountered their mutinous fellow Praetorians going the other way. The escort promptly decided to follow the majority opinion, and switched to the Othonian side, leaving Galba surrounded by enemies. 'What are you doing, comrades in arms?' Galba is said to have cried out. 'I am yours and you are mine!'[14] The Praetorians had never been impressed with Galba's rhetoric, and they were not now. His personal guard unflinchingly killed their aged emperor. As an afterthought they later returned to behead the corpse and present Otho with the head.

The gallant defence of a loyal centurion allowed Piso to escape, though this cost the centurion his life. Nor did Piso get far. He took sanctuary in the Shrine of Vesta, but the soldiery respected the mother goddess of Rome only to the extent that they did not slay him on the premises. Instead they dragged him to the front porch and killed him there. His head joined Galba's on a pole alongside the Praetorian standards.

Otho had his empire and the Guard would get their donative. This had been achieved by Otho's betrayal of Galba and the Praetorians' blatant failure to perform their duty. For such treachery Nemesis was already on the way, improbably embodied in the flabby form of Aulus Vitellius, rival emperor by the grace of the Rhineland legions.

Meanwhile, in Judea ...
Throughout the chaos in the capital, the Flavian faction kept a low profile. They could afford to. If Nero could not risk alienating the man in charge of the armies in Judea, then Galba certainly could not. Vespasian had an estimated 60,000 infantry and horse under his command, the hard core of which was his three legions. These were well under Flavian control.

One legion was commanded by a Flavius Silva, another indication that the Flavians preferred going to war as a family. A second was commanded then or slightly later by Vettulanus Cerialis, which suggests that whatever reason Petellius Cerialis had for not joining his father-in-law in Judea it was not because the two families had ceased to co-operate.[15] The remaining legion was commanded by Vespasian's son Titus.

Vespasian's army was currently under-employed in Judea. Vespasian had started busily in Galilee and had quickly conquered the region. He took under his wing the later historian Josephus, a Jewish general who surrendered to Vespasian after an unsuccessful defence of the city of Jotopata. Like Josephus, the leaders of the revolt in Jerusalem had little stomach for their task. Rather than attempting to relieve Galilee, they had concentrated on preparing their city for a siege.

This inaction infuriated the radical refugees from Galilee, who quickly overthrew the rebel leadership and instituted their own hard-core regime. They were in turn opposed by a new faction and Jerusalem's reserves of grain were destroyed in the subsequent fighting. Therefore, though Vespasian was on his way to Jerusalem, he was taking his time about it. He hoped that many of the rebels would have killed each other off before he got there – and the radical factions were trying hard not to disappoint him.

Naturally, the Flavians in Rome kept their leader updated with news from home. Vespasian was happy enough to accept Galba as emperor. One T Ampius Flavianus became consular legate in Pannonia around this time. If there was a family connection, this may have been a concession made by Galba in return for Flavian support. It would have been an easy gesture for Galba to make, for Ampius Flavianus was elderly and vacillating, so his promotion was consistent with the new emperor's policy of appointing ineffectual generals.

Both Galba and Vespasian shared a common work ethic and a reputation for honesty, but there seems to have been a certain degree of tension between the two. Firstly, Vespasian had a dynamic approach to military operations. This must have been disquieting for an emperor who preferred his generals as torpid as possible. Secondly, the highly bred Sulpician may have considered Vespasian to be somewhat beneath him. Vespasian later suspected that Galba had dispatched assassins to do away with him in Judea.[16]

It is quite possible that when Vespasian sent his son Titus to congratulate Galba on taking office the intention was to also quietly discuss the aged emperor's choice of heir. After all, Vespasian's army gave him 60,000 good reasons why he or his son might be considered suitable candidates. If Titus were to succeed Galba, then there would be little point in Galba assassinating Vespasian. Nor need Vespasian use his army to win an empire that would drop into his family's lap anyway.

If this was the plan, a crushing series of disappointments met Titus on his journey to Rome. First, even as he was leaving Judea came the news that Piso had been made Galba's heir. Then Titus reached Corinth to find that Otho had staged his coup, and furthermore there was another rival emperor in the north.

With their dynastic ambitions thwarted, the Flavians once again settled down to await developments. It was unlikely that whoever came out on top in Rome would want to make an enemy of Vespasian, and meanwhile there were the rebels in Jerusalem to keep him busy. While Titus did not give up his journey to Rome, he certainly delayed it while events in Italy played themselves out. He is said to have asked the oracle on the island of Paphos 'Will I succeed in what I am hoping and planning?' and was satisfied with the answer. Yet for the moment, the heir to the Flavians was keeping his hopes and plans to himself.

Otho versus Vitellius
One of Otho's first acts was to confirm the brother of Vespasian, Flavius Sabinus, in his office as prefect of the city. This was a clear signal that Otho intended to follow his predecessors' policy of keeping Vespasian loyal by showing ostentatious interest in his family. In fact, appeasing Vespasian had become all the more important. Vitellius' rebellion was now common knowledge and there were more than a few who considered both Otho and Vitellius 'alike the worse of humans for shamelessness, idleness and extravagance' (says Tacitus, who evidently shared this opinion). Vespasian may have been a low-born transport contractor and a dealer in second-hand mules, but he was capable, fair and honest, and just then most Romans were frankly not prepared to be overly picky. For all that Otho was master of Rome, he knew that Vespasian could replace him and so was at pains to ensure that the general had no reason to do so.

The army of the western provinces had to choose between Otho or Vitellius. Britain declared early for the pretender Vitellius over the usurper Otho. Gaul had a single legion, I Italica. Founded by Nero from sailors of the fleet, its soldiers loathed both Otho and Vitellius. Forced to choose, they reluctantly settled on Vitellius. The single legion in Spain dithered, torn between affection for the former governor of Lusitania and fear of the size and experience of Vitellius' Rhineland army. In no province was the decision unanimous. Splits ran all the way from the lowest rankers to the high command and the resultant factionalism and feuding were devastating to morale.

Only two groups were unequivocally committed – the Praetorians for Otho, and the Rhine legions for Vitellius. The two organizations each held the other in some degree of contempt. The Praetorians regarded the Rhine legions as uncouth half-foreign barbarians, while the Rhinelanders considered the Praetorians bone-idle degenerates enervated by the easy life of the capital.[17] The ordinary citizens of Rome had on occasion suffered from Praetorian arrogance. One suspects they were waiting with interest to see how these self-styled 'elite' troops fared against battle-hardened regulars. In rather the same spirit, the Roman aristocracy wanted to see what sort of general Otho would make. With his slightly effeminate mannerisms, this splay-footed, bandy-legged dandy in his immaculately tailored clothing and carefully fitted wig hardly looked the part of a warrior emperor. Yet Otho had shown signs of a different character when he stood up to Nero for the affections of Poppea Sabina, a woman he loved. When Nero banished him to a governorship in distant Lusitania as punishment, Otho had governed his province for ten years with moderation and justice.

Otho did not want an armed clash with Vitellius. Even if the Praetorians were a match for the Rhine legions man-for-man (and the Rhine legions were ready to dispute this), Otho was substantially outnumbered. Early negotiations between Otho and Vitellius got off to a conciliatory start, since Vitellius was always somewhat ambivalent about the position his lower ranks had railroaded him into. But peace never really had a chance.

Not Vitellius but the Rhine legions were the driving force of the rebellion. Their emperor and general may have been half-drunk and sleeping off a heavy meal by midday, but Caecina, Valens and the troops were energetic and enthusiastic. Otho's emissaries were spurned, and the emperor in Rome reluctantly concluded that matters would have to be resolved by force.

All was not lost. Otho was acting less like Nero's old favourite and more like an emperor every day. He was conciliatory to the senate. He treated Lucius Vitellius, the brother of his rival, without particular disrespect or favour. Otho obtained the favour of the crowds by executing Nero's hated henchman Tigellinus. Even more crucially, Otho managed to win over the allegiance of the Pannonian legions. Spain, after considerable vacillation, declared for him and Africa followed. Equally gratifying was the news that Flavius Vespasian in Judea and Mucianus in Syria had come down on his side. The fleet too was loyal, and importantly, it was near at hand. The trick for Otho would be to survive until the rest of his allies could reach him. The Rhineland legions were closest of all, and they were already on the move.

In early February Otho started to cobble together an army from what he could raise in Rome. He had two legions – XIII Gemina and I Adiutrix, the latter a legion newly raised from the fleet at Ravenna. Naturally, there was also the Praetorian Guard, which amounted to about another legion. Six thousand men were on their way from the Danube legions. They would have sent more, but the Sarmatian tribes were restless. XIV Gemina Martia

Victrix was also on the way from Gallia Narbonensis, where the legion had been resting after its British heroics against Boudicca. Otho added some troops from Rome's urban cohorts, and supplemented them with two thousand gladiators from the arenas of Rome.

Nero's neglect of the army had led to his downfall and Otho would not repeat that mistake. He himself would take this somewhat rough-and-ready army to war. He ordered many of the Roman Senate to accompany him, including Lucius, the brother of Vitellius and Verginius Rufus, the man who would not be emperor after his men had defeated Vindex. One of the three men in command of the infantry was none other than Suetonius Paulinus, who had last generalled XIV Gemina Martia Victrix in Britain. In Otho's absence, the city was to be governed by the emperor's brother, Salvius Titianus.

Assembling this army and sorting out its command structure took time. Otho was only able to set out in March, by when the Vitellian vanguard was already over the Alps. The plan was for Otho's army to meet the main Vitellian army in the plains of north Italy before it had fully recovered from the rigours of crossing the Alps.

As the army left Rome, the Praetorians were surprised and heartened to see Otho dressed for his role, wearing armour and marching on foot with the standards. There was to be no primping and preening on this march. It was almost as if, having disposed of Galba, Otho was making an ostentatious effort to become the sort of man Galba would have wanted him to be. It was unfortunate that the men themselves showed less military character. A detachment dispersed a pro-Vitellian militia near the Maritime Alps. Afterwards the men decided to pillage the inoffensive town of Albintemilium apparently for no other reason than that it was nearby, and offered richer plunder than the enemy the Othonians had been fighting. Among those who perished in this wanton carnage was a woman called Julia Procilla. Her son, Julius Agricola, the former military tribune of II Augusta (p. 57), hastened from Rome to bury her and sort out her family affairs.[18] In contrast with the headstrong and disorganized Othonians, the Vitelians remained well-disciplined, and the legions' treatment of civilians made an excellent impression on the undecided.

The first encounter with the Vitellian army itself went well for Otho. It took place on the coast, at the border of Gallia Narbonensis. The Vitellians were making a reconnaissance in force, and, as befitted troops on such a mission, were strong in cavalry. This included a unit commanded by one Julius Classicus, a man who was also to play a part in future events. The

Vitellians were defeated by a detachment of the Othonian army supported by the fleet and forced back into Gaul.

Though something of a sideshow to the forthcoming clash of the main armies, this small victory was significant because it secured for Otho the western route to Rome. This meant that the main thrust of the Vitellians would come across the plains of north Italy, where Otho was marching up towards the river Po to meet it.

THE FIRST BATTLE OF BEDRIACUM (CREMONA)

Preliminaries
As expected, the main Vitellian force exited the mountain passes before Otho was able to prevent it. The Vitellian army consisted of auxiliary troops and elements of three legions – I Italica from Gaul, and V Alaudae and XXI Rapax from the Rhinelands. The larcenous Caecina was in command of the advance section with Valens bringing up the rest. As Caecina's forces arrived in Italy they captured a cohort of Danubian reinforcements on their way to join Otho. Encouraged by this development, the Vitellians advanced on Placentia (modern Piacenza), much as Hannibal had done almost three centuries before.[19]

Placentia was a military colony designed to stop enemies from the north from crossing the Po. As such, it was a well-fortified city designed specifically with invading armies in mind. It was essential for Otho to hold this strong point against the invading Rhinelanders. Yet this did not stop the ill-disciplined garrison from rushing out to confront the enemy in the field. There they would have been outnumbered, outmatched and massacred by the Vitellians had not their commander talked his men back to sanity and back behind the walls in time. When the Vitellians arrived and launched a brisk attack on the city, the necessity of strong walls was confirmed. It took two days of hard fighting before the Rhinelanders were persuaded to retreat to Cremona and consider other options for getting across the Po. Had the garrison been caught in the field, Vitellius easily would have secured Placentia and stolen a march on Otho.

As it was, the Vitellians encountered another setback. The auxiliaries meant to secure their lines of communications were severely cut up by Otho's gladiators in a commando-style raid across the river. In retaliation for this raid, and to restore the flagging morale of his men, Caecina decided to ambush the Othonian reinforcements, which were heading for Placentia at full speed. He set his trap at the temple of Castor and Pollux by a village called Locus Castrorum on the Via Postumia.

As the Othonian cavalry approached, a small detachment of Vitellian troops left the village. These faked surprise at the sight of the enemy and fled, intending to draw their enemies deep into Caecina's cunning trap. The Othonians duly advanced and Vitellians hidden in the woods on each side of the road rushed out to take advantage of an enemy now outflanked on both sides.

The Othonian cavalry coolly retreated. Then, as the dust of their manoeuvre settled, the Vitellians found themselves facing the massed ranks of the Praetorians reinforced for good measure by detachments of XIII Gemina and I Adiutrix. Forewarned of Caecina's plans, the Othonians had prepared a small surprise of their own. Suetonius Paulinus and a considerable force were even now swinging across the Vitellian rear to cut off and annihilate the would-be ambushers.

Probably because he was hindered by the terrain, Paulinus was a trifle slow in closing the trap door, and a good number of Vitellians scrambled clear. At the temple they even launched a spirited counter-attack on cavalry following up their retreat. This counter-attack was their undoing, for it gave the Othonian infantry a chance to catch up. The resultant combat partly answered the question of whether the Praetorians could fight. They could, and rather well. Afterwards the pile of the slain Vitellians reached as high as the gable ends of the temple about which the mini-battle had been fought.

The Vitellian survivors fled back towards Cremona, pursued by the Othonians, who mopped up piecemeal reinforcements as fast as Caecina sent them out. Eventually Caecina realized that he was simply feeding men into a meat-grinder and began to muster his entire army. Suetonius Paulinus was no fool and knew that he was outnumbered. Accordingly he ordered his men to halt. The Othonians did so, and with their usual lack of discipline immediately rounded on the commander who had led them in a highly successful action. He had been too tardy in closing the Vitellians into the planned trap. Now he was preventing them from following up their success and destroying the threat from the Rhinelands for once and for all. The wilder elements accused Paulinus of treason and of being a secret Vitellian supporter.

A short lull followed the clash at Locus Castrorum. The Vitellians were waiting for Valens and the rest of their army to arrive. Delay suited the Othonians, who were expecting reinforcements from the Danube legions. The men were still calling for Paulinus' head on a platter. To pacify them Otho called his brother from the administration of Rome and placed him in overall command of the army in the field. The emperor intended to stay just behind the lines at Brexellum and let his generals do their job.

Caecina passed the time by trying to get over the Po with a pontoon bridge while Otho's gladiators tried to stop him. The Vitellians built a defensive tower at the end of their bridge and the Othonians matched it with one of their own. The Othonians sabotaged the bridge with fireships and the Vitellians captured one of the islands in mid-stream. The gladiators tried to get the island back, but were repulsed with heavy casualties by Batavian troops. These auxiliaries very probably included the children of the generation that had so successfully secured the river crossings for the Romans during the invasion of Britain twenty-five years previously. The defeat of the gladiators led to the local commander being replaced. This replacement was a Flavius Sabinus, in this case probably the nephew rather than the brother of Vespasian. The latter remained in Rome.

The Battle
On 8 April Valens arrived with the rest of the Vitellian army. Further reinforcements were being scraped together from the depleted Rhineland garrisons, but basically the Vitellian force was now as large as it was going to get. Though it outnumbered the opposition facing it, in time this army would be outnumbered in its turn by the forces Otho had summoned from the far reaches of the empire. It was essential for the Rhinelanders to settle things without delay.

This was clear to Paulinus, by far the canniest of the Othonian generals. He argued strongly that fighting a battle before reinforcements arrived was to be playing into the enemy's hands. Otho's other advisors felt that their men would not permit them to delay, and the Vitellians should be attacked before they had time to recover from their long march, just as originally planned. This dissent among their commanders further lowered the trust of the Othonian troops in their generals. But if the soldiery trusted their commanders too little, Otho trusted them too much. His decision to leave his generals to do their job weakened morale. The men fighting for Otho needed his presence. And they needed the cavalry and substantial bodyguard Otho kept with him at Brexellum.

Our sources for Otho's pre-battle council of war are unsatisfactory. Nevertheless it is possible to reconstruct the deliberations from the army's subsequent actions. It appears that the immediate target of the Othonians was Caecina's bridge. This represented a partial victory for Paulinus. Destroying the bridge would keep the Vitellians north of the Po. If they were still there when the Danubian legions arrived, then the Vitellians would be severely disadvantaged. If, on the other hand, the Vitellians did get over the Po, Otho had no illusions that the Italian towns or the senate in Rome would fight to the death for him. Most simply wanted the civil war over as soon as possible. Unlike the legions, they were not deeply concerned which of the two wretched options for emperor won it.

Accordingly, the Othonian army, some 30,000 strong, set out against the Rhinelanders, who now numbered some 50,000 men. Otho's generals probably intended to set up camp close enough to the river to make work on Caecina's bridge impossible. Then, in a fortified camp, their smaller force could await the arrival of the Danubians. This is the only explanation of why the Othonians went out equipped for a campaign complete with camp-building materials. These would not have been needed if a decisive battle was contemplated.

Things went wrong almost as soon as the Othonians came in sight of their enemies. Firstly, they soon discovered that rumours of low morale among their opponents were false. The Vitellian cavalry attacked the Othonian column as soon as it came into sight. The attack was repulsed, but the damage was done. Seeing the Vitellian legions forming up, some Othonians attempted to deploy into line of battle. Others continued with the original plan. The muddy ground, tangled vineyards and deep ditches spoiled communications and the effective execution of either operation.

The veteran Vitellians had no such problem. They speedily formed up on open ground near the river. This quick deployment by the Vitellians and the confusion amongst the Othonians meant that the original plan of making a camp was never an option – the Vitellians would be all over the Othonians before they could get the earthworks properly started. The only option was to change the shovel for the sword and fight a pitched battle.

The first infantry clash was on the river flank. Here the Othonian ex-sailors of I Adiutrix met the Vitellians of XXI Rapax. At first the men of I Adiutrix thought that XXI Rapax was leaving the Vitellian line to desert to them and welcomed their attackers with cheers (which worried the rest of the Othonian army, who thought that I Adiutrix was about to desert). When the Vitellian response left no doubt of their error, I Adiutrix counter-attacked with such ferocity that they captured XXI Rapax's eagle. Though briefly bemused by the aggression of a legion that had seemed disinclined to fight moments before, the veteran legionaries of XXI Rapax rallied. They killed I Adiutrix's commander and forced the legion to fall back, exposing the Othonian flank.

On the opposite side of the chaotic battle line, the Rhinelanders of V Alaudae engaged and defeated the Othonian XIII Gemina. This left the outlying part of Otho's army, a detachment of XIV Gemina Martia Victrix, cut off from the rest of their battle line. It would appear from our confused reports that while thereafter the Vitellians focused on breaking the Othonian centre, the soldiers of the XIV Gemina Martia Victrix recognized a lost cause and slunk away as inconspicuously as possible.

Meanwhile, on the river flank where the I Adiutrix had already taken a beating, things went from bad to worse. The gladiators who had been opposing the building of Caecina's bridge tried to ferry themselves across the river. They were met and defeated while in the water by the Batavians, who excelled in this style of combat. Then, once they had disposed of the gladiators, the Batavians hurled themselves enthusiastically on to the flank that XXI Rapax had exposed by beating back I Adiutrix.

This left the Praetorians in the centre, who were matched against the Vitellian I Italica. According to Plutarch's scornful report, the Praetorians fled without striking a blow when faced with the reality of combat. This may be a bit harsh, as the collapse of both wings of their army left the Praetorians in an impossible position. But in any case, the Praetorians broke, and with them went any chance of retrieving the situation. The army fled back toward Bedriacum, taking massive losses from the Vitellians, who followed up hard and only ceased killing when darkness fell.

The Emperor is Dead – Long Live the Emperor!

The father of the biographer Suetonius was Suetonius Laetus, who was an officer in the Othonian legion XIII Gemina. Therefore the events of the immediate aftermath of the battle were probably related to Suetonius at first hand. By this account, Otho would never have overthrown Galba if he was not certain that he could bring matters to a peaceful resolution, and it is evident that only the intransigence of the Rhine legionaries caused the failure of negotiations with Vitellius. News that the army had been defeated in battle was at first received with incredulity by Otho's entourage. This reaction would have been all the more credible if, as surmised here, the intention of the Othonians was not to fight a battle in the first place, but only to set up camp close enough to hinder Caecina's bridge-building activities.

The man who brought the news was accused of lying and of trying to excuse his own cowardice in running from the action. The soldier, already distraught from the rigours of defeat, promptly responded by killing himself. This ended all doubts of his bravery and sincerity.

Yet even after this defeat, Otho's position was far from hopeless. The Vitellian victory had been hard-won. The Rhinelanders were in no shape to press forward at once, and the defeated legions were even now rallying – especially XIV Gemina Martia Victrix, which seems to have escaped serious punishment by virtue of its position on the far wing of the army. The Vitellians remained trapped against the Po and a defensive action might well keep them there, especially as the first of the Danubian legions, VII Claudia, had already arrived in Italy and could be expected in five days. Furthermore additional units of XIV Gemina Martia Victrix had now turned up at headquarters and were looking for instructions.

But Otho had taken things as far as he was prepared to go. He genuinely shared the opinion of the rest of Italy that it was not worth the chaos and bloodshed of a full-scale war just to decide who should be emperor. He was deeply distressed by the pointless deaths of Roman soldiers of both sides in the battle. There would be no more. Until his accession as emperor, Otho had seemed as narcissistic and degenerate as any of Nero's followers. Now he decided quite literally to lay down his life for his country. If restoring peace to Italy meant that Vitellius should be emperor, Otho could accept that, if not literally live with it. The frantic pleas of his soldiers could not move him. Some soldiers sought out Verginius Rufus. If suicide took Otho from the scene, this time the army would force Rufus to be emperor. Rufus fled his house and escaped the soldiers before the lethal honour could be bestowed upon him.

Meanwhile Otho urged his officers to make what terms they could with Vitellius. Then he retired to his tent. He spent the evening conversing with whomever wanted an audience with him and afterward enjoyed a good night's sleep.

Waking at daybreak, he promptly completed the only task on his agenda by stabbing himself with one of the two daggers kept at his bedside for that purpose. Rome's emperor of ninety-five days was buried in a tomb made deliberately modest in the hope that the Vitellians would not despoil it.[20]

The officers of the Othonian army set out to parlay with Caecina and discovered that the younger Flavius Sabinus was already on the same mission. Vitellius was still en route to Italy, so some senior Othonians set out to meet him and put their case to the new emperor in person. Among these was Suetonius Paulinus. This general now used to good purpose the earlier accusations of treachery and lack of commitment to the Othonian cause. He enthusiastically pleaded guilty to all the charges once laid against him and carefully stressed some of the wilder allegations that Vitellius might have forgotten. The effort was unnecessary. Vitellius was not a vindictive man and he spared all the Othonian leaders who appealed to him for mercy. This included Titianus, the brother of Otho.

Lines of Command
This first bout of civil war is interesting for the study of Roman generalship in that none of the chief protagonists was directly involved in the fray. In previous convulsions, Pompey and Caesar, Mark Antony and Octavian had all been at the forefront of their armies. They were physically present at the great battles that decided their destinies.

Yet in this next clash of Roman armies a century later, Nero remained in Rome. Rather than lead out an army against Galba, he sent a general who promptly deserted. Otho accompanied his army to the front but absented himself from the battlefield. It would appear that rather than directly leading their armies the emperors were leaving the job to more experienced subordinates.

Vitellius was not even in Italy when the decisive confrontation took place. Yet it seems he did intend to personally lead one arm of the invading army across the Maritime Alps and into Italy. However, reinforcements from Britain arrived slowly. Due to this and his natural incompetence, the war was over before Vitellius had got organized. He owed his success, just as he owed his initial promotion to emperor, to the energy and ambition of others.

It is unknown what Caecina thought of the emperor he was largely responsible for creating. However, that a dishonest former quaestor in Spain could make the abrupt transition to energetic and successful military commander is a testament to the amount of military training that upper-class Romans still received as a matter of course. It is also a testament to the ability of professional soldiers in the ranks to compensate for inexperience in their commanders. Without these two factors it is dubious that Caecina could have made all the running on the Vitellian side and largely overshadow Valens. Caecina's fellow general was indeed a *vir militaris*, and as a professional soldier he might have expected to take charge of the campaign.

On the Othonian side, one can only speculate what would have happened if Suetonius Paulinus had overall command. He had great experience and exactly the cautious mindset needed to delay the Vitellians until reinforcements arrived from the Danubian legions. However, Paulinus had never had to command troops as unruly and mutinous as the Praetorians. Nor was the Othonian attempt at generalship by committee like anything he had experienced. One suspects that the disastrous upshot of the campaign came as no great surprise to him. He may have spared a thought to his former subordinate, Petellius Cerialis. Cerialis, for reasons unknown to us, had stayed out of the war and undoubtedly congratulated himself on his wisdom in doing so.

That Otho and Vitellius in this bout of civil war preferred to lead from the rear can perhaps be explained by the fact that neither had much military experience and both had experienced subordinates. At this time it was still felt that an emperor should be at least a senator, and preferably a senator of ancient lineage or great prestige. The generals whom these would-be emperors commanded were either professional soldiers such as Paulinus and Valens or opportunists such as Caecina. These men lacked the *auctoritas* to attempt to seize power for themselves. It was safe to give such men command, as they were operating at as high a rank as they could conceivably obtain.

Emperor Vitellius
The victorious Vitellius began his march to Rome with little ostentation or pomp, not because he lacked the inclination for both, but because he lacked the means. Rome's new emperor had been close to bankruptcy before he was sent to the Rhinelands and had left his wife, Galeria, and his two children in a cheap boarding house in Rome. On his return journey local dignitaries fell over themselves to provide him with the luxuries to which he intended to become accustomed. The new emperor's lifestyle became steadily more luxurious as he approached the capital.

Even before he arrived in Rome, Vitellius took the obvious step of discharging the current Praetorian Guard and executing those officers directly involved in the murder of Galba. A second measure (which was to have far-reaching consequences) was to free Julius Civilis, whom we met earlier in Britain, a Batavian auxiliary commander suspected of treason against Otho. At issue was not whether Civilis was innocent, but whether Vitellius could afford to alienate the Batavian auxiliaries, who had so far been loyal and important supporters of his cause.

If the Batavians were to be rewarded by a tribal leader regaining his liberty, XIII Gemina, which had been among the strongest supporters of Otho, was to be punished. Vitellius intended to celebrate victory games in Cremona and he set XIII Gemina to building an appropriate amphitheatre. For the next month, the legionaries laboured to the jeers and mockery of the townsfolk. I Adiutrix was sent out of the way to Spain and XIV Gemina Martia Victrix dispatched once more to Britain.[21] XIV Gemina Martia Victrix were distinctly unhappy with the current regime. Matters were not helped by a bad command decision before they departed for their overseas posting. The legion was temporarily quartered with the Batavians in Augusta Taurinorum (Turin). A vicious feud broke out between the pro-Vitellian Batavians and the Othonian XIV Gemina Martia Victrix. The subsequent political discussion left much of the city a smoking ruin.

The Danubian legions that had been advancing on Italy to support Otho resentfully withdrew on hearing that their cause was lost before they had been able to support it. (According to Vespasian's biographer Suetonius, not everyone left Italy, and much was to come from this, as will be related below.) Vitellius now refilled the empty ranks of the Praetorians with his own loyalists. The military situation was now as stable as he could get it.

Forty days after his cause had triumphed at Bedriacum, Vitellius arrived at the scene of victory. To the bitter resentment of the nearby XIII Gemina, the Cremonians had not, as was customary, cleaned up the battlefield. The Othonian dead lay unburied so that the scene might be preserved for the emperor's delectation. Vitellius jovially refused to be offended by the stench of unburied corpses and made the famous comment that 'a dead enemy always smells good'. XIII Gemina had supplied many of these 'dead enemies' and appended that remark to their growing list of reasons for doing something about Vitellius. The self-restraint of Vitellius' army broke down with the realization of victory. His troops plundered rich estates as though occupying a hostile country.[22] As with the defeated Othonian legions, the landholders of Italy suffered in silence – but they did not forgive.

Chapter 5

Rebel With a Cause

AUT CAESAR AUT NIHIL **(EITHER CAESAR OR NOTHING)**
Vitellius courted the people of Rome with some success. Pleasing news came also from Africa, which accepted his claim to be emperor. Perhaps made careless by so much success, Rome's new master did little to reach out to Otho's former loyalists. Yet many who had felt deep disquiet on seeing Otho come to power felt nothing but admiration for how he had exercised and then relinquished it. This group now transferred their disquiet to Vitellius, with added resentment for the loss of the unusually promising emperor Otho had been shaping up to be.

Also, from top to bottom in Roman society there were many who were totally unimpressed by Vitellius. For every embittered Othonian with a grudge there were many more, in the senate and across the Roman Empire, prepared to give their support if the Othonians came up with someone suitable to replace their lost leader.

Some of the more perceptive may have noted that one of Nero's malignant legacies was that a suitable emperor need not even want the job. Nero had executed anyone he considered a possible rival, so being nominated – however unwillingly – as an imperial candidate was a death sentence unless the candidate was prepared to take his nomination further.

Corbulo had demonstrated that loyalty was no protection – perhaps even a 'mistake'. Thus the job of an imperial general became much more difficult and dangerous from the mid-60s AD onwards. A general had to be successful and command the loyalty and respect of his troops, but not to the extent that he became a potential emperor, either in the current incumbent's mind or in the minds of his soldiers. It was a delicate balance to maintain, and subsequent Roman history is littered with the corpses of generals who failed to maintain it ... and with the corpses of emperors who failed to note that a popular general was about to go critical.

Vitellius was the earliest example of this trend. Once his legions had nominated him, it probably seemed safer to become emperor than to risk being eliminated by Galba as a potential threat. But what had worked with

Vitellius would work with any potential Othonian candidate in future. Anoint a man with leadership of the anti-Vitellian cause and he could either risk his life trying to become emperor or risk his life by rejecting the nomination. Only Verginius Rufus ever carried off the third option of running away from the job.

FLAVIAN DELIBERATIONS

Some of these considerations must have exercised the minds of the main players in the year AD 69. What potential rivals to Vitellius existed? Would they prove loyal to the new emperor? If a rival emperor was proclaimed, how safe was he? How safe was it to support him, and how dangerous would it be not to support him? And above all, what of Flavius Vespasian?

Vespasian came from a relatively ignoble background, but his was a senatorial family. In fact, his brother had just been confirmed by Vitellius as prefect of Rome. Vespasian had done well in Britain, adequately as governor in Africa, and even better as commander of the Jewish war. The Flavians had powerful connections in the Roman senate, with allies such as the ancient family of the Petellii. Above all, Vespasian had three legions that were currently under-employed.

Most of Judea was conquered. Now Vespasian's soldiers were encamped under the walls of Jerusalem. Here in Judea's barren hill country the logistical situation meant that a very large army was more of a hindrance than a help to siege operations. Three legions and auxilia required some fifty metric tonnes of grain and almost a million litres of fresh water every day. Therefore it is probable that Vespasian was already contemplating the redeployment of soldiers not vital for the siege. Former Othonians had a few suggestions to offer about that.

A number of high-ranking Romans quietly slipped out of Italy and made their way east. Despite the imperial injunction against senators visiting Egypt, some joined Tiberius Alexander, the highly pro-Flavian prefect running that country. Others became guests of Licinius Mucianus, the governor of Syria, a man who made no secret of his friendship with Titus, the son of Vespasian. Licinius Mucianus was well qualified to become emperor and probably could have counted on Vespasian's support if he had decided to do so. But Mucianus had no interest in the job. However, he was very willing to join Tiberius Alexander in backing Vespasian for it.

Vitellius appointed a man called Aponius Saturninus to command in the Danube. Saturninus was probably the only pro-Vitellian in the area. The legates of the Danubian legions had supported Otho and knew that Vitellius was even now considering their replacements. III Gallica had been recently transferred to Illyria from Mucianus in Syria and openly declared its support for Vespasian.

Yet even if by some miracle Saturninus kept the Danubian legions out of any future Flavian rebellion, Syria, Judea and Egypt could supply nine legions. Nor could anyone doubt that after recent events the arena-building XIII Gemina of Cremona would happily add to that number.

It is true that a large proportion of the legions Vespasian needed to march on Rome were also needed where they were to guard the frontiers of the empire. But both sides fighting a civil war would be equally crippled by this requirement. Vespasian would have to worry about the Parthians and Sarmatians, but Vitellius' Rhineland legions had to contend with the restive tribes of Germany.

Overall, Vespasian had the political support to become emperor. He had the soldiers too. Furthermore, it was a moot point whether seizing the empire was less dangerous for Vespasian than waiting for Vitellius pre-emptively to remove him just in case he tried. On the other hand, the Rhineland legions were probably the best fighting troops in the empire. Also a bid for power would be dangerous – perhaps fatal – for those Flavians in Rome, who included Vespasian's brother, Sabinus, his son, Domitian, and his former son-in-law, Petellius Cerialis.

However, Vespasian was not really given much choice. The groundswell of support for his nomination for emperor grew quickly and uncontrollably. One of the clearest indications of this was that Vespasian did not even have time to arrange a secure message warning his nearest and dearest to get out of Rome in the very near future.

If the uprising against Vitellius had a definite starting point it lay with two thousand Danubian soldiers of VII Claudia and VIII Augusta. These were among the Danubians who had reached eastern Italy at the time of the battle of Bedriacum. These men did not return to base on hearing of Otho's death.[1] They were uncertain of the fate which awaited Othonian loyalists and, like the eastern legions, were deeply unimpressed by Vitellius as emperor. VIII Augusta was one of the oldest legions in the Roman army. Some of its soldiers had taken part in the invasion of Britain, and the veterans remembered Vespasian from this time. So now the legionaries inscribed his name on their standards – and only the emperor's name was thus displayed. Word reached Tiberius Alexander in Egypt that Vespasian had armed support in Italy. The Egyptian prefect promptly mustered his troops and swore support for the rebel cause. By the first of July, northern Italy, Egypt, the Danubian legions and presumably Rome knew that a rebellion headed by Vespasian had broken out. Vespasian himself was brought up to speed three days later when he emerged from his quarters and the guards saluted him as emperor.[2]

REBELS IN ROME
One can only speculate at the feelings of Vespasian's son Domitian when he heard that his father was leading a bid to overthrow Vitellius. These feelings might well have been tinged by some degree of bitterness. Vespasian was in Judea, backed by the Syrian, Egyptian and Judean legions. Domitian was in Rome, and completely in Vitellius' power. There was very little chance of Vitellius surviving should Vespasian succeed. Therefore the better things went for Vespasian, the worse they were likely to go for Domitian, since Vitellius might well want to take a few senior Flavians down with him. And there was nothing Domitian could do about it.

Flavius Sabinus and Petellius Cerialis were in the same boat. The fact that Petellius Cerialis was still in Rome when Vespasian's revolt broke out speaks volumes for how suddenly civil war flared anew. Vitellius might want Flavius Sabinus and Domitian on hand as hostages for Vespasian's good conduct, but there was no reason for Petellius Cerialis to be in Rome. Given sufficient warning, he could have quietly left the city up to a month beforehand. In fact he had even more reason for wanting to be out of the city than Vespasian's immediate family. Cerialis was exactly the sort of Flavian whom Vitellius would execute to warn Vespasian that the danger to Sabinus and Domitian was real.

But though the senate had already accepted Vitellius as emperor, Vitellius himself had yet to arrive in Rome. Progress through Italy became ever slower. Central Italy was more able than the north to accommodate the imperial urge to eat, drink and be merry in every town and villa along the road. Much of what passed for government fell to Caecina and Valens. But relations between Vitellius' senior henchmen had never been more than cordial and now were souring rapidly. Each competed with the other for followers and for Vitellius' favour. Anyone opposed to an order or instruction from one general could easily get it countermanded by the other.

News of Vespasian's revolt initially had little effect on the power-drunk Vitellians. The first reports from the Danube frontier came with soothing assurances from Saturninus. Only III Gallica was in arms and steps were being taken to stabilize the situation with the other legions. Saturninus did not mention that these steps would take him over to the rebel side, thus achieving complete harmony of purpose between soldiers and general.

The entry of Vitellius into Rome furthered the disquiet of senators and the civil population. The Rhineland legionaries little resembled the sophisticated Praetorians whom the Roman citizenry knew. Some legions had been on the German frontier for decades. All these long-term Rhineland legions had become more than somewhat German in manner. The legionaries had strange, uncouth accents, wore animal skins over their armour and tended to respond to mockery with lethal force.

With the people uneasy about the new arrivals, Vitellius could not alienate the senate. He conscientiously attended meetings on even minor matters. Helvidius Priscus, a famously stiff-necked senator of republican leanings, publicly challenged one of his rulings. Vitellius laughed it off as 'a mere disagreement between senators'. Given the strength of Flavian support in the senate, Vitellius avoided any overt moves against the senior members of the clan. And among the more junior Flavians, Petellius Cerialis had mysteriously disappeared.

Cerialis had decided that Vitellius' arrival was his cue to abandon Rome. He intended to seek out the rebels before the emperor had noticed he wasn't there. As a refugee, Cerialis faced two problems in his flight. The first was that if he tried to leave Italy, he was bound to be stopped either at a formal checkpoint, or by one of the less formal groups of Vitellian soldiery plaguing the countryside. As the close relative of a rebel leader, Cerialis was likely to suffer somewhat if discovered at a formal checkpoint. He would suffer greatly if captured by irregular Vitellian soldiery. These men had none of the political sophistication Vitellius was showing by keeping Sabinus and Domitian at liberty.

Italy was not an easy place to get out of. By now the seasonal Etesian winds were blowing westward across the Mediterranean. This made it easy to travel to the pro-Vitellian west, but much harder to sail eastward to safety in Judea or Egypt, even assuming that it was possible to board ship without discovery.[3] The alternative was to go by land to the Danubian legions. The problem here was that either Vitellius or a competent subordinate had noted a steady flow of messages through the Pannonian Alps from Vespasian's supporters to prominent Italians and senators. Now the passes to northeastern Italy were blocked and patrolled. Captured messengers were sent to Rome for interrogation and execution.

Given that Rome was unhealthy, and that escape was very difficult, Petellius Cerialis took almost the only remaining option. He disappeared into the countryside. The passing of different armies across Italy had severely disrupted rural life. Villas had been plundered, crops and oxen requisitioned, and herds swept up to feed soldiers on the march. A usually stable society in which everyone knew everyone else had now a goodly number of adventurers, escaped or masterless slaves, deserted Othonian ex-legionaries and dispossessed farmers and smallholders. In the guise of a displaced shepherd, the would-be emperor's former son-in-law intended to live rough in Campania until help arrived from the east.

THE WAR MACHINES GEAR UP
Since Cerialis knew Vespasian, he would have suspected that help might be a while coming. Where Cerialis was impetuous to the point of being foolhardy, Vespasian was stolid, unhurried and methodical. The conquest of the Roman Empire would be achieved in the same deliberate manner as the subjugation of Judea.

Firstly, the same west winds that penned Cerialis in Italy were usually the signal for the merchant fleet to start the annual voyage from Alexandria to Rome. This fleet carried the city's essential grain supplies, and this year it would not sail. Tiberius Alexander kept his ships in port, only allowing out those that sailed up the coast of Palestine to supply the Flavian legions. To increase the pressure on Vitellius, Mucianus made preparations to bring the Roman fleet from Pontus on the Black Sea to blockade the harbours of Italy.

For political more than military reasons, it was decided that the Danube legions would advance with at least the same number of eastern soldiers. Veterans were recalled to the colours and messengers hurried along the great trunk roads of the eastern empire. They carried urgent requests for estimates of how many men each legion could spare without denuding the frontier defences. Other messengers crossed the frontier to Parthia. They politely – and successfully – warned the king against attempting, in Armenia or elsewhere, to exploit Rome's internal turmoil for his own advantage.

Next came the question of money. Mucianus donated lavishly from his private fortune and pressed client kings and wealthy individuals to follow suit. (Many of these donors were later to discover that Vespasian was famously stingy with the imperial money chest, and few ever saw their money again.) Titus was raised to command of the war in Judea, with Julius Tiberius of Egypt promoted as his advisor. Mucianus was put in charge of preparing an advance guard for the invasion of Italy. Vespasian himself took over in Egypt, on guard against an invasion by the African legion near Carthage which had declared for Vitellius.

It was typical of Vespasian's approach to warfare that he first secured his lines of supply and stabilized his finances. Then he next established his command structure. Then he turned his attention to the legions that would be doing the actual fighting. Good news came from the Danube, where the legions fell one after another behind his cause. There had been little doubt of VII Claudia, and XIII Gemina were still smarting from their defeat at Bedriacum and their humiliation in Cremona. They were eager for a return match with the Rhinelanders. III Gallica in Moesia had always been pro-Vespasian, and the rest of VIII Augusta went along with their comrades already in Italy. In short, the empire east of the Alps was under Vespasian's command without a blow being struck.

To counter the storm from the east, Vitellius had his Rhinelanders, and legions in Britain, Africa and Spain. Yet not all the Rhinelanders were available, for Hordonius Flaccus on the German frontier reported that the Batavians were restless, stirred up by that same Julius Civilis whom Vitellius had so prematurely freed (of which more will be related later). Men were needed to guard other frontiers as well. Vettius Bolanus could spare few from Britain, where XX Valeria Victrix had recently mutinied. Anyway, Queen Cartimandua was having further domestic ructions with her husband (cf p. 46) and the Brigantine situation was threatening to explode once more.

Legion XIV Gemina Martia Victrix had only just returned to Britain from Italy. After their defeat at Bedriacum, the once pro-Othonian legionaries had no intention of supporting Vitellius. Nevertheless, Bolanus did what he could for his new emperor. He sent substantial detachments from IX Hispana and took the opportunity to strip XX Valeria Victrix of its malcontents. II Augusta presented a special problem. Vespasian had once commanded the legion and the veterans would not fight against him. In the end, Bolanus sent Vitellius the newer recruits to the legion.

Like Vitellius, the Flavians also were looking for recruits across the west. Vespasian's emissaries urged former Othonians to take up arms against Vitellius. Among those who readily responded were the discharged Praetorians and Julius Agricola, who had just buried his mother and was returning to military matters.

For Vitellius, the Danubian legions were a real and present danger to north Italy. It was vital to secure Cremona for precisely the same reasons that Otho had tried to block the Vitellian advance there. Therefore as the summer advanced, so did Caecina, now consul, as he led the emperor's army northwards. In truth, many of the legionaries were happy to leave Rome. There had been little room for tens of thousands of men in a city unused to military occupation, and many of the Rhinelanders had been recruited locally in Germany and were unused to the heat of Rome in July. Overcrowding and an unfamiliar diet had caused illness. The exotic delights of the capital had sapped discipline and morale. Even without the threat of Vespasian, the Rhine legions would have had to move north again soon.

The Flavian war councils debated their next move. Some were in favour of a long game. Rome could be starved by blockade while the full strength of the eastern and Danubian legions was mustered. Then a single march would take Italy. This is what Vespasian had planned and what Mucianus wanted.

The strongest opponent of this policy was one Antonius Primus. This upstart commander was in many ways the mirror image of Caecina on the Vitellian side. Caecina had become a Vitellian to escape justice. Primus had already felt the heavy hand of the law on his collar. Condemned for forgery, he had been expelled from the senate and exiled from Italy. For reasons now unknown, Galba had restored Primus to favour. Primus was now legate in command of the legion Galba had raised, VII Galbiana. Somewhat ungratefully, Primus had written to Galba's murderer, Otho, offering him support against Vitellius.

If Vitellius got hold of this letter, the best Primus could hope for was to be exiled again. So Primus became a fervent supporter of Vespasian. Like Caecina, he compensated for his lack of scruples with energy, boldness and considerable military skill. And like Caecina, Primus offered his overall commander some degree of security. Even in these desperate times neither senate, people or army would consider either of these moral bankrupts as suitable for any position higher than that which they held already.

Primus delivered a stirring speech to his fellow legates. He wanted an immediate advance with the cavalry and such of the Danubian legions as were already on hand. Not everyone was convinced of the strategic soundness of this plan. Nevertheless, they allowed Primus to go ahead and lead an expedition into Italy. If he succeeded, all well and good. If he failed, the main army advancing under Aponius Saturninus could probably cover the retreat of the advance guard while everyone would be rid of its annoying commander.

One advantage of speed immediately became apparent. XIII Gemina had been ordered out of Cremona after building the hated amphitheatre and was on its way to the Danube. To no one's surprise, the legionaries did a smart about-turn on hearing of Vespasian's rebellion. They contacted Primus' advance guard and hastened to join it near Padova (modern Padua). Further Flavian reinforcements made a welcome appearance with the arrival of VII Claudia, which also had not got far on its return march to the Danube frontier. Primus already had III Gallica, and by now most of VIII Augusta was also in his camp.

On the Vitellian march to Cremona, Caecina showed none of his usual flair and initiative. The reason was simple – he was contemplating a further change of allegiance. To his chagrin, Valens, the 'military man', had proven adept at playing the political game. Valens now stood higher in the emperor's esteem than Caecina. Therefore Caecina had been taking advice on his best interests from Flavius Sabinus, Prefect of the city of Rome and brother to Vespasian. One of Caecina's first actions on arriving in northern Italy was to confer with the prefect of the fleet at Ravenna. This was another Vitellian who was having second thoughts about his loyalty.

After some initial sparring, Primus and Caecina eventually faced off across the Po about 100 miles from Cremona. Despite the rabid eagerness of the soldiers to begin killing each other, both commanders had negotiation in mind. As a further prompt to Caecina, the commander of the Ravenna fleet switched allegiance to Vespasian right on cue. If Caecina could now deliver his legionaries as well, Primus and the Flavian army would have a secure river crossing and an almost unopposed march on Rome. The early push to Rome would be triumphantly vindicated.

There was a complication. Primus' legionary reinforcements were accompanied by Flavianus and Aponius Saturninus, commanders of Pannonia and Moesia respectively. Both of these men outranked Primus, who was still officially only legate of VII Galbiana. However, Primus had already gained the loyalty of the entire army. They liked their current general and intended to keep him. A rash attempt by the governors to assert their authority led to scenes of violent disorder in barracks.

Totally misreading the temper of the troops, Flavianus began issuing orders arrogantly. At the last he saved himself from a lynching by grovelling on the ground and from there tearfully begging for the mercy of the soldiers. They contemptuously ejected him from the camp. Saturninus quickly identified the anti-authoritarian trend. He hid himself in the ashes of the heating system and made a barely more dignified escape. Both men eventually made their way to Vespasian. They were warmly commended for their sacrifices for the Flavian cause, but did not get back their lost command of the legions. For now Primus had supreme command in Italy and a free hand to negotiate with Caecina.

These negotiations were secret because Caecina had no chance of selling a change of allegiance to his men other than as a *fait accompli*. Therefore, once he had come to terms with Primus, Caecina called his senior officers. He informed them that the legions were under new management and had them swear loyalty to Vespasian. The legionaries only found that they were now a Flavian army when someone spotted that the name on their standards had changed from Vitellius to Vespasian. They did not take the discovery well.

Not even the legendary oratory of Caecina was up to the task of making his men swallow his treacherous about-face. His persuasion worked to some extent though, for instead of lynching him, the men merely threw Caecina in chains. Then, led by enthusiasts from V Alaudae, the legionaries restored the Vitellian standards. For good measure they massacred a detachment of sailors from the fleet at Ravenna. These men were on detached duty and therefore behind with current events. They turned up in three light galleys, unaware that their commander had switched sides, or that the Vitellian legions had briefly become Flavian but now were not.

This massacre probably confirmed the Flavian sympathies of the rest of the Ravenna fleet. This presented a risk that Primus might turn the Vitellian flank by using the fleet to move troops down the coast. So the new commanders of the Vitellian force, Cassius Longus and Fabius Fabullus, praefectus castrorum and legate of V Alaudae, decided to finish the journey to Cremona by forced marches. This would speedily unite their army with the advance guard of I Italica and XXI Rapax, which Caecina had sent ahead with much of the cavalry. A forced march would have the additional benefit of giving the unsettled troops little time or energy to do anything else. Hopefully once the army was combined at Cremona, it would be joined by reinforcements from north of the Alps, where the garrisons were being stripped to dangerously below the bare minimum. (In fact, no further reinforcements were forthcoming. The Rhine garrisons had their own preoccupations, as will be seen below.)

Primus received word that Caecina's switch of allegiance had failed to win hearts and minds. It was time to see if the swords of his legionaries were more persuasive than Caecina's honeyed words. The Vitellians were on the move towards Cremona, so Primus immediately marched his army toward the same destination. Having the Postumian Road to Bedriacum on his side of the river Po, he made very good time. This shorter route and better road allowed Primus to arrive a day earlier than the Vitellian army. The Vitellian advance troops of I Italica and XXI Rapax were already guarding Cremona, camped outside the city. Primus immediately decided to try his luck against these two legions before the rest of the Vitellian army arrived. His foragers spread out across the farms in the nearby countryside. Possibly some of these foragers were from the XIII Gemina. These men well remembered the taunts of the people of Cremona while they had been building the amphitheatre there.

This may be why the foraging amounted to devastation. It was certainly comprehensive enough to draw the Vitellian legions out of their camp to drive off the pillagers.

Primus was leading some four thousand cavalry, deployed to cover the foragers should they run into problems. On news that the enemy legions were on the move, he ordered the foragers recalled. He also ordered his own legions to advance into battle. A problem immediately developed with what should have been a well-synchronized manoeuvre for veteran troops. An impetuous officer in the cavalry took it upon himself to charge the Vitellian advance guard. After a temporary success, his unit was routed, and the glory-hunter's fleeing men sucked others into their panic-stricken flight down the road. Primus' cavalry force was dissolving. But the Flavian commander knew how to act decisively. He literally stopped a fleeing standard bearer dead in his tracks by running the man through with a spear. Then he rallied a small clump of men around the standard.

This group steadied the retreating cavalry nearby. They were aided by a good defensive position and foragers returning from the fields. The pursuing Vitellian troops hit this knot of resistance piecemeal and their disorganized attack was chopped to pieces. This completed the rally of the Flavian forces and the battle started to go the other way. The Vitellian vanguard was driven back against I Italica and XXI Rapax, which by now had advanced four miles out of Cremona. The confused legionaries tried to hold their formation in the face of their routing and terrified comrades. They were unprepared for a wedge of veteran Danubian auxiliaries following up close behind the fleeing men, and their line was broken before it was properly formed. The Vitellian legions did the only thing possible. They disengaged, making their way back to camp and city amid scenes of considerable chaos.

If he had been able to follow up, Primus might have finished the battle then and there. But he had no way to attack fortified positions with only exhausted cavalry and foragers to hand. He had to await the arrival of his legions. These reached him at 4pm, some five hours after the action had begun. Primus' men were all for attacking the city at once, but captured stragglers from the Vitellian advance guard persuaded them otherwise with disquieting information. The Vitellian legions marching to Cremona had covered over thirty miles in the past day. If they carried on their march, they would arrive in a matter of hours. If the Flavian army did attack Cremona and failed, it would be caught between the rock of Cremona and the hard edge of the Vitellian reinforcements. This sobered the aggression of the men to the point where they were ready to accept Primus' orders to stand down. They would prepare for a pitched battle on the morrow.

THE SECOND BATTLE OF CREMONA

Primus pulled his army back two miles. In the process of falling back to their new position, some ex-praetorians walked over the very ground on which they had been defeated seven months previously. Unlike that untimely and disorganized engagement, Primus intended everything to go like clockwork for the rematch. At the point he chose to make a stand, the via Postumia was somewhat higher than the surrounding fields, and Primus ordered XIII Gemina to use the embankment as a rampart to anchor his line. On the left of this he put the two Seventh legions, first Primus' own unit, VII Galbiana, and then VII Claudia. As it happened, these two legions had a large drainage ditch covering their frontage. There was no such advantage for VIII Augusta, which was deployed on open ground to the right of the road, with III Gallica on the flanks. III Gallica's battle line was split by a clump of impenetrable scrubby woodland, so a unit of former Praetorians was deployed with the legion to compensate for any problems this might cause. The remaining Praetorians were kept in reserve. Auxiliaries and cavalry secured the flanks.

By now the sun was already setting on an October afternoon. Though he had deployed his men into battle order, Primus was not really expecting to fight. His deployment was something of a dress rehearsal for the line of battle planned for the next day. It was also a sensible precaution, because it was too late to fortify a proper camp and the Vitellian reinforcements were still advancing. It would be unwise to take anything for granted until the enemy settled down in Cremona for the night.

Primus' caution was well-advised. The Vitellian army reached Cremona. It slowed slightly as the men were fed supper on the march by the literally relieved townsfolk, but the legions kept coming. It became clear that their intention was to smash the Flavian army before bedtime. That a Roman force might consider battle at the end of a long day's march is a tribute to the training regimen of the Roman army. In fact, every Roman legion twice a month did an excursion to practise for just such an eventuality as that which they were now putting into practice. The second battle of Bedriacum was to be a night action between a Flavian army of somewhat tired men and a Vitellian army considerably more tired still.

'It would have been more advisable to rest up for the night,' remarks Tacitus, who, like most Roman senators, was a keen amateur tactician.[4] However, the Vitellians had no real leaders and no real plan. Caecina had provided convincing evidence that the top management of the legions might prove treacherous, so the rank and file had no intention of pausing to allow time for further betrayals.

The deployment of the Vitellians was something of an ad hoc affair. Still, it was yet another impressive demonstration of how well legions could deploy into line of battle despite a rudimentary command structure and no effective leadership. Nevertheless, it was understandable if, under the circumstances, the final formation was less than perfect.

The centre of the Vitellian line was formed by the British detachments of IX Hispana, II Augusta and XX Valeria Victrix. XVI Gallica and XXII Primigenia squared up against Primus' VIII Augusta and III Gallica. The Vitellian IV Macedonica and XV Primigenia took on the two Flavian Seventh legions on the other flank.

It is almost impossible to estimate the number of men on each side. Most of these 'legions' were divided between units still doing their duty on the frontier and others who had taken the time out to fight a civil war. At a very rough guess there were some 20,000 to 25,000 fighting for Vitellius and somewhat fewer – 15,000 to 20,000 – for Vespasian. While the Danubians had the advantage of the terrain, and were somewhat fresher, the Vitellians had the edge in experience. Furthermore, their ranks were fleshed out by soldiers of I Italica and XXI Rapax. These were still disordered from their precipitous retreat earlier in the day, and they joined the advancing column with a unit here and a unit there, fitting in wherever they were needed.

Whatever else it may be, this was no tactician's battle. The moment they had dressed their line, the Vitellians hurled themselves at their opponents with a vigour that compensated for any lack of subtlety. In the darkness before moonrise, fighting was savage, confused and bloody. Both sides were Roman, with the same weapons, tactics and dress. As the battle lines became ragged, it became hard to tell friend from foe. Challenges given and answered soon made the watchwords of each army known to the other, and troops following their standards deep into enemy ranks occasionally discovered to their terminal embarrassment that these standards were not thrusting triumphantly forward, but had been captured by the enemy.

At the centre of it all, the Flavians latest recruits, XIII Gemina, did well. The legion was helped by combat experience, considerable animosity towards the Rhinelanders and the elevation of the road on which they fought. VII Galbiana had fewer of these advantages, and the untried legion reeled under the assault of its battle-hardened opponents. Like a good general, Primus was carefully following the course of the battle. When he saw VII Galbiana giving ground, he ordered the Praetorian reserve to move across the rear of the battle line and back up the faltering legion. Whatever their performance in the first battle, the Praetorians now gave a good account of themselves. The line thereafter moved back and forward but remained firm.

The Vitellians of XV Primigenia had with them a siege engine of considerable size. How they had procured this or brought it along on their forced march is unknown. But they now put it into operation – one of the very rare instances of heavy artillery being used in an ancient battle. The stones smashed into the massed ranks of the Danubian legionaries, who were totally defenceless against the havoc the weapon wrought. Two soldiers acting on their own initiative picked up shields with the markings of XV Primigenia from the ground. Disguised by these, they infiltrated the Vitellian lines until they reached the engine. They fell upon it, slashing cords and irreparably damaging springs until the Vitellians noticed and killed the pair of nameless heroes.

Moonrise brought a quarter-moon over the backs of Flavian army. This threw their shadows before them and confused the aim of the Vitellians, who were unsure if their pila were hitting shadow or substance. Vespasian's men, with their targets clearly outlined in the moonlight, had no such difficulty. Stories of tragedy and heroism were told of that night: Atilius Varus, centurion of VII Galbiana, helped recapture the legion's eagle and then defended it single handed, slaughtering all who tried to seize it once more, and only succumbed to his wounds once help had arrived. A recruit of the Seventh noticed something familiar about the veteran of the XXI Rapax he had just cut down. He was appalled to find the father whom he had followed into the army dying at his feet.[5] Others saw old comrades on the other side and pleaded with them to switch allegiance. Occasional impromptu truces broke out along the line where soldiers on opposing sides stopped fighting long enough to share a quick meal together. Afterwards they picked up their swords and re-engaged in combat.[6]

The legions were deadlocked. Two components of the finest military machine in antiquity were each slowly grinding the other to mincemeat. With neither side able to win through numbers, superior equipment or skill, all that remained was morale. Through the night Primus played a general's part, moving among the soldiers, encouraging and inspiring them. He bucked up III Gallica, reminding them that though recently arrived from Syria, they had already achieved much against the Parthians and Sarmatians. When appeals to pride failed he tried mockery, asking the Danubians whether they had ever intended to truly fight or had hoped the enemy would quail from a dirty look. The Praetorians he witheringly addressed as *'pagani'* (country bumpkins)[7] and asked them where they would go if defeated – 'what general, what camp will want you? Without victory, all that remains is death, because frankly, you cannot be more disgraced.'

The battle raged until dawn. By then both armies were exhausted. Not a legion had buckled, no one had fled the field, and after a night of slaughter there seemed nothing for it but to carry on into the day. Then, out on the northern wing, the men of III Gallica turned, gave a resounding cheer and held up their swords in greeting. The rumour swept through both armies that Licinius Mucianus had arrived with reinforcements and the III Gallica were greeting old comrades from Syria.

In fact III Gallica were, as was their daily habit, saluting Sol Invictus, the newly risen sun. They had adopted this tradition while in Syria. But the Rhineland and British legions had no such custom; nor did the Danubians. For them there could only be one explanation for III Gallica's behaviour – help had arrived. Primus may have known what was happening, but he carefully allowed his men their illusions.

In the confident expectation that they were about to be reinforced, the Danubians launched their attack with fresh vigour. The Vitellians were as tough as they came, but had marched all day and fought all night. They knew they were in no shape to take on fresh enemies. They had no general to rally them as Primus had done, and exhaustion takes a mental as well as a physical toll. The walls of Cremona that they had scorned yesterday suddenly seemed irresistibly inviting to the wavering soldiers. Singly, then in groups and units, the army broke and ran. They were defeated, in the end, by dawn.

AFTERMATH

The battle was won, but the fight was not over. The Vitellians had not been mistaken that both Cremona and their camp offered security, and a good proportion of their army managed to find shelter behind the ramparts of one or the other.

This left Primus with a dilemma. If he pulled back to Bedriacum with the enemy force largely intact, then the entire battle would need to be re-fought in the near future. It was almost impossible to ask soldiers without entrenching tools to set up a siege camp while they were still recovering from a night's battle. And this was apart from the near certainty that the Vitellians would attack as soon as Primus' army started digging. That left one final option – storming positions that the garrison of I Italica and XXI Rapax had been carefully fortifying since their arrival. Even allowing that the Vitellians were even more exhausted than his own men, how could the general ask soldiers who had just won him a hard-fought victory to throw themselves immediately into a further engagement that promised to be every bit as bloody and difficult?

Few armies in the world would have done it. Yet Primus discovered that with his legionaries, the problem would have been trying to stop them. Infuriated by the missiles the ballistae in the Vitellian camp were already lobbing at them, the men were clamouring to finish the job. Primus hastily organized his forces for an impromptu attack. Foragers were sent to scour local farmsteads for any digging implements they could find. While these were being fetched, the army moved to its assault positions. Primus planned to ignore Cremona and first take out the more vulnerable legionary camp. Each legion was assigned a point of attack and encouraged to be the first over the camp's ramparts.

Now, once again, the irresistible force of a veteran Roman army smashed into the only immovable object known to it – another Roman army. XIII Gemina had been at the forefront of those following up the Vitellian retreat. Now the legion launched itself at one of the gates of the enemy camp. To meet the storm of missiles that greeted them, they pulled their shields over their heads so that they overlapped in the famous *'testudo'* (tortoise) formation. Yet their enemies had been there before, and done that. They knew the best way to break a testudo was by pushing down with long poles into any gaps that appeared and following this up with a bombardment by any heavy objects available until the formation broke.

This worked on XIII Gemina, though that legion did not give up the attack. However, VII Galbiana, led by Primus in person, kept such a tight formation that it was impervious to ballista missiles. Finally, in desperation, the Vitellians heaved the ballista itself over the ramparts and on to the testudo. This worked for a moment, but at the cost of taking some of the rampart with it. The testudo immediately reformed. So strong was the Roman testudo that a chariot could be driven across the top of it. The legions now put this strength to good use by forming a second storey on top of the first layer of shields. This put the men standing on that level with the men on the wall.

Meanwhile, VII Claudia had taken a more conventional route and taken down a tower with their siege artillery. The legionaries now formed a wedge and drove into the breach, while III Gallica, in the thick of the action, went at the gate with axes. And it was a man of III Gallica who gained his legion the honour of being first over the ramparts.

The Vitellians recognized that their position was hopeless, but they were not yet ready to abandon the fight. By design, the army opposing them was weakest on the side of the camp facing Cremona. Primus did not want a sally from the city hitting his besiegers from behind. The Vitellians now forced their way out of the camp and into the city. They took huge casualties in the process, as it was impossible to disengage.

Only when they were behind the walls of Cremona did the Vitellians begin to despair, for Primus and his indefatigable army immediately began mustering for another assault. The testudos reformed and siege artillery began hurling flaming missiles over the ramparts. The Vitellians were men who had – without rest – just completed a forced march, fought and lost a night-long battle, and then unsuccessfully defended their camp from assault. Having immediately afterwards to stop a city from being stormed was too much even for them. There were legions – for example X Gemina in peaceful Spain – which had seen less action in six decades than they had managed in the past twenty-four hours. Accompanying the army was Caecina, still a prisoner in chains. He pointed out the hopelessness of the situation to the senior Vitellians as they despairingly mustered their defence. As the one man of the army guaranteed a favourable reception by Primus, Caecina suggested that he be allowed to negotiate a surrender.

Perhaps because they had themselves been treated with relative generosity by the Vitellians after their defeat at the earlier battle of Bedriacum, the initial fury of the Flavian legions cooled fast. The men rapidly remembered that their defeated enemies were, after all, fellow Roman soldiers. Caecina negotiated easy terms for them, and indeed for himself. He had pushed his luck to the limit by arriving at the enemy lines in the full garb of a Roman consul, complete with his attendants. Fortunately for him, the Flavian army was too glad to get the fighting over with to worry about the pretensions of those who arranged the peace. Besides, they were itching to get started on Cremona.

Cremona had been enthusiastically pro-Vitellius throughout the campaign. The Flavian army considered it a hostile city. The men undoubtedly took their lead from XIII Gemina, who remembered well the insults and abuse from the townsfolk as they laboured at their amphitheatre. Finally, Tacitus suggests, probably correctly, that Primus and his officers had inspired their exhausted men into their last desperate effort by promising them a free hand with the helpless city once they had taken it.

Cremona was sacked with as much violence as any barbarian encampment. The suffering of the townsfolk was actually made worse by the fact that no Italians would accept their fellow-countrymen as slaves. This left no reason for the plundering legionaries to take prisoners who could be sold for profit.

Everyone was fair game without respect to age, gender or class. The next four days were an orgy of massacre, rape and looting. This horror continued until relatives living outside the city sent urgent messages that they were prepared to ransom surviving family members. The offer came too late for an estimated 50,000 victims. To their disgrace, even some Vitellian legionaries joined their former enemies in pillaging the city that had supported them. The pillaging and killing only really stopped when Cremona was too wrecked to sustain the presence of an army any longer. Then the legions turned south towards Rome.

FLAVIUS SABINUS IN ROME

Vitellius was recovering from a bout of illness when he received news of the defection of the fleet at Ravenna. The bad news trickling in rapidly swelled to a doleful flood with news of the defeat at Bedriacum and the sack of Cremona. Vitellius' henchman, Valens, had been in Etruria at the time. Realizing the need to bring reinforcements to Italy without delay, Valens wrote to Vitellius asking him to mobilize the soldiers he had kept in Rome as replacements for the disbanded Praetorians. Then Valens himself took ship for Gaul to raise Gallic levies and bring the Batavians into the conflict. Yet news of the defeat at Cremona had preceded him. The Batavians wanted nothing more to do with Vitellius and had already marched home. The countryside was divided between those yet loyal to Vitellius and former Othonian loyalists who had embraced the Flavian cause. Unsure of whom to trust, Valens put to sea again. There he was captured by ships sent by a Flavian commander.

Spain always had been tepid towards Vitellius. Now the legion raised by Galba from the fleet, I Adiutrix, declared for Vespasian. VI Victrix and sleepy X Gemina followed their lead. Gaul promptly followed Spain, removing any hope for Vitellius from that quarter. In Britain, II Augusta had never been enthusiastic about opposing its old commander. Once the governor had sent the least pro-Vespasian element to reinforce the Vitellians in Italy, the remainder of the legion was solidly behind Vespasian. The newly arrived men of XIV Martia Victrix were former Othonians who loathed Vitellius. Together these two legions convinced the IX Hispana and XX Valeria Victrix to switch allegiance. Bolanus had major problems with the Brigante on the northern frontier. He apparently decided that the important thing was to keep the empire secure for whomever ended up ruling it. If the legions wanted Vespasian, Vespasian it would be. Within weeks of the sack of Cremona, Vitellius had lost the west.

With north Italy in Flavian hands, Primus replaced the most rabidly Vitellian officers of the Germanic legions and prepared to hurry them out of the country. The Rhinelanders were needed for a rapidly escalating crisis on the German frontier. The Flavian VII Claudia was also sent back to shore up the Danube frontier.

Primus set out for Rome. But however well things were going for his cause, his personal star was fading. His victory had aroused the jealousy of Mucianus. Vespasian's backer saw himself as the second man in the new imperium and was not prepared to tolerate a usurper. Secondly Vespasian showed, not for the last time, that his bluff, wrinkled countenance masked a politician of Machiavellian skills.

He must have known that the conquest of Italy was never going to be painless. Primus' plan to strike fast and early had caught the Vitellians off guard, but it had also discombobulated those in charge of pay and logistics. The heavy autumn rains of that year so bogged down the northern countryside that supply trains would have had great difficulty reaching the army, even had someone had the foresight to lay them on. So the legions were forced to live off the land, and the land suffered badly in consequence. As an experienced general, Vespasian had probably foreseen this.

Eventually, Italy would have him as emperor. Best, then, that the Italians blame someone else for the devastation inflicted on the countryside in the course of making him so. It eventually dawned on Primus that he was being set up as a scapegoat, especially since Italy and the Roman Empire generally were appalled by the fate of Cremona. He wrote to Vespasian pointing out 'He had fought for his emperor not with messages and letters, but with hand and arms.'[8] This letter displayed Primus' justifiable pride in his achievements, but his opponents called it proof of his arrogance.

Nor was Primus to be sole master of the legions for much longer. Petellius Cerialis now joined the army from Campania with whatever cavalry he had been able to muster while there. To Primus' chagrin, many delegations from Italian cities made their way directly to the emperor's former son-in-law, and only afterwards to Primus, the overall commander. What Cerialis had been up to in the months leading up to Primus' advance is unknown, but the manner of his escape from Rome had added to his reputation. When Saturninus and Flavianus once threatened his overall command, Primus had them run out of the camp by his soldiers. The men would do no such thing with the popular and charismatic Cerialis. Fortunately Cerialis was not looking to take over from Primus. He merely sought and received command of much of the cavalry.

Vitellius had at first been stunned by the enormity of the disaster at Cremona. News of the capture of Valens roused him and he took personal command of operations. Yet another legion was raised from the fleet. This supplemented the still-formidable cohorts of the Rhineland legionaries he had recruited into his new Praetorian Guard. Edicts were sent to rebellious provinces offering them lavish bribes and remission of taxation. Citizenship was offered to all provincials who would support the Vitellian cause. The treasury was scraped bare to keep the people of Rome loyal with lavish games and circuses.

Perhaps a bolder commander would have risked everything by attacking the cold, underfed and somewhat demoralized army of Primus. Though outnumbered, the former Rhinelanders of Vitellius' Praetorian Guard were fresh and highly motivated veteran fighters. They stood a chance. But if Vitellius even contemplated this, he changed his mind when news came that the fleet at Misenum had joined its colleagues at Ravenna and defected to Vespasian. Now there was no way to save Italy from blockade. Without grain, Rome would eventually turn against Vitellius. His end was a matter of time.

For a while, optimism had been kept alive. Lucius, the brother of Vitellius, recaptured Terracina (which had fallen to Vespasian at the same time as the fleet had rebelled at Misenum). There was also a rumour that Valens had escaped captivity and was even now in Germany raising new armies. Yet Lucius hesitated to bring his soldiers back to the crisis developing in Rome. And the captors of Valens responded to rumours of his escape by brutally executing their prisoner. His head was sent on a tour of pro-Vitellian soldiery in Gaul, who responded to this dashing of their hopes by deserting in droves to Vespasian.

Fresh messages reached Rome. Primus urged Vitellius to save himself by surrender. He offered the unlikely promise that the former emperor would be allowed to retire unharmed to Campania and live out his days with his family in a villa on the coast. Other messages to Flavius Sabinus were more realistic. Primus pointed out that things in Rome were going to get ugly, and Sabinus and Domitian should get out of the city by any means possible. Domitian was in favour of the idea. However, he worried that the guards set over him were almost as enthusiastic about an escape as he was himself. Domitian had a suspicious nature. (In later life this was to mature into what would be considered paranoia – except that by then people really were out to get him.) So now Domitian fretted that his guards had been ordered to encourage an escape so that he could be legitimately killed while making it.

Flavius Sabinus also declined to leave Rome. He claimed that he was too old and infirm to join an army on the march. In truth though, the brother of Vespasian had an ambitious plot cooking and had no intention of abandoning it. If all went well, the advancing army would find that Rome had been claimed for Vespasian by a coup from within, led by Sabinus and a coterie of seditious senators. Nor, claims Tacitus, was the emperor unaware of the plot. Vitellius was ready and willing to hand over the empire, if only he could do so safely. But he was virtually a prisoner of his court. Too many in Vitellius' entourage were not going to yield new-found power and privileges unless they absolutely had to. Others were uneasily aware that a new government might not look kindly upon their abuses of power.

Vitellius took himself from his palace to the forum. There he publicly attempted to renounce his imperial dignity. But like his entourage, the people would not allow it. This left Rome with something of a dual government. The unwilling Vitellius was emperor by popular demand and by command of his subordinates. The power-brokers of the senate knew that this was at best a temporary sham, and hastened to pay court to Sabinus. The rabidly pro-Vitellian soldiery took exception to this, and they were the most heavily armed faction in the divided city. Either Sabinus did not bother to court these men, or, more probably, they were not prepared to listen.

The Vitellian soldiers mauled the retinue of Sabinus in an armed clash. It became clear that the senior Flavians were no longer safe. Sabinus and his supporters hastily withdrew to Rome's citadel of last resort, the Capitoline hill. Suddenly Rome's ancient citadel was under siege again, for the first time in almost five hundred years.

Once he was holed up on the Capitoline, it was evident that Sabinus was not planning to go anywhere. Therefore the guard set over him was lax. Sabinus had Domitian and other family members smuggled on to the hill to join him. He then sent messengers post-haste to Primus, demanding urgent help. Yet even if they set off immediately by forced marches, the Flavian legions would arrive too late. The only hope of relief would be a dash to Rome by the cavalry. Fortunately Petellius Cerialis had been leading a strong reconnaissance force into Sabine country and was well positioned to force his way down the Via Salaria to Rome.

Tacitus has harsh words to say about this. Cerialis was being 'rash' and 'headstrong'. Attempting to take a city with a thousand cavalry was folly. Though it had long outgrown its formal boundary, Rome still had walls. These were maintained mostly out of respect for tradition and because the gates helped to control the flow of people and goods into the city, but they were walls nevertheless. Within those walls were a hostile populace and a considerable body of Vitellian soldiery. The idea that Cerialis could fight his way through these obstacles and rescue Sabinus and his family was quixotic at best.

This is probably true. But it overlooks the fact that the attempt had to be made. The lives of Vespasian's son, brother and nephew were on the line. Even if Cerialis was prepared to explain to his emperor why he had not even tried to save his family, he was politician enough to know that the Roman people too would look askance at a failure to even make the attempt. Besides, who knew how solid were the sentiments of the people and soldiers in Rome? It might be that the arrival of Cerialis and his horsemen at the gates of Rome was the signal that the Flavian element had been waiting for. Cerialis could not provide a conquering army, but he might be the catalyst that turned Rome into a Flavian city at the crucial moment.

Certainly the odds were against it, but what had he to lose? If Cerialis ran into solid opposition, he had a cavalry unit, and Primus following up at speed behind him. At worst he could make a fighting withdrawal back to the Flavian legions. In the process he would obtain valuable information about the enemy's morale and battle-readiness. And finally, if Rome could be taken by a single cavalry charge, there was no one better to try it than the self-confident Petellius Cerialis.

There was need for haste. Within a day, the Vitellian soldiery were preparing to assault its own Capitol. The insanity of civil war led them to attack even the temple of Jupiter Optimus Maximus, the hallowed place where for centuries Roman armies had finished their triumphal marches through the city. Sabinus and his rough-and-ready crew of defenders stood little chance against trained soldiers, though they tried. Access was blocked by impromptu barricades of statues thrown down across the narrow roads. At some point in the struggle, a torch was thrown, and the ancient temple of Jupiter, the most sacred building in all Rome's empire, caught fire. Sabinus was no warrior and his shambolic defence was quickly overwhelmed. He and Atticus, a pro-Flavian consul, were captured, and many other leading adherents to his cause were cut down.

Sabinus had made no attempt to flee, but he successfully ensured his son's escape. Nor did the Vitellian soldiery pay much attention to panicked acolytes fleeing the burning temple of Jupiter. Had they done so, they would have discovered young Domitian escaping in disguise.

Cerialis was met just outside Rome by a mixed force of infantry and cavalry. Given the haste of his mission, he had no time to scout the terrain, or skirt the block of armed men. A confused engagement followed. It was fought amid gardens and winding alleys where the defenders had all the advantages. Cerialis had no choice but to fall back. He would have done so anyway, as the Vitellians probably took pleasure in informing him that his rescue attempt was in vain. Sabinus had been executed.

DEATH OF (ANOTHER) EMPEROR

Vitellius had been present when Sabinus died. He was now little more than a figurehead. He did not so much order the execution of Sabinus as watch him lynched by a mob of soldiers. The men knew that their commander had little stomach for a fight. With this killing they nailed his colours to the mast. No Flavian general would negotiate with the killers of the emperor's brother.

This was proven when Primus and his legions arrived and set up camp outside Rome. A delegation came from the city bearing a letter from Vitellius himself. The delegation was led by a respected philosopher and given further sanctity by the inclusion of several Vestal Virgins. Vitellius asked for no more than a day of truce, so that 'everything' could be sorted out with a minimum of fuss. The reply was polite but implacable. By killing Sabinus and firing the Capitol, Vitellius and his men had placed themselves outside the rules of war. There would be neither negotiation nor mercy. Appropriately, it was now late December. The festival of the Saturnalia was due. The only Roman public festival that featured the mortal combat of gladiators would this year feature the clash of bitterly opposed armies.

Primus did want to wait until after 20 December, mainly to cool the ardour of his troops. Cremona had been bad enough. For Rome to be pillaged in the same way would get Vespasian's reign off to a disastrous start. However, his men would not countenance delay. Again, Primus took the only option available. He would at least guide what he could not control, so that morning he organized the assault on Rome. He divided his army into three columns, one driving into the city along the Via Flaminia and another pushing down the banks of the Tiber towards the gardens of Sallust. A third would follow the footsteps of Sulla in 82 BC, and advance on Rome up the via Salaria to the Colline gate.

A body of the Roman citizenry had organized themselves into a 'legion'. This was in truth an untrained militia that stood absolutely no chance against veteran soldiers. It was scattered with a single cavalry charge, presumably led by Cerialis. Other city folk were less firm in their commitment to Vitellius. They watched the developing battle as though it were laid on for their special entertainment. Lining the rooftops, they cheered for the Vitellians as the home team, and showered the advancing Flavians with roof tiles and bricks. Yet when the stubborn resistance of the Vitellians was broken by the superior numbers of the Flavian army, the same people loudly pointed out the houses and wine shops where the defeated men had taken refuge. Many partook of some discreet looting wherever they thought they could get away with it.

Only the defenders at the Gardens of Sallust held back the Flavian legions. But even here, they were forced to fall back when Primus' men secured the Campus Martius. On the fields where the people of Rome had once mustered to elect their consuls, the struggle for power now took a more primitive form. With their flank turned, the Vitellians fell back, and the struggle raged among the bath houses, shops and temples of the usually peaceful city.

The last stand was at the Praetorian barracks that the Vitellian legionaries had so proudly occupied but a few months before. This was a well-appointed Roman camp, which had been recently given further fortification. In the past, Roman camps had withstood Gauls, Britons and hordes of rampaging Germans. But this camp faced far more dangerous opponents. Legionaries knew every detail and weakness of such camps and possessed the skills, motivation and equipment to crack open the defences.

> With unheard-of energy the victors, with the veteran legions leading the assault, used all the means with which they had mastered even fortified cities. The testudo and ballista, flaming missiles and earthworks all came into play as the soldiers told each other that this last triumph would crown all the labour and battles that had led to this moment ... though doomed, the Vitellians were determined to die hard. Many breathed their last on the towers and ramparts. Then, when their enemies finally smashed down the gates the last men standing rushed into battle, determined to die with honour, their faces to the enemy, and their death wounds in front.[9]

Vitellius did not lead this desperate last stand. He was utterly at a loss as to what to do. His first plan was to slip out of the palace to his wife's home on the Aventine, there to await someone senior to whom he could surrender. Then perhaps realizing the danger in which this would place his family, he returned to the palace. He found that his officials had locked and then abandoned the complex. As the sounds of the assault on the camp resounded from the nearby Viminal hill Vitellius wandered the corridors alone, finally barricading himself into a small room (by some accounts a kennel) with a watchdog tied to the door.

Here he was eventually found and dragged out. A sword was thrust under his chin so that as he was pulled through a crowd of cursing soldiery he had to face their abuse and blows and see his statues being pulled down. A Rhinelander who had escaped the fighting was distraught at this treatment of his emperor. He attacked the group around him, with the apparent objective of putting Vitellius out of his misery. The berserk attack injured the tribune leading the prisoner, but no more. From the Palatine hill Vitellius was dragged across the forum. His tormentors planned that his final destination would be just short of the Capitoline hill. Here was Rome's prison, the Tullianum, and outside that the Gemonian steps where the bodies of executed criminals were displayed. Here, just hours ago, the body of Sabinus had been contemptuously thrown.

In his last moments Vitellius showed himself after all a Roman, prepared to die as a Roman should. When a tribune finished a particularly vicious bout of personal abuse, Vitellius replied spiritedly 'Yet nevertheless, I was your Emperor.' These last words provoked the crowd beyond all restraint. The mob fell upon him and beat him to death.

AFTERMATH
Keeping the victorious soldiery in check was less difficult than in Cremona, but it was an effort nevertheless. Whereas XIII Gemina had a vendetta with the Cremonans, the legions had nothing personal against the citizens of Rome in general. There was also the respect due to the ancient capital of the empire. Primus, Cerialis and the other generals knew well that Vespasian would later have to live among these people. Therefore they made a major effort to make sure that the occupation of Rome left no lasting legacy of hatred. Domitian was found safe, which mitigated the army's anger at the death of Sabinus, and the young prince was escorted safely to his home. Everywhere it was an edgy night in Rome. Armed men prowled the streets and cut down enemies real or imagined. Not a few soldiers used the cover of night to engage in freelance looting and robbery. Yet overall, as the people of Rome well knew, things could have been much, much worse.

The next day Domitian addressed the senate. He gave a measured speech in which he assured that body that the year of anarchy was now ended. The rule of law had returned. A letter was read from Vespasian, and the new emperor's reasonable and pragmatic address set the tone for the new era. A grateful senate responded by making Vespasian and his son Titus consuls for the coming year. In the meantime Domitian was appointed praetor with consular authority.

Troops were sent south to wipe out the last remnants of Vitellius' empire and Terracina was re-re-captured. Lucius Vitellius surrendered, deceived by the false promise that his life would be spared.

Within a fortnight it seemed that Rome had awakened from a chaotic bad dream. The legions had withdrawn. The only combat still taking place was vicious infighting in the senate, where a new pecking order was being established and questions such as how to pay for the rebuilding of the Capitol were being thrashed out. Mucianus arrived. With the direct authority of Vespasian behind him, he rapidly undercut the pretensions of Primus. Though he had received consular honours for his part in the war, Primus felt himself hard done by and left Rome to take matters up with Vespasian personally. But Primus had served his purpose. The new emperor was welcoming and appropriately grateful, but his gratitude took no material form. Primus now vanishes almost completely from history, apart from a casual aside by the poet Martial in AD 100, which tells us that Primus was alive and healthy well beyond his sixtieth year.[10]

No sane man contemplated a sea voyage in December, so Vespasian was forced to remain in Egypt until the summer of AD 70. The invasion from the province of Africa never materialized. The legion there defected to the Flavian cause around the end of the year. Despite the end of the war, the new emperor had much to do. A combination of Nero and a civil war had left the state bankrupt. Lawlessness was rife in the provinces. Denuding the frontiers of troops had resulted in disastrous barbarian invasions along the Danube. The most serious problem of all was in Germany, where a revolt by the Batavians threatened Rome's entire northern frontier.

Part IV
Petellius Cerialis Takes Charge

Chapter 6

Desperate and Dastardly Deeds Along the Rhine

THE BATAVIANS IN AD 69
At this point it is necessary to step outside the flow of the narrative and recap the events of AD 69 from the viewpoint of the Batavian cohorts of the Roman army. This recap shows how the tumult engulfing the empire affected a particular unit, and this is of interest in itself. However, what happened to the Batavi in AD 69 was to change the life (and very nearly cause the death) of Petellius Cerialis, so understanding this year from a Batavian perspective is important for understanding later events.

The eight Batavian cohorts in the Roman army had a significance much greater than their numbers. In providing soldiers as auxiliaries to the legions, the Batavians demonstrated their loyalty to Rome. This was important because the tribe had a strategic role in keeping the northwestern frontier stable.

When Romans first met this tribe, the Batavians occupied a 100km-long fertile island at the point where the river Waal divides from the lower Rhine en route to the sea. In fact the name of the people (who were an offshoot of the Germanic Chatti tribe) probably derives from *bat awjo*, meaning 'good island'. Perhaps because of the ructions and tribal dislocations caused by Roman incursions, the Batavians moved to that region of what is now the Netherlands still called the *Betuwe* today. It is uncertain whether this move was forced by pressure of tribal migrations or was an opportunistic expansion, or a mixture of both.

The Batavi were renowned as warriors even among the ferocious Germans.[1] Nevertheless, their location on the Island could not have been comfortable. It was at a point which allowed the Romans easy access to lower Germania, and the Germans found it a good position from which to raid the Roman lines.

Because they occupied a crucial hotspot, some accommodation had eventually to be reached between Batavians and Romans. By the start of the imperial era this accommodation took the form that the Batavians did not have to pay taxes. Instead, they would supply the army with a set number of men every year.

In the year AD 69 the Batavi were both aggrieved and unhappy. We have seen (p. 42) that the Batavian cohorts had served with distinction in Britain. As auxiliary non-citizen soldiers, they were paired with the Roman XIV Gemina Martia Victrix, and with that legion they were summoned from Britain in AD 66 or 67 to take part in a war Nero was planning in Albania.

The Batavi were, for reasons now lost, very unhappy with this move. Therefore, when news of the revolt of Vindex reached Nero, it seemed logical for the imperial authorities to pull the Batavi back along with elements of the XIV Gemina Martia Victrix to deal with the revolt.

The troops were ordered to Italy to shore up Nero's faltering regime. However, Nero underestimated the degree of animosity the Batavi had for him. The auxiliaries actively hindered their colleagues in XIV Gemina Martia Victrix from reaching Rome in time to do anything constructive. This distanced the Batavi from their legionary colleagues, and this distancing became literal as the Batavi later separated themselves from XIV Gemina Martia Victrix and moved west. This suggests that they had always intended to join Vindex in his revolt. As the Batavi neared Gaul and found that Vindex had perished, they attached themselves to Galba's cause instead.

This commitment had the effect of securing from Galba the freedom of Julius Civilis, as mentioned above (p. 98). Civilis had many years of experience as an officer in the Batavian cohorts. He had almost certainly met Vespasian while both were engaged in the conquest of Britain. In later years he might well have met Petellius Cerialis in Britain as well.

However, in AD 68 Civilis was out of the army and in Gaul. There he and another Batavian, Julius Paullus, were suspected by Nero's minions of fomenting rebellion with Vindex. Galba freed Civilis (he was too late to save Paullus, who was executed) and took him to Rome as part of his retinue – and partly, one suspects, as a hostage for the continued good behaviour of the Batavi.

Soon afterward, Otho wrenched power from Galba. The Batavi were deeply upset and suspicious of the new regime, a suspicion that Otho tried to mitigate by sending Civilis back to the auxiliaries with a position of command. By one reading of a (somewhat garbled) text in Tacitus, Otho might also have offered the cohorts Roman citizenship in an attempt to keep their loyalty when news came of Vitellius' rebellion.

At this time the Batavi had appointed themselves watchdogs over the tribe of the dangerously disaffected Gallic Lingones, and were within that territory. This put them relatively close to home. The Batavians were allied with the Cannenfates, a tribe that shared their island with them. The Cannenfates were more peaceful, albeit only in comparison to their rabidly warlike neighbours. However, it was a Cannenfatean tribal leader, a man called Brinno, who decided to make the most of the prevailing troubled times. He planned to clear the Romans from the Island, making it a purely Germanic habitation once more.

The Batavians on the Island were very willing to help. They had been exasperated by an excessive levy of their menfolk for the army of Vitellius. There were reports that particularly comely young men had been targeted by lecherous recruiting officers, and not for service at the front. Outrage at this practice caused many to join the uprising, and the nearby Frisian people were roped into Brinno's project. The smaller Roman forts on the Island were quickly seized, and by the end of May only the larger forts at the Island's upper end remained in Roman hands.

This left the Batavian cohorts in an ambiguous position – they were an integral part of the Roman army, yet of a people partly in rebellion against Rome. Fortunately they could count on the understanding of the Roman soldiery, many of whom were in more or less the same situation. Despite the ambiguous loyalty of the Batavian cohorts, the Vitellians had no inhibitions about recruiting the auxiliaries to their cause. The Batavi had never forgiven Otho for killing Galba, and so agreed to switch sides. Nevertheless, they were both confused and unenthusiastic, especially since their legionary colleagues in XIV Gemina Martia Victrix had committed to Otho. The auxiliaries showed their uncertainty in a series of riots to which this tumultuous force was anyway prone.[2]

At least some Batavian troops were at the first battle of Bedriacum between Vitellians and Othonians, but these were probably the extra levies imposed earlier by Vitellius. It is certain that most of the veteran Batavian cohorts stayed in Gaul. They were needed to control the Maritime Alps and the Lingones. (In fact, the Batavi and the Lingones were rapidly subsuming their differences into a common antipathy to Roman governance in general.) The insipid loyalty of the Batavi decided Vitellius to send them back to Britain. The auxiliaries would be accompanied by XIV Gemina Martia Victrix. This formerly Othonian legion had been defeated at Bedriacum and now reluctantly served the new regime. Given the differing loyalties of the Batavi and the legionaries of XIV Gemina Martia Victrix, and the readiness of the Batavi to riot at the drop of a helmet, bringing the two units together resulted in a completely predictable explosion (described on p. 99).

132 Imperial General

The Batavi received the blame for the riot. XIV Gemina Martia Victrix proceeded to Britain as described earlier, but the Batavi headed for the German frontier. It is unclear whether they had been disbanded or otherwise punished 'for truculence', but they were certainly highly disaffected and mutinous.

On the Island, Tacitus claims that Civilis had been behind Brinno's rebellion all along.[3] Certainly, the Batavian leader's subsequent actions had more than a whiff of duplicity about them. Claiming that he intended to suppress the Cannenfatean uprising, Civilis took a cohort of the now unemployed Batavi to the Island. He almost certainly had the blessing of Hordonius Flaccus, commander of the Rhine army at Moguntiacum. Flaccus was Flavian by inclination, yet in command of a surly force of pro-Vitellius soldiers. Both commander and soldiers were feeling uncomfortably vulnerable. Manpower along the Rhine had been stripped to the bone to support the imperial ambitions of the legions. The entire German frontier was a powder keg. So the last thing Flaccus needed was the public relations disaster of Roman legionaries fighting their former allies on the Batavian island. He would have been delighted when a Batavian volunteered to do the job.

Rebellion
Sadly, Civilis never intended to suppress the rebels. Once he reached his homeland, he joined their cause. Civilis justified his actions by claiming to raise the standard of rebellion for Vespasian. Indeed the Flavian general Primus had written to Civilis after the riot with XIV Gemina Martia Victrix. He suggested that Civilis did exactly as he was doing, and Flaccus may have discreetly suggested the same.

So ostensibly as Flavian partisan, although probably as an anti-Roman nationalist, but in any case as a rebel, Civilis squared off against the remaining Romans on the Island. He had three columns of soldiers with him: one of Frisians, one of Cannenfates and a third of his own Batavi. The Romans prepared to evacuate in the face of this superior force. Flaccus had sent ships ready to take the men off the Island once they had burned their forts. These ships were currently grounded nearby, as the Romans intended to use the hulls to break the first wave of the Germanic attack. For a while the strategy allowed the Romans to at least hold their ground. Then, unexpectedly, a Roman unit changed sides. This was the Cohors Tungri, a unit of Belgic auxiliaries amongst whom the agents of Civilis had undoubtedly been busy beforehand.

Further treachery prevented the ships from managing the evacuation. Many of the sailors were Batavians. These deliberately hindered the efforts of their Roman colleagues or blatantly ran their ships aground in front of Civilis' army. Soldiers and sailors alike were encouraged to join the general trend of deserting to Civilis, with the fig-leaf offered to the turncoats that they were not rebelling against Rome, but volunteering for Vespasian. Anyone with a dissenting viewpoint was slaughtered. Civilis finished the action with a handy fleet of twenty-four ships to complement his growing army.

The Gallic contingent among the Romans was offered a choice – to stay under arms with Civilis or to return to their homes, preferably to raise rebellion there as well. Civilis had high hopes of rebellion at least among the Gallic Lingones. These had never liked Vitellius in the first place, and had developed an affinity with the Batavi, who had been quartered with them for so long.

With a full-scale war threatening to overwhelm southwestern Germany and draw in formerly peaceful areas of Gaul, Hordonius Flaccus was forced to act. He had six legions at his disposal, deployed at bases along the Rhine. At his base in Moguntiacum he and two legions – IV Macedonica and XXII Primigenia – were furthest from the action. I Germania at Bonna (Bonn) was closer, but the nearest legions were approaching their winter quarters near Xanten, a base generally known as Castra Vetera (the Old Camp). These legions were commanded by a man called Minius Lupercus. Accordingly, it fell to Lupercus and his men to suppress the uprising.

Lupercus would normally have had two legions with which to do the job: V Alaudae and XV Primigenia. But the war in Italy had drained the frontier of manpower, and how many men were actually on hand is unknown. The fact that Lupercus was forced to supplement his force with Germanic auxiliaries and even Batavian cavalry suggests that he was desperate enough to use even soldiers of dubious loyalty.

To no one's surprise, the Batavian cavalry defected the moment they saw the standards of Civilis. The other auxilia faded into the woods, abandoning the legionaries to their fate. That such a betrayal was not unexpected probably explains why the two legions were able to keep their formation and make a fighting retreat to Castra Vetera.

The remaining Batavian cohorts now presented Flaccus with an ultimatum. Before the march on Rome, Vitellius had purchased their loyalty with the offer of double pay and an extra bonus. It was time, the cohorts said, to deliver on this promise – if they were not paid, their contract with Vitellius was void.

It was on occasions such as this that a Drusus or a Germanicus or any of Rome's inspirational commanders of the past might have rallied the Batavi to their traditional loyalty. It was still possible that the cohorts might respond to a judicious bribe combined with the threat of the remaining Rhineland legions.

Mucianus in Rome would later demonstrate how this might be done. The soldiers of Lucius Vitellius had surrendered near Terracina. They had done so without a fight, as their commander had ordered. They were upset by Lucius' subsequent execution, and though now nominally re-incorporated into the imperial army were on the verge of mutiny. Mucianus said he would talk to the men and ordered them to parade in undress uniform, without weapons. As the Vitellian loyalists fell into their ranks, they observed that a full Flavian legion was drawn up facing them – in full battle array. The way back to the barracks was blocked by equally well-armed auxiliary troops. In his address to the ever-more terrified men, Mucianus mused upon whether they could ever really be trusted to bear arms. He may have made a passing reference to the blood-soaked day in 82 BC when Sulla had killed some six thousand pro-Marian troops he had penned into the Circus Maximus, not far from the present parade ground. No direct threats were made, but by the end of Mucianus' chat with the troops, the ex-Vitellians were begging for a chance to show their loyalty to the new emperor.

Sadly, Hordonius Flaccus was a general of a different and lesser calibre. He had, after all, been selected by Galba precisely because he was indecisive and ineffectual. So at this moment of crisis, Flaccus did what he did best. He prevaricated, gave confused orders and then countermanded them. When his faltering attempts to negotiate were contemptuously rejected by the Batavian cohorts, Flaccus ordered I Germanica at Bonna to prevent the Batavi from crossing the Rhine to join Civilis and the cohort that had already deserted. Had I Germanica done as originally ordered, and Flaccus himself followed up to trap the Batavi between his army and this legion, he might well have cowed the mutinous cohorts into some semblance of obedience. But at the last moment Flaccus lost his nerve and ordered that the Batavi be allowed to exit the frontier unopposed.

'Order, counter-order, disorder' goes the modern military maxim. I Germanica went on to prove that this was true in their day as well. Having prepared to resist the Batavi, and then been told not to do so, they were unsure of what to do when the renegades approached their camp. The Batavi made it clear they were not looking for a fight and simply wanted to pass by with a minimum of fuss. However, they added that they were prepared to cut their way through the legion if they had to.

I Germanica was stripped down to three thousand men, and these were mainly raw recruits hastily added from camp followers and local peasantry. No legion that meekly stood aside when ordered to do so by cohorts of auxilia would get respect from the rest of the army, and the new levies of I Germanica were itching to prove themselves. Hoping to overwhelm the Batavi by sheer numbers, they swarmed from the camp and surrounded the auxiliaries.

The Batavi were battle-hardened regulars and not in the least intimidated. They formed into columns and secured flanks and rear. Then they cut through the inexperienced and shambolic opposition like a knife through butter. The crush as the legionaries attempted to get back into their camp killed many. These casualties were added to heaps of the slain whom the Batavi left in the trenches below the ramparts.

No attempt was made to stop the renegades thereafter. Colonia Agrippinensis (Cologne) shut its gates to them, but had no legions to offer resistance in the field. The legions of Lupercus at Castra Vetera also allowed the Batavi to pass unhindered. This was either because they were still licking their wounds after their previous rough handling by Civilis, or on the direct orders of Flaccus, who had by now well and truly lost the confidence of his men.

Grim Days At Castra Vetera

By autumn Civilis had an army of over fifteen thousand men. The hard core were the Batavian cohorts. If we assume that the first cohort was a milliary unit of 1,000 men[4] and the others[5] numbered 500 men apiece, then this hard core was composed of 5000 very tough and experienced fighters. The remainder were Cannenfatean rebels, Frisians and opportunistic Germanic warriors who had come from the wild lands beyond the frontier to join the fun. These Germans found crossing the Rhine very easy, for an exceptionally dry summer had greatly lowered the depth of the river. So they came in their thousands. 'Here were the standards of veteran cohorts, and beside them totems of wild animals, taken from their sacred groves in the forests,' remarks Tacitus. This bizarre conjunction must have confirmed the impression of the bemused legionaries that in AD 69 the world had turned upside down.

Civilis still clutched the fig-leaf of loyalty to Rome, or at least loyalty to the Flavians, since this would anyway put him in conflict with every Roman on the Rhine frontier. Accordingly, Civilis went through the motions of swearing his force to loyalty to his chosen emperor, and sent an offer to the troops at Castra Vetera that they should do the same. V Alaudae, Julius

Caesar's famous 'Larks', and the proud XV Primigenia were hardly going to take orders from a semi-civilized horde of rebels and barbarians.[6] They replied in no uncertain terms to that effect.

They knew that the Roman army of the Rhine had still I Germanica at Bonna and IV Macedonica and XXII Primigenia at Moguntiacum. They may also have known that XVI Gallica was on the way to reinforce them. Thus Civilis was faced with six Roman legions – a force normally strong enough to face down any threat. But the two legions at Castra Vetera were below half-strength and I Germanica was not only under strength but made up of raw troops disillusioned after being roughly handled by the Batavi. The remaining legions also had sent large detachments to fight in Italy and were themselves well below strength.

Lupercus and his fellow legionary legate, Numisius Rufus, threw themselves into the task of preparing Castra Vetera to stand siege. Their basic problem was that they were attempting to defend a permanent legionary base. Castra Vetera was supposed to hold two legions, and since entire provinces had been conquered with less, no one had thought that two legions might actually need defending. Consequently the camp was not situated for defence, but on a gentle slope. The walls were not intended to hold back ravening barbarian hordes but to prevent soldiers from slipping out to enjoy the illicit pleasures of the town that had grown up around the barracks. (The town was now being demolished. This was partly to prevent it falling into enemy hands and partly to provide a clear field of fire from the ramparts.)

Furthermore, the walls, such as they were, had been built to contain two full legions. Yet the defenders of the camp could barely muster enough men to make one under-strength legion. In itself, this was no insignificant fighting force. But the Batavian cohorts alone were probably a match for them in numbers, ability and experience. And that was without the other 10,000 Germans Civilis had at his disposal.

The only hope for Lupercus was to stand siege and hope either that Flaccus somehow pulled himself together and sent reinforcements (unlikely) or that the hazy Teutonic grasp of logistics would cause the Germans to starve before the defenders did. (This was usually probable, but not with the Romanized Civilis commanding operations. And the Romans had not planned on being in Castra Vetera so early in the year. They too were low on food.)

The Roman legionaries set to reinforcing the ramparts and did a superb job. After all, they were experienced field engineers whose lives were at stake. The walls were a formidable obstacle by the time Civilis turned up. However, nothing could be done about the scanty number of defenders who had a camp perimeter of almost 3km to defend. To add to already poor morale, the defenders were aware that Civilis was an experienced Roman commander. He knew exactly what problems the legionaries were facing, and how best to exploit these.

The rebel army first set about constructing a very unbarbarian set of entrenchments about the camp and paraded in full strength before the ramparts, all the better to demoralize the defenders. It then it hurled itself at the walls. The attack was a combination of *furor Teutonicus* – berserk Germanic fury – and Roman sophistication. Near-naked German warriors threw themselves at the ramparts. But they threw themselves atop fighting bridges constructed on the best principles of Roman technology, complete with engineers who tried to undermine the walls even as their barbarian colleagues tried to take them from above.

On the Roman side, Lupercus had been thorough. The opening rebel artillery barrage spent itself uselessly on the earthworks and ramparts that the legions had spent the past weeks reinforcing. Roman catapults smashed the German siege works to smithereens and burning spears thrown from the walls set fire to what was left. The earthworks had deep trenches studded with 'lilies' – sharp iron or wooden spikes hidden in shallow pits that impaled unwary attackers. Also, the supposedly demoralized legionaries fought hard. Civilis' attempt to take the camp by storm was a failure. A second attempt a few days later fared even worse. After that, the Germans attempted to intimidate the defenders by camping close to the ramparts. This merely provided the Romans with a set of tempting targets for their wicked high-power 'scorpion' crossbows.

Civilis was not discouraged. He styled himself another Hannibal or Sertorius, since like these two great opponents of Rome, he had lost an eye. As he told his men, even if the Romans could hold their walls, the camp was packed with refugee non-combatants, and the legions had barely enough food for themselves. It was time to see if the Romans could fight hunger as well as they could fight his warriors.

It hardly helped morale at Castra Vetera that the rescue effort was being organized by Hordonius Flaccus. This general's own men openly reviled him. Many suspected (possibly with good reason) that Flaccus had been working with the Batavi to co-ordinate the series of defeats they had suffered. Everyone knew that the Flavians were encouraging the rebellion of Civilis. The Batavian revolt tied up the legions in the north and prevented vital reinforcements reaching the Vitellian army in north Italy. Flaccus first denied that he had received messages from the Flavians. Then he admitted that he had received a messenger. He pretended to be indignant at the contents of the message and ordered the bearer sent as a prisoner to Rome. His men were more than sceptical about the entire performance.

The Roman army had reached as far as Colonia Agrippinensis (Cologne) in its attempt to relieve Castra Vetera. Now it halted, bogged down by internal argument and dissent. The legate of XXII Primigenia was a man called Gaius Vocula. Exasperated by his general's shaky grip on events, he finally took matters into his own hands. He harangued his men into subordination and executed the most noisy troublemakers. Shown firm leadership, XXII Primigenia immediately steadied, and thereafter the army generally looked to Vocula rather than Flaccus for direction.

Matters improved further when elements of XVI Gallica arrived with a healthy contingent of Gallic auxiliaries. However, with the army's leaders pro-Flavian and the rank and file passionately Vitellian, tensions ran deep. A minor setback caused the men to turn on the legate of the newly arrived XVI Gallica. The men nearly lynched the unfortunate man, and Flaccus along with him for good measure. Again Vocula came to the rescue, calmed the legionaries and executed the ringleaders of the incipient mutiny.

Then news arrived that the Vitellian army had been crushed at Cremona. The tidings hit the army like a thunderbolt. The legionaries realistically accepted that their cause was doomed. Vocula and Flaccus managed to persuade the troops to swear allegiance to their new emperor, but it was hardly an inspiring ceremony. Morale was at rock bottom.

Everyone in the Rhineland was now technically on the same side, yet the war was not over. Civilis refused to accept that he and the local Romans were all Flavians together and went from being a Roman rebel to a Batavian rebel. He decided that Castra Vetera could be safely besieged by his Germanic warriors and sent off his Batavian cohorts. These were ordered to destroy a relief column heading for the camp – a column all the more threatening because it was led by Vocula and not Flaccus.

Vocula was a strong commander. But he was a poor general and he failed to set advance pickets. The Batavians were both audacious and fast moving. Vocula only discovered that the enemy were nearby after their sudden onslaught had nearly overwhelmed his camp. The Gallic auxilia promptly deserted, leaving the confused and demoralized Romans to be cut down in great numbers ('more like a massacre than a battle', says Tacitus). Then for a moment the fortunes of war abruptly shifted in Rome's favour.

A small contingent on the way to reinforce the main Roman army had heard the conflict erupt and hurried to the scene. They fell upon the backs of the attacking Batavi, who were understandably disconcerted by this new development. Seeing their enemies confused and surprised, the legionaries abruptly remembered their trade. From the effect they had on the Batavi, the legionaries believed that the reinforcements were much stronger than they were, and Vocula's men were determined not to be disgraced by them. They rallied, dressed their ranks and started slaughtering the Batavi. It was a complete reversal of fortune, and proof of Napoleon's later dictum that morale is more important than numbers.

Civilis' cavalry escaped with the prisoners and standards they had captured in the first round of the fighting, but the infantry cohorts were destroyed as a fighting force. Roman casualties were higher, but Civilis had lost the hard core of his army.

The rebel commander had nevertheless captured sufficient prisoners and Roman standards to hide his defeat, at least temporarily. So he informed the Romans at Castra Vetera that the relief column had been as comprehensively defeated as it almost had been. He paraded prisoners and standards before the ramparts as proof, but the cynical legionaries refused to believe him. The deception was further undermined when one of the prisoners shouted out the truth. The Germans immediately gave the man's words extra credibility by cutting him down to silence him.

Nor could Civilis disguise the smoke from burning German homesteads that announced that Vocula was closing in on the camp. Within days, the relief column was at hand – deliberately camped close enough to allow the besieged legionaries to see Roman standards. Vocula wanted to give his men time to recover from their march, but the men were buoyed up by their recent victory. Since they were by now in the habit of paying minimal attention to their commanders, they simply drew themselves into battle order and attacked.

The battle was too close-fought to justify such optimism, but at the critical moment Lupercus in Castra Vetera sallied from the fort with his legionaries. Civilis, leading his Germans from the front, was thrown from his horse. Word went through the German ranks that he was dead. This caused many Germans to assume the day was lost. They fled and others followed until the entire German army was streaming from the field. A very much alive and furious Civilis then had little choice but to follow his army in retreat.

The relief of the Castra Vetera was only temporary. Vocula was so desperately short of supplies that he could not afford to follow up the fleeing

German army. Indeed, once the Germans had successfully ambushed his casually guarded supply train he could not even afford to remain where he was. He had to withdraw. He took with him a thousand of the defenders of Castra Vetera, and presumably all the civilians who were sheltering within the walls. It was a sign of how desperate the supply situation had become that Vocula was prepared to thin an already depleted garrison so that the remainder could last longer on minimal rations.

As he prepared to withdraw, two mutinies took place. So low was Roman morale, and so little trust had the men in their commanders, that the men leaving the camp objected to going and the men staying in the camp objected to remaining. However, the mutineers in the camp soon had little choice but to follow orders. Once Vocula had withdrawn to rejoin Flaccus at Moguntiacum, Civilis returned and set up his siege works once more.

Things Get Worse
In the main army at Moguntiacum, things kept getting worse. Long ago, Vitellius had promised a bonus for the troops he had left on the frontier. As one of his final acts before his death in Rome, he had arranged for this bonus to be dispatched. When the money arrived at the frontier, Vitellius' act of solidarity with his troops aroused a surge of loyalty among the soldiers. In a clumsy attempt at propaganda, Flaccus distributed the bounty in Vespasian's name. He fooled no one and infuriated many.

One evening a mob of soldiers got drunk on wine purchased with their bounty. Filled with nostalgia for their lost cause, and fury with those who had betrayed it, they dragged Flaccus from his tent and lynched him. Then they raised Vitellius' standards again, so that in the Rhinelands a portion of Vitellius' lost empire came briefly to life once more.

As a general, Hordonius Flaccus had been an unmitigated disaster. In his defence, he had been selected precisely because he was an ineffectual and uninspiring character. Even a flamboyant and self-confident leader such as Primus or Caecina might have quailed at the task confronting Flaccus. The soldiers on the frontier were too few to carry out their function. They were facing a confident enemy, yet were themselves demoralized and suspicious of their leaders. Defeats were blamed on incompetence and treachery. This is partly because, from a Vitellian viewpoint, Flaccus was incompetent and treacherous. However, lack of discipline and a refusal to obey valid orders meant that the legions were responsible for many of their own woes.

Given a strong lead and prompt action by an experienced commander, it is unlikely that the Rhine frontier would have unravelled as it did. Primus and Caecina were each in their own way inspirational commanders who had a clear concept of their mission. They had the character to fill the men with their own enthusiasm. Flaccus, on the other hand, was the wrong man in the wrong place at the wrong time. He paid for it with his life.

Vocula was a man of stronger character, and with Flaccus gone he managed to bring the legions back to their loyalty to Vespasian. It was a grudging and tenuous loyalty at best. Rumours flew about the Rhinelands that the Capitol in Rome had burned to the ground, as indeed it had. In a superstitious age, many took this as an omen that the empire of the Romans was likewise about to perish.

Among those was a Gaul called Classicus, commander of the Roman auxiliary cavalry. After the defection of the Batavi, the cavalry auxilia mainly consisted of Classicus' fellow Treveri tribesmen. Classicus now pulled his troops out of the Roman camp and announced that he had made a separate peace with the Germans. To Vocula's horror, many legionaries were inclined to follow the example of the Treveri. Vocula gave an impassioned speech in a desperate attempt to hold the wavering loyalty of the men. It failed. The dispirited commander withdrew to his quarters, intent on suicide. He was beaten to it by a renegade from I Germanica, who murdered him instead.

Classicus seized the moment. He dressed in the full regalia of a Roman officer and rode unopposed into the Roman camp. The men brokenly accepted his claim to be the senior commander present. They followed his orders and put their legates in chains. Even a year ago, no one would have believed this could happen. But now two Roman legions – I Germanica and XVI Gallica – swore allegiance to a Gallic rebel as their leader. They were followed by the men at Castra Vetera. The defenders of the camp were down to eating the grass between their paving stones, so their defection had more excuse.

However, the Germans remembered the rough treatment they had received at the ramparts when they had attacked the camp. V Alaudae and XV Primigenia were not welcome in their ranks. When the legions, as ordered by Civilis, departed from Castra Vetera the Germans fell upon them and massacred the men. V Alaudae, Caesar's 'Larks' – once one of the elite legions of the Roman army – was practically destroyed as a fighting force, and most of XV Primigenia also perished. Lupercus, who had led the defence, was captured and given as a slave to a Germanic priestess whom Civilis favoured. The German commander had dyed his hair red and vowed not to cut it until Castra Vetera had fallen. Now he went gratefully to the barber.

The fall of Castra Vetera was enough for the Lingones, the Gallic tribe with whom the Batavian cohorts had originally been quartered. Their tribal leader, Julius Sabinus, repudiated his alliance with Rome. He set himself up as emperor with the bizarre claim that, because he bore the name Julius, he was a descendant of Julius Caesar. In collaboration with Classicus of the Treveri, northern neighbours of the Lingones, Julius Sabinus established an 'Empire of the Gauls' with its capital at Augusta Treverorum (Trier). He immediately began preparations for a campaign against the Sequani, a nearby tribe that remained loyal to Rome. For this campaign, Julius Sabinus took command of the men who had surrendered to Classicus. I Germanica and XVI Gallica officially became legions of the new Gallic empire.

The commander of the Batavian cavalry who had defected to Civilis in the action that had landed the legions at Castra Vetera in the first place (see p. 133) had since fallen out with his tribal chief. He had been exiled, escaped and mustered his horsemen and three Gallic tribes to fight Civilis and the rebel Gauls. But Civilis had exactly the flair and personality that Hordonius Flaccus had fatally lacked. The German leader simply refused to fight the Gauls who marched against him. He rode boldly into their ranks with a sheathed sword and announced he was willing to join them 'as your general or your comrade'. Impressed by his audacity, the Gauls accepted Civilis as their general, and the mutinous Batavian cavalrymen had to flee for their lives.

PETELLIUS CERIALIS TAKES CHARGE

Not since the dark days of the Varian disaster in the Teutoberg forest had Rome suffered such a catastrophe. Indeed, many argued that this was an even more severe misfortune. Varus had lost three legions. In the latest disaster four legions had been lost. V Alaudae and XV Primigenia had been destroyed by the Germans, while I Germanica and XVI Gallica had managed the only thing even worse than that by going over to the enemy.

Vespasian had not yet arrived in Rome, and Mucianus could not wait for him to do so. If the Rhine frontier was not secured, Gaul might be lost, along with Upper Germany and Noricum. Someone had to resolve the crisis in the Rhinelands before the entire Roman Empire north of the Alps fell to pieces. But which general should be given the job?

Even if Primus had not already left on his mission of complaint to Vespasian, there was no way that Mucianus would give command to his bitter rival. Whoever went to sort out the Rhinelands had to be a man immediately identified with the new regime: a general, yet not someone like Suetonius

Paulinus, who had compromised with Vitellius. Someone with the character to inspire loyalty in his men, yet never lead those men against Vespasian.

These job selection criteria left a shortlist of one – Petellius Cerialis. Mucianus was not unaware of certain character flaws in his choice. The man had attempted to take Rome with a cavalry charge and had tried to stop Boudicca's hordes with a scratch force of half a legion. He could benefit from some judicious counsel. So the cautious and unassuming Gallus Annius was appointed alongside the dashing and impetuous Cerialis. (In the event Gallus Annius was so cautious and unassuming that he completely vanished into his fellow general's shadow.)

Taking Stock
The first thing the Roman authorities needed was accurate intelligence to establish the extent of the disaster. This information was not easy to come by with Italy still disorganized and Germany in chaos. But eventually it was established that the six legions of the Rhineland garrison had fallen into three equal categories. Two legions – V Alaudae and XV Primigenia – were effectively destroyed. I Germanica and XVI Gallica had mutinied and defected to Julius Sabinus and the Empire of the Gauls. XXII Primigenia had withdrawn to Moguntiacum and joined IV Macedonica. The latter legion was passionately pro-Vitellius. Nevertheless, the legionaries were unimpressed by offers from Civilis and Julius Sabinus to join their uprising. Instead the tepidly Flavian XXII Primigenia and the Vitellian IV Macedonica combined forces and between them held together what was left of the Rhine frontier.

If these two legions held Moguntiacum for Rome, not much else in the area was Roman. Most of the Rhinelands towards the sea were held by Civilis, his Batavians and his Cannenfatean allies. Colonia Agrippinensis had become 'an allied city' of Civilis. The colony had no large garrison, and the alternative to being an ally was being flattened as an enemy.

Further south in Augusta Treverorum Classicus and Julius Sabinus ruled their 'Empire of the Gauls'. This empire consisted mainly of five Gallic tribes, led by the Treveri and the Lingones.

As Petellius Cerialis set out for Germany, some good news arrived. Julius Sabinus, the Caesar of the Lingones, had tried to expand his new empire. Since the morale of his two new legions was too low for any practical purpose, he kept them on garrison duty well away from any trouble spots. Instead, he used his fellow tribesmen to launch an ill-advised war against the nearby Sequani. This tribe not only remained loyal to Rome but were so fiercely loyal that they completely crushed their attackers in battle. Sabinus vanished, and was believed to have immolated himself in a country villa.[7]

The Batavian cavalry were still not reconciled with Civilis. Their leader was now conducting a guerrilla war against the Cannenfates. Militarily, this force could inflict little more than pinpricks. But it forced Civilis to deploy much-needed forces to stop the situation from getting any worse, and forced some Belgic tribes to reconsider their alliances. Finally, Civilis moved west to deal with the annoying defectors personally. This took him far from his headquarters at a time when he should have been preparing for the arriving Roman force.

All of these minor points helped Cerialis. But they paled in comparison to his major advantage. Having just won a civil war, his side had a seriously large army available. The major disadvantage was that the soldiers in that army had been energetically trying to kill each other a few months previously.

With Spain secure, VI Victrix and X Gemina had been summoned from that province. Ahead of them came Galba's I Adiutrix, the legion Vitellius had sent back to Spain after it was defeated in the first battle of Bedriacum. I Adiutrix would be marching against the Batavi alongside XXI Rapax, whom they had last seen face-to-face in combat at Bedriacum. Also in Cerialis' army was VIII Augusta, which had also met XXI Rapax at Bedriacum, and defeated it in the second battle. Then there was XIII Gemina, which after defeat in the first battle had built the amphitheatre at Cremona, and after victory in the second battle had demolished the arena along with the rest of the city. In the company of three legions that had recently been trying to kill them, the men of XXI Rapax must have felt rather friendless.

While parts of the army were divided amongst themselves, XVI Gemina Martia Victrix was particularly schizophrenic. The Vitellian element would soon be reunited with their pro-Flavian colleagues, as the rest of the legion had been summoned from Britain. At least both factions would be united in enmity for the Batavi, from whom they had parted in riotous circumstances in Turin (p. 99).

Cerialis also had XI Claudia, a legion of Othonian sympathies that had sent detachments to Italy. These elements had been defeated at the first battle of Bedriacum and had helped to win for Vespasian in the second, and were now joined by the rest of the legion. Backing up this already formidable force was a new legion – II Adiutrix – formed from sailors of the Ravenna fleet whose mutiny had so greatly aided Primus in his advance into Italy.

Petellius thus had five legions at his back with two more on the way. When he arrived in the Rhinelands he could add to his force IV Macedonica and

XXII Primigenia, each still loyal to Rome, albeit to their particular version of it. Had Civilis not been gallivanting about the German forests in search of his errant cavalry commander, he might have realized that his rebellion now faced a truly formidable challenge of nine legions – one of the largest Roman armies ever assembled.

This number went up to eleven legions. I Germanica and XVI Gallica contemplated the massive force bearing down on them and decided that they were, after all, thoroughly loyal to Rome. The men slew the ringleaders of the revolt (the man who had killed Vocula had been cut down by Roman loyalists even before this). Then they sent representatives begging Cerialis for mercy. Cerialis probably received the news with mixed feelings. I Germanica were a despicable mob who had disgraced every cause they had joined. Their addition to the Roman army probably weakened rather than strengthened it. But XVI Gallica had some veteran soldiers who – with careful management – might be useful in the coming weeks.

In fact, careful management would decide Petellius' success or failure. Anyone with eleven legions could be master of the world, provided he could successfully master those eleven legions. Hordonius Flaccus had proven that eight legions were too few if they were poorly led and motivated. Vocula had shown that, without proper logistic support, four legions were too many. So for Petellius Cerialis the main challenges would not be the enemy. The challenges would be keeping the men loyal, off each other's throats, and off the throats of their officers. A key element for a contented army would lie in keeping this massive force properly fed and supplied. This was no small issue for a man whose logistical experience was limited to a single legion. Fortunately, the Roman commissariat was both professional and experienced.

Another challenge would be to ensure that the formerly Vitellian units of Cerialis' command (XXI Rapax, IV Macedonica, XXII Primigenia, I Germanica and XVI Gallica) did not find themselves another would-be emperor and re-launch the civil wars.[8] The secret to managing this trick would be to keep the minds of the once-mutinous rabble firmly focused on the enemy. This, rather than his famed impetuosity, explains why Petellius Cerialis took a vigorously proactive approach from the moment that he arrived in his sphere of operations in May AD 70.

Not all of his massive army came with him. The wretched I Germanica and XVI Gallica were still in limbo while Cerialis decided their fate. Some legions needed to be sent to wind up the empire of the Gauls and sort out the subsequent chaos. Also the entire frontier needed shoring up before opportunistic tribes elsewhere took advantage of the collapse of the Rhine army.

Therefore VIII Augusta peeled away from the main line of march, took up station south of Moguntiacum near Argentorate (Strasbourg) and there secured a vital crossing point on the middle Rhine. XI Claudia went even further west to Vindonissa (Windisch) in Upper Germania, thus securing the passes to the province of Raetia. This left both these legions on the northern border of the loyal Sequani tribe, so they could at the same time defend the frontier and assist the Sequani if required. Cerialis had chosen to send away loyal legions while keeping XXI Rapax under his personal supervision. This is no surprise, but it is indicative of his confidence that he intended to manage the former Vitellians of the Rhineland with fewer friendly legions to back him up.

Perhaps with logistical issues in mind, Cerialis also dismissed the local Gallic levies that had been raised for the emergency. The legions could handle the war, he announced. Let the Gauls go home and concentrate on keeping the peace. To ensure that the Gauls did indeed stay peaceful, elements of XIV Gemina Martia Victrix were sent to help pacify the restless tribesmen. This legion was ideal for the job, as it was best that it operated in separate cohorts while Flavians and ex-Vitellians were slowly re-integrated. Lest single cohorts seem tempting to would-be rebels, the legionaries spread the news that the two additional Spanish legions (VI Victrix and X Gemina) were also on their way to Gaul with orders to crucify anyone who still felt like causing trouble.

This dispersal of the legions was not without risk. For his strike force Cerialis was left with the raw recruits of II Adiutrix (and look how well the raw levies of I Germanica had turned out), the solidly loyal XIII Gemina and their old foes from Bedriacum, XXI Rapax. After his arrival at Moguntiacum, Cerialis had the doubtful pleasure of welcoming IV Macedonica and XXII Primigenia to his command. This left him with one loyal legion, one untried legion and three legions of veteran former enemies.

It turned out that the Moguntiacum legions were pleased to see Romans of any shape or description. The past weeks had involved a tense stand-off with the local German tribes and not a few skirmishes escalating almost to minor battles. Therefore Petellius Cerialis enjoyed a warmer welcome than he may have expected considering that his field army was now mostly ex-Vitellian.

Both Cerialis and Civilis raced to deploy their armies before the other was ready. Petellius Cerialis wanted to add yet more ex-Vitellians to his main army by including I Germanica and XVI Gallica before Civilis could demolish those still-fragile units. The two legions had withdrawn to the lands of a friendly nearby tribe near Augusta Treverorum.

Since Augusta Treverorum remained a centre of resistance for Classicus and the rebel Treveri tribe, Petellius had now two good reasons for making this his first target. The defeat of the Treveri would continue the repair of the frontier very handily, and the two errant legions could be re-inducted into the Roman army. The Sequani to the southeast had defeated the Lingones, whose lands were between themselves and the Treveri. Thus, once the Treveri had been dealt with, all would be secure south and east of Bonna. This would leave the remaining enemy (mostly Civilis and the Batavi) nicely concentrated in Lower Germania between the legions and the North Sea.

The Treveri attempted to stop Cerialis' army a day's march from Augusta Treverorum at Rigodulum (modern Riol). Here they blocked a river crossing and fortified the overlooking hills. Cerialis gave neither his own men nor the rebels any time for contemplation. The legionaries had just enough time to drop their marching gear and catch their breath before the assault on the rebel earthworks began. Cerialis was relying on the superior experience and discipline of his men to break the inexperienced opposition, but above all he was relying on superior numbers.

Even the cavalry were ordered into the fray, though experienced officers might have been appalled at the prospect of charging uphill against an entrenched enemy. Their general's infectious self-confidence persuaded the men to charge, and Cerialis was so sure of success that he sent more cavalry sweeping around the back of the hills. Their orders were to catch enemy fugitives bolting from the Roman force.

There may have been a brief moment of self-doubt as the legions came under heavy missile fire on their approach, but the men held firm and without hesitation closed to hand-to-hand combat. In the event, Cerialis' confidence was justified. The legions steamrollered through the Treveri. They were much more numerous, better armed, better trained, and above all, they were men with a point to prove to their new commander. As the Treveri buckled, their leaders fled into the arms of the cavalry Cerialis had positioned to catch them.

Augusta Treverorum fell the next day. The men were keen to get down to some serious looting, but Cerialis kept them firmly in hand. The different fates of Cremona and of Augusta Treverorum are remarkable. Augusta Treverorum was much more a captured enemy city than Cremona had been. But Cerialis was no Primus, and with Vespasian's rule already looking secure, the general had less need to pander to the crudest impulses of his men. Besides, there was immediately on hand an example of where disobedience led. The cowed and humiliated rabble of I Germanica and XVI Gallica now haltingly faced the scorn of the army with which they were reunited.

> The attention of the army was diverted to the pitiful appearance of these legions ... bowed down as they were by the knowledge of their guilt, none dared raise their eyes from the ground. No friendly greetings were exchanged between the troops as they met, nor could [the disgraced men] even bring themselves to answer those who would console or encourage them. Instead they hid themselves in their tents, as though ashamed to be seen in the light of day. The men were panicked by the thought of punishment, but even more they were overwhelmed by guilt and humiliation.[9]

How he handled these rebel legionaries would do much to determine Cerialis' standing with his (largely ex-Vitellian) army. Would clemency be seen as weakness and an excuse for license? Would severity provoke resentment and indiscipline? The general had to tread a fine line.

He opted for a *tabula rasa* – a clean sheet. He informed the men that he was grateful that destiny had seen fit to preserve two Roman legions for him through those turbulent times. What was past would be forgotten and the men were to consider that day as the first of their military service. They would be admitted to the camp (being forced to camp outside the walls was a common punishment for a disgraced unit) and strict punishment would follow any discussion of who had defeated or had been defeated by whom in the recent past. Cerialis also strongly hinted to his erring legions that punishment was due, but would be deferred and even forgotten if the legionaries worked off their debt to Rome by valiant performance on the battlefield.

With the peoples of the Treveri and Lingones, Petellius was equally mild. He could afford to be. Their leaders were dead, fled, or in Roman hands. Cerialis did not even bother to accept the surrender of the Lingones in person. He sent one of his officers, Julius Frontinus, who recorded the occasion with pride in a rare autobiographical mention in his later book *The Stratagems*.

> In the war fought under the auspices of Caesar Domitian and begun by Julius Civilis in Gaul, the very wealthy city-state of the Lingones had revolted to Civilis. [The inhabitants] feared that it would be plundered by the approaching imperial army of Caesar. But directly contrary to their expectations, the inhabitants were left unharmed and their property intact. They returned to allegiance [with Rome], and handed over to me command of seventy thousand warriors.[10]

Young Frontinus had an interesting career ahead. He was to remain under Cerialis' command even after the Batavian war, governed Britain and later became curator of Rome's aqueducts. He wrote a detailed treatise on these, which has survived to the present day.

The Gauls had rebelled in the belief that the Roman state was disintegrating into anarchy. Nothing could have more convincingly proven them wrong than the huge camp of disciplined legions, all of whom, despite their orderly appearance, were patently eager for the Gauls to start something. Cerialis addressed the thoroughly cowed Gauls in a speech Tacitus has moulded into the definitive statement of contemporary Roman imperial policy: Rome had always defended Gaul from Germany, Cerialis claimed. Civilis' claim to be freeing the Gauls from the Roman yoke was a lie.

> Liberty is always the pretext – for no man ever tried to make himself master and others his slaves without using the word ... We conquered, and have used our rights as conquerors only to make you carry the cost of being at peace. The peace of nations is defended by armies, and armies are supported by pay. Though you pay this tax, you share in empire. Gauls command armies and rule provinces.

Turning to the root cause of the rebellion – Nero – Cerialis chided the Gauls:

> Despite being far away, you benefit as much as we from worthy emperors. When a ruler is cruel (and there will be vices as long as there are humans) those nearby suffer most. Endure this, as you might endure a time of famine, flooding or any other natural evil.[11]

Without the Romans, Cerialis asked, did the Gauls expect peace, benevolent government and no taxes? Gaul was prosperous; Germany and Britain less so. This would be corrected within months if the Gauls ever succeeded in gaining their own government, since Britain and Germany would first revolt and then invade Gaul. Finally, as recent events had proven, it was not that easy to shrug off Roman rule. 'If your recent fortunes have taught you anything, it is that rebellion and ruin are not preferable to submission and safety.'

Unsurprisingly, the tribesmen leapt at Petellius' offer to let bygones be bygones, and professed themselves delighted once more to be citizens of the empire, protected by the legions from the German threat.

And that threat was growing. Civilis and Classicus were mustering troops from all that remained of their domains. Cerialis complacently let the enemy muster. He made no attempt to defeat any components of the enemy force before they joined the main army. Tacitus is critical of this decision, but Cerialis evidently felt he had little to fear from a German army of whatever size. *He* had eleven legions. If Civilis wanted to gather his men so that the Romans could break them in one battle, this was certainly preferable to chasing odds and ends of the enemy army around Germany's forests and bogs.

Ambush
Civilis continued to attempt the subtleties that had worked so well with Flaccus. He sent a letter assuring Cerialis that Vespasian was dead, though Rome was suppressing the news. Cerialis probably was not expected to believe this, but it gave him a credible excuse if he should decide that his eleven legions could be better employed in making himself emperor than fighting the Batavians. By leaking the 'news' of Vespasian's 'death' to the Roman army, Civilis also no doubt hoped that the men might spontaneously decide to support Cerialis, rather as Vitellius had been railroaded to the imperial purple a year previously.

Cerialis did not pretend he had not seen the messenger nor heard the message. Instead, he made the whole matter known immediately. He laughed off the letter and very publicly sent both message and messenger under guard to Rome. The men followed their commander's lead. They showed neither interest in sedition nor in the offers of cash to deserters, which Latin-speaking Batavian ex-soldiers shouted across the lines.

The confused and mutinous force of a year ago was gone. Under new management, the army remained focused on executing its orders, and the disconcerted Batavian leaders were well aware that their execution was part of those orders. The uncertainty was in the German camp. Tacitus tells us that Civilis wanted to wait until reinforcements arrived in the form of wild tribes from the German interior. Classicus pointed out that more Roman legions were also on the way. It would be best to attack while most of Cerialis' army was ex-Vitellians. Their morale must be fragile, and it might collapse at the first setback.

A surprise attack had almost undone Vocula. Though Cerialis had added a wall and ditch to his camp, the Germans had noted that watch-keeping was sloppy. Who was going to attack so many legions? For good measure, the Batavians had determined that Cerialis was in the habit of spending nights away from camp. Apparently he found the attractions of a local lady's villa more seductive than his own praetorium.

A massive ambush was planned. It is to the credit of Civilis and Classicus that they managed to move well over ten thousand German tribesmen over the river Moselle and through the hills around the camp without alerting the Romans. Tribesmen of the Ubii, Tencteri and those Lingones who had refused to surrender to Rome worked together in silent harmony with the surviving Batavian veterans. In silence the legionary camp was surrounded. Its commander was absent. The Romans were unaware that anything was amiss. And then the night turned into thousands of screaming German tribesman charging at a dead run. The night watch could not hold the walls alone, and by the time the rest of the legionaries had scrambled from their tents into some semblance of armour, the defences were already breached.

The Roman cavalry received particular attention from the German horde and was routed early in the engagement. Civilis put a special guard on the bridge over the river to ensure that fugitives from the camp could not find shelter in Augusta Treverorum. This guard also ensured that Cerialis, who was already in the city, could not get back. At first, when informed that there was work waiting for him back at headquarters, Cerialis tried to calm the excited messengers. They assured him that there was abundant reason for panic. Convinced, Cerialis left the villa at once without even bothering to get properly dressed.

Fully exposed (so to speak) to enemy missiles, the general gathered his bodyguard. He first set about personally rounding up those fugitives who had forded the river and added them to his immediate command. Then with these men Cerialis attacked the bridge and captured it after a brief, brutal fight. After what Tacitus calls this 'daring yet successful effort', Cerialis left the best of his scratch troops to hold his hard-won line of communication and rushed to the camp. A terrifying sight met his eyes. The battle raged among the tents and the trenches, and those soldiers who had managed to rally around their legionary standards were pathetically few. Many others – the heroes of I Germanica at the fore – were less intent on fighting than finding whatever route to safety they could.

Over the noise of battle, the roar of an indignant Cerialis could be heard.

It's not Flaccus, it's not Vocula who you are deserting here. No one can suspect me of treachery. I've got nothing to apologize about except that I trusted you. I thought you had forgotten you were allies of Gaul. I believed that you were Romans again ... Add me to the list of your commanders – you have killed them or let the enemy kill them – every single one. Go on, tell Vespasian that you deserted your general on the battlefield. Or go and tell Civilis and Classicus – they are right here. There are legions coming that will avenge me and punish you.[12]

The officers of the legion passed on the message to those who had not heard it, reminding the men of I Germanica that this really was their last chance. Obediently, the legion struggled into something resembling battle formation. Seeing that I Germanica had ceased coming apart, the other legions held steady. The battle was still far from evenly balanced – the Germans had the initiative and the Roman battle-line, so far as it existed, was a confused and ad hoc affair. Many of the participants (including the commanding officer) were improperly dressed, or indeed not dressed at all. Even with the inspirational Cerialis to rally the men, the situation looked bleak.

It was time for heroes, and it was the ex-Vitellians of XXI Rapax who stepped up. The battle-hardened veterans fought until they had slightly more room to manoeuvre. Then they formed a compact wedge that drove across the German line, forcing the startled warriors into retreat. In turning, the Germans saw torches and Roman horsemen silhouetted on the ridge above the town. These were carried by the routed Roman cavalry cautiously making their way back to find out what was happening. However, the Germans knew well that their ambush had been a pre-emptive attack designed to finish off the ex-Vitellians before VI Victrix and X Gemina arrived from Spain. And now they had – or so it seemed to the alarmed Germans. Another disadvantage was that having breached the Roman walls, some wild tribesmen found themselves confronted with more booty than they had seen in their lives. They then spent more time fighting each other for it than they spent battling the Romans.

This did not matter whilst the legions were on the defensive, but when the army rallied the confused Germans were driven helter-skelter from the camp. Nor would Cerialis let them rest. His blood was thoroughly up. All through the next day, he drove his men against the backs of the fleeing enemy. He allowed neither German nor Roman a moment's grace. When the Germans fell back on their camp, the Romans promptly fell upon it as well, and conquered it before the Germans could organize a defence. Before night fell again, the disconsolate survivors of the men who had hoped to destroy Cerialis' camp could only watch as the Romans plundered their own.

The Push To Lower Germany
The night battle for Cerialis' camp probably took place in early June. It marked the point where the reconstruction of the Rhine frontier was well and truly begun. When news of the Roman success reached Colonia Agrippinensis, the 'allies' of Civilis reacted decisively. The Batavian commander had billeted troops in the city both to ensure the loyalty of the inhabitants and to protect his wife and daughter, who were living there. However, the inhabitants of Colonia Agrippinensis included a considerable number of retired legionaries. These had been planning a coup and were waiting for the chance to put it into operation. The Germans were invited to a huge party with abundant wine. Once enough Germans had passed out within, the building where the party was hosted was locked and set on fire. Any survivors were massacred. The people of Agrippinensis arrested the family of Civilis and sent messengers rushing to Cerialis pleading for him to reach the city before Civilis came for revenge.

Civilis was indeed infuriated by the capture of his family. But the rebel commander had other problems. The final units of XIV Gemina Martia Victrix had just arrived by ship from Britain, and Civilis was eager to get back to his base on the Island before the British legionaries beat him to it. In fact, his anxiety was unnecessary. The new arrivals from XIV Gemina Martia Victrix had no orders to finish the war with a pre-emptive strike. Cerialis intended to win the war by the methodical reduction of rebel territory, just as Vespasian had done in Judea. Therefore, instead of rushing to the Island, XIV Gemina Martia Victrix made a leisurely sweep southeast through Gaul, bringing rebel tribes there back to their allegiance. As XIV Martia Victrix approached, one tribe – the Nervi – showed their loyalty by a spirited attempt to throw the Germans off their lands for themselves. The neighbouring Tungri rapidly followed this example.

The Germans responded actively. The Cannenfates shared the aquatic expertise of their Batavian comrades and launched a lightning attack that captured or sank many of the ships that had brought XIV Gemina Martia Victrix from Britain. Then Civilis' cavalry gave a bloody nose to the Roman horse Cerialis sent to reinforce the British legionaries. However, these successes were transient, and mainly intended to give Civilis a breathing space as he withdrew to Lower Germany to make his stand.

Cerialis now used his vastly superior numbers to good effect. He drove north with his preferred legionary corps of XXI Rapax and II Adiutrix. To this he added VI Victrix once it had arrived from Spain. Yet even as this force kept the pressure on the Germans, Cerialis had other legions free, which he dispersed along the Rhine frontier and in northwestern Gaul to keep the peace. (I Germanica was left at Augusta Treverorum.) His adroit use of manpower meant that Cerialis' core army was small enough to be flexible, and the logistical burden of supporting the rest of his vast force was spread across much of northwestern Europe.

While everything was going smoothly on the battlefront, a political issue briefly developed on the home front. As Corbulo had discovered, court intrigues in Rome were potentially every bit as deadly as the enemy in the field. Rome was now solidly in Vespasian's power, even if the emperor himself was still en route to the city.

Mucianus had put to death the young son of Vitellius, a brutal act that ill repaid Vitellius' own restraint with regard to Domitian. Perhaps because of this, young Domitian wanted to change his image from helpless hostage to conquering general. He left Rome and advanced to the Alps, sending messages ahead to Cerialis that he was coming to Germany. There he would present himself to the troops and take command of the war. What Cerialis made of this hare-brained proposal one can only imagine. To complicate things further, other messengers arrived from Mucianus urgently telling Cerialis that he should in no circumstances agree to anything of the sort. In the end Cerialis did what many another general in the field has done when confronted with impossible or contradictory orders from headquarters. He ignored them as politely as he could.

Eventually he was informed that after the victory outside Augusta Treverorum, the remainder of the war was a mopping-up operation. This could, after all, be entrusted to inferior generals such as himself. Domitian would remain in Lugdunum 'overseeing' operations from a distance, ready to step in if the situation deteriorated. Everyone pretended that this was not simply a face-saving compromise to prevent young Domitian from looking a fool, but at the time few were deceived. Domitian reacted to the snub by ostentatiously abandoning politics altogether and devoting himself to literature and art.

This compromise had a further benefit for Mucianus. A generation ago, the epic deeds of Germanicus on the Rhine had given that general superstar status in Rome, and a degree of popularity that these days could only safely be bestowed on the emperor. If Cerialis seemed to be doing too gloriously well, it was very useful to have Domitian on hand to mop up some of the credit. (And indeed, once enough time had passed to cloud memories of exactly what had happened, Domitian shamelessly did just that.) For his part, Cerialis handled what could have been an embarrassing contretemps with polite diplomacy. Domitian appreciated this, and Cerialis' relations with the emperor's son remained cordial.

Castra Vetera Revisited
Civilis now decided to challenge the Romans on ground of his own choosing. To make certain that Cerialis would confront him, Civilis chose the legionary camp at Castra Vetera. Petellius Cerialis accepted the bait with alacrity – this was a chance to avenge the murdered legionaries of V Alaudae and XV Primigenia.

Cerialis would have known that the wide stretch of field near the camp made a suitable battleground. True, the surface was slightly boggy, but as mid-summer was approaching, it should be dry enough for his purposes. The general paused on his march to Castra Vetera only long enough to reunite the long-sundered sections of XIV Gemina Martia Victrix under his direct command and to add a host of auxilia to replace the defected Batavi.

On arrival at Castra Vetera, Cerialis discovered that his battlefield was not slightly boggy – it was a veritable lake. Civilis had diverted the Rhine across the fields to make it so, knowing that his water-wise Batavi would be at home there while the more heavily equipped legionaries would struggle. And so it proved. Despite the unfavourable ground, there was no question of Cerialis refusing battle. It was not in the man's character, and the legions had become infected with his get-up-and-go approach. The men threw themselves at the Batavi and watched appalled as the front ranks sank into the watery morass. The Batavi had previously mapped out the bogs and shallows of their manmade swamp, and their more lightly equipped troops operated with impunity where the Romans floundered. Remarked Tacitus, 'it was more like a naval engagement than a regular battle'. The Germans swarmed around the Roman flanks and rear, but two problems denied them any chance of victory.

Firstly, they could splash around the Romans in relative safety. But to defeat the legionaries, they had to come to grips with them. When they did that, the exasperated legionaries cut them to pieces. Secondly, outflanking the Romans took the Germans outside the bog, and on dry land they were outclassed. In short, the Romans were discomfited and frustrated, but as long as they kept their discipline in these unusual circumstances they were in no serious danger. Eventually Petellius realized that he was making no headway and pulled his troops back to *terra firma*. The Germans were too wise to follow and their advantage was lost.

This was technically a victory to the Germans, but it proved something important to Cerialis. Though bewildered by their situation, the men had kept faith in their commander. They had held their ranks, neither charging rashly nor fleeing in confusion. As a result they had withdrawn from what might have been a disastrous situation with no more than light casualties and some embarrassment. The mutual bond of trust between soldiers and general was strengthened – a trust neither Vocula nor Flaccus had come close to enjoying.

Both sides prepared to resume the conflict the next morning. As the troops drew up, each general addressed his men. A general's pre-battle speech was more than a simple pep talk. Like the sacrifices, it was a ritual, one of a series that by its formality and order helped the men into combat mode.

On the German side, Civilis assured his army that the Roman Empire remained a chaotic shipwreck. The Germans were facing a demoralized and disintegrating foe. For the Romans, Cerialis chose to address each legion individually. No commander in a major battle could bring his entire army into hearing range. Therefore the usual habit was to address personally whichever units were likely to bear the brunt of the fighting, and let word of mouth carry the speech to the rest of the army.

But this morning Cerialis rode to each legion and gave each a customized speech. XIV Gemina Martia Victrix were reminded of their victories in Britain, and the memory of Galba was invoked for VI Victrix, in whose camp Galba had first been proclaimed emperor. II Adiutrix were reminded that this battle was their baptism of fire. Today they would set the standard for future generations. For XXI Rapax, the message was simple – Cerialis pointed to Castra Vetera and told the Rhinelanders to take back the camp and their pride.

Cerialis had spent the previous evening reflecting on that day's battle. As a result of his musings, the cavalry and auxilia now made up the battle line. Behind these, screened from the enemy, the legions were deployed not in line, but in columns. This narrower frontage meant that the legions could operate without spreading into boggier parts of the battlefield. Furthermore, a simple half-turn could convert each column into a battle line facing an outflanking force.

Ideally, the Romans did not want to get drawn into the marsh at all. Therefore the battle started with an exchange of missiles during which most Germans lurked just out of pilum range, hoping to draw the Romans into the morass. When their enemy failed to take the bait, the Germans launched a furious assault on the auxiliary line.

Roman auxilia were not heavy infantry only in comparison to the yet more heavily armed legionaries. Against most opposition they were at least as heavily armed and armoured, and quite capable of standing their ground. In this battle Cerialis intended them to blunt the ardour of the initial German attack. Once they had achieved this, the auxilia fell back through the legionaries.

Roman discipline and training allowed them to rotate their front-line fighters. The front-rank Germans had no such drill. Now they were already tired from their opening clash with the auxilia. All the legionaries now had to do was hold the Germans until their front ranks (which were invariably composed of the best and fiercest warriors) dropped from exhaustion. Then they would slowly and inexorably push forward. It was a strategy which would be immediately recognized by any soldier who had been in Britain for the final defeat of Boudicca by Paulinus.

Petellius Cerialis had not taken lessons only from Paulinus. Like any general with aspirations to greatness, he had read the campaigns of Alexander the Great. Alexander had liked to use his infantry to pin the enemy frontally whilst the cavalry swept around to attack the flanks. In his Germanic re-enactment of Alexander's battle strategy, Cerialis used a German deserter to guide his horsemen around the combat. Both the Pauline and Alexandrine strategies meshed perfectly. The German front line started to buckle just as the cavalry charged home on the flank. With disaster pending to the front and side, the tribesmen unhesitatingly turned and sprinted for the Rhine. The slow start to the battle meant that victory had come in the late afternoon, and following it up proved difficult. Had the fleet been available to Cerialis, the Germans would have been slaughtered in the water. But the fleet was still in chaos after its defeat by the Cannenfates. Had the ground been better, the cavalry would have fallen on the rear of the fleeing enemy. But the cavalry had bad memories of the bog from the previous day. Now an unexpected and heavy rain shower made things even worse. Most of the German army escaped.

Nevertheless, this was another victory for Cerialis, and his stock with the men rose accordingly. VI Victrix erected a monument to their victory, as presumably did the other legions. The monument by VI Victrix has recently been discovered by modern archaeologists. (It gives the name of the legionary legate as Sextus Caelius Tuscus. Fragments of armour and weapons have also been retrieved from the battle site.)

Among the German casualties in the battle was the reputation of Civilis, which was sorely wounded. Tribesmen who had joined to loot the corpse of the Roman Empire now realized that this 'corpse' was alive and kicking. Therefore some of the men Civilis had not lost in the battle simply lost faith in their leader and dispersed back into the forests. Fortunately for Civilis, these losses were partly compensated by tribesmen of the Chauci. These had arrived too late to participate in the fight, but stayed on to reinforce his warriors.

Still, the rebel leader accepted his defeat. His capital, Noviomagus (Nimenjen), could no longer be defended. Civilis salvaged what he could and burned the rest. Then he pulled back to defend his nation's heartland, the Island of the Batavians. Here he once more displayed the military engineering skills he had learned from the Romans by setting his men to maximize the flow of the Rhine into the south fork of the river. Afterward the water on the side facing the Romans was deep and strong, but on the German side it was a mere trickle. (Civilis was taking a page from the book of Drusus Germanicus, who had once built a mole across the river to achieve the opposite effect.)

With his base as secure as he could make it, the indomitable Batavian returned to the offensive. Since a head-on collision had failed, Plan B was a series of co-ordinated attacks on different parts of Cerialis' dispersed army. The legions under their charismatic leader had shown disappointingly firm morale. Perhaps those further from Cerialis' direct command might prove more fragile. And even if this were not the case, Civilis knew his man from his time in Britain. The steady, methodical approach that Petellius was using was contrary to his natural inclination. Perhaps a sudden flurry of attacks would fluster a general known for his impetuosity into doing something rash.

After the victory at Castra Vetera, XIV Gemina Martia Victrix had been rotated out of the field army to garrison duty in Upper Germany. The replacement for XIV Martia Victrix was X Gemina from Spain. X Gemina had been posted to at Arenacum on the Rhine, and it was there that the first blow of Civilis' counter-strike fell.[13] With their customary skill at ambush, the German raiders caught a foraging party gathering wood. With the foragers were a number of officers who were out either hunting or scouting. These too fell in the ambush, so the Romans lost five centurions, the camp prefect and their bodyguard. But the rest of the legion withdrew to camp, which the raiders knew better than to assail.

Civilis quickly switched his focus before Cerialis could respond to the attack on X Gemina. The next attack was at Batavorum, 'the market of the Batavians'. This was a town just off the Island the Romans had captured. The army was working on a bridge there, perhaps in preparation for a final push into the Batavian heartland. The Germans here were charged with destroying the bridge. Perhaps warned by the ructions at Arenacum to the east, the Romans were alert and the assault failed, though an indecisive fight went on until nightfall.

Cerialis was at a fort he had established at Grinnes, close to the Waal and Meuse rivers. This fort was targeted for a surprise cavalry attack led by Civilis himself. The charge ripped through the Roman ranks. Fortunately Cerialis himself was an experienced cavalry commander. He personally led the counter-attack, which reversed the tide of battle. As his men fell back, Civilis distinguished himself by his efforts to stem the retreat. In fact, he so distinguished himself that the Romans promptly identified him and sent a hailstorm of missiles in his direction. Under intense fire, the Batavian leader had to abandon both the fight and his horse and swim the river to safety.

In the end the attacks designed to confuse and demoralize the Romans had the opposite effect. The solid rebuffs they had delivered left the Romans confident that they had the measure of the opposition. Civilis still had a large and competent army in the field, but perhaps the war was after all what Domitian had been told it was – a vast mopping-up operation.

Dodgy Doings on the River
To date, the campaign was as significant for what had not happened as for developments on the ground. There had been no mutinies, no desertions, no sedition in camp, no problems with supply – in short, none of the problems that had bedevilled the Rhineland army over the previous year. Competence engendered confidence, and under Cerialis' decisive and inspiring command the legionaries settled, with what one imagines was considerable relief, back to their accustomed task of killing Germans.

For all the mutterings in Rome (which Tacitus repeats and embellishes) that Petellius Cerialis was too hasty and lacked the character to command so huge an operation, no one could deny that things were going extremely well for the general. 'Haste characterized his plans, though success characterized the results,' writes Tacitus petulantly. 'Fortune carried the day when technique failed.'[14] Yet it is hard to see how Cerialis could have done better. Not only was he restoring the German frontier as quickly and competently as even the headiest optimist could have wished, he was doing so with minimal fuss. But Tacitus knew his man (in fact, he probably knew him personally). The coming days were to support his uncharitable opinion.

For Rome the Batavians on their island were far from the major issue of the war, though Civilis might be excused for seeing things differently. The revolt of the Rhine legions and the subsequent revolt of Gallic tribes to the south and west had ripped apart Rome's frontier defences from the North

Sea to the Alps. True, the Roman perspective of the empire's borders was nowhere near as rigid as it was later to become. Nevertheless, the Romans still remembered the invasion and near-conquest of Italy by Germanic hordes two centuries previously. Cerialis' orders gave priority not to defeating the Batavi, but to re-establishing the Rhine frontier. This is what the general now set about doing.

The legions were back in place at strategic locations along the Rhine, and the frontier was stable and defended. Now the commander wanted to ensure that his men were properly dug in for the approaching autumn and winter. The untidy remnants of his fleet were now back under his direct command, so Cerialis took advantage of this to travel upriver to Bonna to inspect the legionary winter camps under construction. A feeling that the Batavi were a spent force gave the inspection something of the feeling of a holiday jaunt – a moment of relaxation before getting down to the serious business of storming the Island.

The Germans observed the slapdash security around the Roman camp. They particularly noted that this carelessness extended even to the ship that Cerialis had made his travelling headquarters.

One moonless night, two German units slipped past the Roman pickets into the camp. One group began cutting the ropes holding up the eight-man Roman marching tents. Before those underneath had worked out that this was no prank, the Germans killed them as they struggled free. This daring murder by night could only go on so long before it was inevitably discovered. Thereafter the Germans raised an ear-splitting battle-cry, which brought the legionaries tumbling out of their tents, memories of the night battle at Augusta Treverorum fresh in their minds.

Instead of a German horde, the soldiers saw much of their fleet slipping away down the Rhine. The Batavi, with their usual aquatic skill, had formed the second group of infiltrators. These had quietly cut the mooring cables of the Roman ships. Then, with the Romans distracted by the chaos in their camp, rowing boats sailed alongside with grapnels and took the undermanned ships in tow. Among the ships captured in this daring raid was that of Petellius Cerialis. The horrified legionaries on the shore were watching an attempt to abduct their general from under their very noses.

The Germans in the raid had been too few to cause serious damage to the Romans in the camp. Nevertheless, it took some time for the uproar to die down. Amongst the characters milling about on the river bank, many were under-dressed and all were confused about the best way to retrieve their general. It took time before attention was paid to a near-naked individual who furiously explained that Cerialis had not been abducted. He had not been taken with his ship because he had not been aboard the ship when it was taken. The speaker knew this for certain because he himself was Petellius Cerialis, Imperial General, albeit temporarily separated from his insignia of rank and the rest of his wardrobe (which *were* aboard the ship now vanishing down the Rhine).

To Cerialis' embarrassment, the full story gradually got out. The general had left his ship during the night. He had found his bed there less attractive than the bed of Claudia Sacrata, a lady of the nearby Ubian tribe. This tribe had recently defected back to Rome, and Cerialis had been personally welcoming this lady back into the bosom of the empire. He had been ashore and occupied with other than military matters when his ship was taken.

The sentries used this as their defence when their sloppy guard keeping was questioned. They claimed that once their general had left the camp with romance in mind, they had deliberately turned a blind eye to clandestine coming and goings. They had assumed these were concerned with their commander's nocturnal activities.

Civilis must have been disappointed not to have netted Cerialis in his night-time operation. He gave the flagship to his favourite priestess, that Veleda who still presumably had as a prisoner the unfortunate Lupercus, former commander of Castra Vetera. Apart from Cerialis' command ship, the rest of the fleet had been taken for a reason. The Romans had been using the Rhine as a supply route and barges were carrying grain and fodder for the legions. Civilis wanted to intercept them.

Now he drew up every ship the Batavians owned or had captured and flaunted these in a maritime parade before the indignant Romans. If the intention was to provoke the general into rashness, it succeeded. Civilis had finally got under Cerialis' skin. Though his ships were now outnumbered by the Batavi, the furious Cerialis gathered up everything he had left and prepared for battle.

Civilis prepared to meet the Roman warships at the wide confluence of the Mosa (Meuse) and the Rhine. For the Batavians, it was a crucial battle. The autumn was fast approaching and the weather deteriorating. If they could destroy the Roman fleet and supplies than they would probably be safe for at least the coming winter. In this time new alliances could be forged with German tribes in the interior, and messages of sedition circulated in Gaul. Defeat, with Cerialis in his present mood, meant that the Romans would be on the Island within days.

Petellius Cerialis was well aware what the Batavians had to gain and what he had to lose. Strategically speaking, this naval battle that meant much to the Batavians could at best be meaningless for him. Victory on the water would not greatly improve his position. A better way to protect his convoys was to destroy the Batavi as a military threat. Cerialis did not want to sink ships that the enemy had captured and which he wanted back. He may also have been aware that the Batavians were growing tired of the war. The rebellion had gained them little and had cost dearly in money and manpower, and now war threatened their homeland itself. It was time for Cerialis to bring the war home to the people on the Island.

On the day of battle, the Roman war fleet came downriver with the current and met the Batavi sailing upriver with the wind behind them. The Roman ships were fewer, but they were well piloted and larger. Nor did they stop to fight. With a brisk exchange of missiles, the two lines of ships passed through each other, and left Cerialis and his legions on the other side of the Rhine. Where Civilis had wanted a naval battle, Petellius had sought only to land his legions. Afloat, the Batavi had a chance. Once the legions were ashore, the Island was at Cerialis' mercy.

Of mercy there was little over the coming days. The ghosts of V Alaudae and XV Primigenia demanded that vengeance be taken in full, and it was. The only houses left intact and the only lands unravaged were those of Civilis himself. The Batavi were well aware that this was a deliberate tactic intended to drive a wedge between themselves and their leader. But ruined men with homes in flames now faced a winter without livestock or crops. They could not help noticing that the man who had got them into this mess was the only one not currently suffering from it.

If famine faced the Batavi, then their one consolation was that for the moment Cerialis was in something of a pickle himself. While his men had been devastating the Island from end to end, autumn had arrived early, bringing with it heavy rains. By the end of August, the Rhine was in full flood. Thanks to the engineering work of Civilis, that flood was strongest and most impassable on the Roman side of the river. Cerialis was cut off from reinforcements and supplies. He had situated his camp on low ground (there being little of any other kind on the Island). Now it was steadily vanishing into the advancing waters of the Rhine. It began to dawn on the impetuous general that he might have done better to wait after all.

If impetuosity was one of Cerialis' distinguishing features, another was a cheerfully indomitable approach to danger and obstacles. His camp was surrounded by a desperate and vengeful enemy. Hunger was increasing among his men. So Cerialis told the Batavians that he was ready to accept their surrender.

Envoys were sent from his camp, each with a specific message. Civilis was informed that Cerialis knew that his people were turning against him, and that many felt that the war had come about because of his private feud with the Romans. The destruction of two legions was a grievous offence. But even that might be mitigated if Civilis was instrumental in rescuing the legions now stranded in the Roman camp.

Cerialis also sent messages to Civilis' pet priestess, Veleda. He pointed out that the Batavians appeared to have lost the favour of their gods. Fate now favoured Rome, and the priestess would be well rewarded for reconciling her fellow tribesmen with that fact.

Other messengers made it across the floodwaters to inform tribes allied to Civilis that now was the moment to make peace. Rome was in the mood to draw a veil of forgetfulness over the entire ghastly year of AD 69. Notwithstanding Cerialis' current embarrassment, Rome had one of the largest armies ever assembled still in place along the Rhine. This was ready, willing and able to do serious damage to anyone who was still holding out the following spring. As was traditional, those tribes that yielded first would get the mildest terms; the last hold-outs the hardest punishment. Many tribes had surrendered already, more were capitulating – it was time to take the best terms while they were still available.

The Batavians were assured that Rome still valued their manpower and future contribution to the empire. Cerialis understood that the Batavians may have considered they were Flavians fighting against the forces of Vitellius. It was a stretch, but perhaps the destruction of V Alaudae and XV Primigenia was not so different from the carnage pro- and anti-Vitellian armies had been wreaking on each other in Italy at the same time. And the ruination of the Vitellian forces on the Rhine had strangled reinforcements to the army in Italy.

But by this argument, the war now was pointless. The empire was united under Vespasian. All that the Batavians would achieve from further resistance was to be crushed like bugs. They should take advantage of the present, but very temporary discomfiture of the legions on the Island and make peace on whatever terms they could. With Romans and Batavians working together, supplies could be brought in over the weaker, northern branch of the river and the impending famine of the coming winter could be averted.

Thus Cerialis offered the substantial carrot of peace and reconciliation, and the very large stick of eight vengeful legions. Unsurprisingly, Civilis and the Batavians opted to negotiate.

AFTERMATH

At this point we are let down by Tacitus, or rather by the guardians of his legacy. We know that peace talks were conducted on a bridge deliberately broken in the middle. This allowed Petellius Cerialis and Civilis to meet almost face to face, but with a gap and swirling waters underneath to avert any attempts at treachery. We know that Civilis launched into an impassioned defence of his actions, but halfway through the preamble of that defence the text breaks off, doubtless because some monk found a better use for the parchment on which it was written. We have no other source but Tacitus for detailed events on the Rhine frontier. When his narrative runs out, so do details of the exact ending of the campaign in Germany.

However, the broad outlines are clear. Cerialis had seen the miserable aftermath of Paulinus' war against Boudicca, where Roman vindictiveness had set back the development of Britain by over a decade. In Germany, Rome needed a solid frontier, not a prolonged guerrilla war against resentful and unproductive tribesmen. Therefore Cerialis would have offered the Batavians the same generous terms given to the rebel Gallic tribes.

We know that the Rhine frontier was secure and stable after the settlement. Soon after that, Batavian cohorts were again making a valued contribution to the Roman army. Whether a fine or an indemnity was imposed is unknown. The Batavians continued to occupy a strategic point on the frontier, and this meant that their loyalty was considerably more important than whatever monetary contribution they could make. (Especially as the Romans had already pillaged or destroyed most Batavian assets in the weeks before the peace.)

What Civilis was offered personally we do not know. The rebel leader effectively vanishes from history. So too does his priestess Veleda, though we can assume that disgorging Lupercus (if he was still alive) was a non-negotiable clause in the peace agreement.

Overall, therefore, Petellius Cerialis emerges well as a diplomat. He avenged V Alaudae and XV Primigenia and did it without permanently alienating the Batavians. He restored the rebels to their allegiance with Rome and nullified the legacy of Civilis. Germany had been a huge and growing disaster area at the end of AD 69. At the end of AD 70 the region was stable, well defended and returning to prosperity. The difference to the conclusion of Paulinus' war in Britain could not have been more marked. And Cerialis undoubtedly got his ships back.

The reckoning with the Batavians had been concluded. It was time to deal with the legions. The murders of Flaccus and Vocula could not go unpunished. The sole achievement of I Germanica – to stop running away at Augusta Treverorum – was far too little to atone for the legion's many sins and failings. The unit that probably contained the worst legionaries ever to serve under the eagles of imperial Rome would not get the chance to make amends. It was disbanded forthwith.

Almost as guilty was the fellow legion of deserters, XVI Gallica. But at least those legionaries could fight. Rome needed fighting men. The bad apples of the legion were purged and replaced with Italian recruits. The name the legion had disgraced was abandoned, and it became XVI Flavia Firma ('firm for the Flavians'). As a further unsubtle reminder that its disloyalty had not been forgotten, the unit was transferred far from Gaul (where many soldiers had home and family) and re-based in the east. There it remained, and was still guarding the Euphrates frontier almost three centuries later.

IV Macedonica had simply been on the wrong side. The legionaries had spent the war at Moguntiacum keeping what was left of the frontier together in difficult circumstances, albeit for the wrong emperor. Nevertheless, the legion would benefit from a fresh start. It was renamed IV Flavia Firma and moved to Dalmatia (which actually was closer to the legion's historic roots). The new commander was Julius Agricola, a favourite of Cerialis. Vocula's old legion, XXII Primigenia, was allowed to continue at Moguntiacum, which it had held with VI Macedonica in the difficult days after the defection of I Germanica and XVI Gallica. In fact, XXII Primigenia was to remain in Moguntiacum for the following three centuries.

XXI Rapax remained in Germany for the next twenty years. Apparently unable to learn from history, the legion supported the rebellion of its governor against Domitian when he became emperor. As punishment, XXI Rapax was sent to Pannonia. In AD 92 the legion was destroyed by the Sarmatians.

Petellius Cerialis went back to Rome and there was rewarded with a consulship by his grateful emperor and relative, Vespasian. However, Vespasian had one more job for his general. When Cerialis reappears back in the spotlight of history, he is back where he started ... coping with rebellious tribesmen in Britain.

Chapter 7

Aftermath: Return to Britannia and the World Restored

AN UNHAPPY GOVERNOR

Vettius Bolanus, governor of Britain in AD 69, could not have slept well that year. His was a diabolically tricky situation. Britain had declared loyalty to Vitellius after the fall of Otho appeared to have settled the question of who was to rule the empire. In due course, XIV Gemina Martia Victrix had arrived, bruised and disgruntled from Bedriacum. Then Vespasian had rebelled and the loyalty of Vespasian's old legion, II Augusta, became somewhat strained. IX Hispana still remembered the command of another Flavian, the young Petellius Cerialis. Unsurprisingly, Bolanus needed every Vitellian loyalist he could find or create to keep the province loyal to its current emperor. Yet it was those very loyalists whom Vitellius desperately needed on the continent to face the Flavian legions coming from the east.

This created something of a split personality in each of the legions serving in Britain. There was the Flavian faction, most of whom Bolanus had perforce to keep in Britain, and the Vitellian faction, which the governor had to send to Italy. The only way that Bolanus could keep a grip on his army in Britain was to hint that he was something of a closet Vespasian fan himself. He also avoided antagonizing the legionaries with strict discipline. The news from Germany of the problems of Hordonius Flaccus probably increased both the sleeplessness of Bolanus and his eagerness to appease his legions.

BRIGANTIA DEFECTS

Yet the problems of Bolanus paled in comparison to those of Cartimandua, queen of the Brigante. Cartimandua had now ruled the Brigante for almost two decades. During this time she had been a fast friend of the Romans and an essential part of the Roman long-term strategy for Britain.[1] This Roman strategy was basically to keep Brigantia as a loyal client kingdom in the north; then, with that frontier secure, to concentrate on subduing the unruly tribes of the west (and the unruly Iceni of the east, as it turned out). It is quite possible that no conquest of northern Britain was even contemplated before AD 69. Brigantia was not profitable.

Brigantia had no mineral wealth and the loam and clay of Britain was unlike the light, sandy soils of much of the Mediterranean. In the age before the invention of the horse collar, such heavy soil presented a challenge to ploughs and yielded poor crops. Nor did the Romans think much of the agricultural opportunities of the relatively short, wet British summer. Add to this the lack of mineral wealth, and Rome was prepared to occupy only the relatively profitable southern parts of the island. The barren, windy Pennines could be left to Cartimandua in exchange for Roman and Brigante leaving each other in peace.

This was particularly the case as Britain was a more expensive acquisition than any other Roman province, apart from perhaps Judea. Every legion in service drained the imperial fisc, and even with the Brigante happy, Britain had four legions (II, IX, XIV and XX). The larger, economically dynamic, Iberian peninsula was host to just one legion. Greece did not have any. So Roman strategy in Britain concentrated on securing the south of the island. Once that was done, two or possibly three legions could be taken out of the province and either redeployed elsewhere, or, even more profitably, disbanded.

The fatal flaw in this scheme was that it depended on the Brigante staying friendly. And the Brigante had never really been friendly – Cartimandua had been. Her tribe was vast, with multiple sub-tribes spread across northern Britain from northwest of modern Humberside to Cumbria. Each of these sub-tribes had its own minor chieftain with his own views on Roman–Brigante relations. At least one of these groupings was under the direct influence of Venutius, and Cartimandua's ex-husband had little love for either his former spouse or the Romans.

It will be recalled that it had taken the direct involvement of a Roman legion to reconcile Venutius with Cartimandua in AD 50 (p. 45). Given Venutius' anti-Roman sentiments, it is unlikely that Cartimandua had endeared herself any further in AD 51 when she handed over to the Romans the refugee Caractacus, champion of British independence. Therefore when Rome's empire was thrown into confusion after the death of Nero, like the leaders of the Batavians, Venutius scented an opportunity.

Cartimandua had not remained in power as long as she had simply by being the descendant of Brigantia's royal line. She was intelligent, viciously cruel, and both cunning and unscrupulous. Since much of Venutius' authority came from being her ex-husband, Cartimandua took as her consort Venutius' shield-bearer, Vellocatus. Tacitus depicts this as being a simple romance, but is almost certainly wrong. A shield-bearer in a British tribe was no more simply the arms-bearer of the chief than a chamberlain in later Roman society was in charge of the royal bedding. Each was a position of considerable prestige and held by a man of commensurate rank. So in taking up with Venutius' shield-bearer, Cartimandua almost certainly masterminded the defection of a considerable faction of Venutius' supporters.

This proved insufficient protection. The queen's security was mainly based on the power and prestige of Rome. And in AD 69 Roman power and prestige alike had an image problem. Bolanus may have been (correctly) perceived as too weak to persuade his army to go to war against as large and numerous a tribe as the Brigante. In any case, large detachments of the Roman army in Britain had been sent to the continent to fight in the civil war. The remainder was already overstretched. If ever there was a time for Venutius and his followers to eject Cartimandua from power, that time was AD 69. Bolanus did what he could and sent a mixed force of horse and foot to reinforce the Queen, who probably had her royal court in Stanwick.[2]

It may be that this Roman force had the opposite effect to that intended. Far from reinforcing the queen, it turned public opinion against her. In consequence, all that the Romans could do was to pull back to their own lines, taking Cartimandua with them. As Tacitus crisply summarized matters, Bolanus got the queen, Venutius got Brigantia, and Rome got the war.[3]

FRESH BLOOD

News of the Flavian victory at Bedriacum reached Britain. Vespasian's old legion, II Augusta, and those elements of XIV Gemina Martia Victrix still in the province took the lead in forcing a change over to Flavian rule. In an administrative purge, many Vitellian supporters were removed or transferred. Amongst these was Roscius Coelius, the commander of XX Valeria Victrix. He was replaced by Julius Agricola, who was (in the impartial opinion of his devoted son-in-law, Tacitus) Cerialis' most competent subordinate.

Vespasian had first-hand knowledge of British affairs. The instant transformation of Brigantia from friendly client state to hostile northern power confirmed his distrust of rule by client kings. The emperor ordered a new strategy. Britain would now fall under direct Roman rule as far as was physically possible.[4]

Bolanus had sat on the fence between Vitellians and Flavians with sufficient dexterity to retain his office after the transfer to Flavian rule in the province. However, a new man was required for the challenges ahead.

These challenges were, firstly, to re-introduce the British legions to Roman military discipline and, secondly, to re-integrate the troops that had been away fighting in Italy for the Vitellian side. Once a coherent fighting force was in place, this would be employed to conquer the Brigante with minimal expenditure of manpower and money (especially the latter, as the empire was practically bankrupt). Thirdly, and finally, the forcible folding of the Brigante into the empire had to be done with tact. Even if the newly expanded province was not delighted with direct Roman rule, it must at least acquiesce to the fact.

There was an obvious candidate for the job – Petellius Cerialis, the former son-in-law of the new emperor; a man who, as commander of the remnants of IX Hispana, probably had intense diplomatic contact with Cartimandua during the tense days of the Boudiccan revolt. Since then Cerialis had enjoyed hands-on experience in reconciling Vitellian legionaries with Flavian rule. Furthermore, he had not only defeated the Batavi, but had managed this so diplomatically that it is quite possible that a fresh levy of Batavian troops accompanied him to Britain. (Batavian troops later did sterling service in Britain. In an interesting postscript, a Flavius Cerialis turns up as commander of the Ninth Batavian cohort in Britain during the reign of Trajan in AD 105. This man is almost certainly the son of a Batavian nobleman given Roman citizenship by Petellius Cerialis.)

XIV Gemina Martia Victrix was not to return to Britain. The legion joined I Adiutrix at Moguntiacum. Instead, Britain got II Adiutrix, the legion formed from the sailors of the fleet at Ravenna that had deserted to Primus in AD 69 (p.00). This legion was already under Cerialis' command, having capably assisted him in the Rhineland. II Adiutrix now took over garrison duty from IX Hispana at Lincoln. It has been plausibly suggested that the legate of II Adiutrix was Frontinus, who had served with Cerialis in Gaul (p.00).[5] Cerialis took back direct command of IX Hispana. This legion, along with Agricola's XX Valeria Victrix, was to be the main strike force in the Brigantine war.

Unlike the campaign against the Batavians and the campaigns of AD 69 where we have almost day-to-day information, we lack even some rudimentary details of the war against the Brigante. Yet archaeological evidence has helped with the almost total lack of information in the literary sources. Some evidence of Cerialis' movements can be gleaned from the remnants of marching camps that the legions habitually established in hostile territory. We can also make further presumptions based on how the Roman army of the day waged war.

THE CAMPAIGN

We can start from the assumption that Cerialis was not interested in fighting for strategic territory. His intention would have been to crush the Brigante as a political entity. Therefore his army's advance would concentrate on the principal town (*oppidum*) of each minor sub-grouping of the Brigante. The overall target would be the capture of Venutius' main base at Stanwick. Each minor tribe would receive the same ultimatum – renounce Venutius, or have your towns devastated and lands pillaged. To make this threat all the more effective, Cerialis divided his forces. As far as we can tell, he and IX Hispana took an eastern route across the river Humber and up through what is now West Yorkshire. As the western arm of Cerialis' strike force, Agricola and XX Valeria Victrix made their way along the Southern Pennines.

Cerialis gave Agricola considerable freedom of movement, possibly putting him in the same role as Vespasian had performed for Aulus Plautius during the original conquest of Britain. As a semi-autonomous leader of a force designated to pacify an area outside the overall commander's sphere of operations, Agricola had his commander's trust and a wide degree of latitude.

It seems certain that the operation conducted by the now thoroughly experienced Cerialis worked like clockwork, since Tacitus would have relished telling of any errors or setbacks.[6] Instead of any criticism, the picture that emerges is of two Roman legions, each competently commanded, proceeding methodically northwards from central and eastern Britain, pacifying rebellious tribes as they went along, and regularly encountering and defeating *ad hoc* warbands defending their tribal *oppidum*.

From the *Agricola* of Tacitus, we know that the Britons put up a spirited resistance. Tacitus mentions 'numerous battles, some of them bloody'. The same chapter adds that the British liked to fight in their tribal divisions. 'Our greatest advantage in coping with the strength of these tribes is that they seldom act in concert.'[7]

This suggests that as Cerialis made his way northward, he succeeded in detaching at least some sub-tribes from their allegiance to Venutius. For propaganda purposes, it is unlikely that Cerialis introduced the idea of direct rule by Rome at this point. More probably (unless Cartimandua was desperately unpopular), he would have claimed that his intention was to restore the queen to her throne. This, after all, was something the Romans had done before without interfering with Brigante liberty. Sadly, we do not know even this much – in this poorly documented campaign, Cartimandua does not appear at all, and, like Venutius, she is also is absent from the record thereafter.

Excavations at the presumed Brigantian capital of Stanwick show that the site was an already impressive hill fort in the early AD 60s. It then expanded to a full-blown fortified town with ramparts two miles in length. Thereafter an even more ambitious expansion was planned, which would take the overall fortified area to 600 acres. However, some last-minute modifications were made that improved defence at the expense of convenience. Then work was abandoned altogether and some new developments were destroyed. It is evident that something dramatic happened at this point, and though the chronology is uncertain, what happened was probably Petellius Cerialis. This theory is given extra credence by the discovery of a set of Roman marching camps proceeding across Stainmore towards Stanwick. This can only have been Cerialis' IX Hispana on its way to get Venutius.

The legions came together in the north, so it appears that they encountered Venutius in a final battle. Stanwick was too large to defend against a full Roman legion, so it is probable that the Brigantine leader withdrew and made his stand near the modern Scottish border. There are hints that the Brigante allied with a yet more northerly tribe. Either Venutius fled to this when defeated or he died in the final confrontation with Rome. In either case, like Civilis in Batavia, Venutius simply drops from the record.

AFTERMATH
The aftermath of this campaign was totally different from previous Roman interventions in Brigantia. If Cartimandua was restored, she was a Roman puppet. She was only briefly to rule her restored kingdom before all pretence of anything but direct rule by Rome was removed six years later. Cerialis used this transition period to make permanent an army base on flat ground beside the river Ouse near the border of the Brigante proper and the closely associated tribe of the Parisii. This fort was given the Celtic name of Eboracum. It had secured the Vale of York for Cerialis' advance on Stanwick and was of sufficient strategic value to become one of the few forts that Cerialis founded in Brigantine territory.

It is highly probable that Cerialis also established some sort of base at Carlisle, as this would allow the army to be supplied by the fleet as it advanced from Eboracum. Though there was certainly a Roman presence here in later years, we do not know if the Roman occupation of the site was continuous from AD 71 onwards, or if Cerialis' base was temporary and re-established later. But even if he did not found Carlisle, one of Petellius Cerialis' most enduring achievements in Britain was the founding of

Eboracum. As York, the city became one of the greatest in northern England.

The foundation of Eboracum was not only a military measure: it was also part of a deliberate policy of Romanizing the province. While we know almost nothing of Cerialis' three-year governorship of Britain, apart from the sketchy details of the Brigante campaign, we do know that he was the first in a series of competent administrators who finally set Britain on course to become one of the richest provinces in the empire by the end of the third century AD. Cerialis had seen for himself how arrogant treatment of the Britons had led to the disastrous rebellion of Boudicca and how the vindictive policy of Paulinus had created nothing but misery afterward. Experience and character both made Cerialis a generous conqueror who aimed at peace and reconciliation.

The two governors of the province who followed Cerialis were Frontinus and Agricola. Both were former subordinates of Cerialis, and both – particularly Agricola – were keen Romanizers.[8] If this had been a marked deviation from the policies of Cerialis, no doubt we would have been informed of the fact. Instead Tacitus informs us that 'The administration of Cerialis would have eclipsed the administration and fame of any other successor, but Julius Frontinus who took up and sustained his work.'[9]

After the defeat of the Brigante, military activity turned west to the Silures of what is today Wales. With the subjugation of that tribe, Britannia settled into a period of prolonged peace and prosperity. Warfare did not cease. Under Agricola the legions pushed ever further north, eventually fighting a battle at Mons Graupius in modern Scotland. Mons Graupius was won almost entirely by four cohorts of Batavian infantry, which charged uphill to scatter the enemy whilst the legions remained in reserve. It is arguable that this victory very briefly brought the entire island under Roman dominion. But Caledonia was never occupied, as Rome urgently needed the troops elsewhere.

By that time, Petellius Cerialis was long gone. A decade previously, in AD 74, he had handed over command of the province to Julius Frontinus and left Britain, never to return.

ORBIS RESTITUTUS – **THE WORLD RESTORED**
The empire of AD 74 was very different from that in the violent and wretched decade of the 60s. The far-from-fabulous sixties had started with Nero becoming increasingly erratic and tyrannical after he had his mother Agrippina murdered. Arrogance and mismanagement at the top translated to

arrogance and mismanagement by subordinates. This resulted in the catastrophic rebellion of Boudicca in AD 61. The uprising devastated the province, destroyed half of IX Hispana and had a similar effect on the career of Petellius Cerialis. The embers of the British rebellion were still smouldering when an equally violent uprising broke out in Judea.

Apart from these headline events, there had also been a continuous and growing threat to the Danube provinces, where huge Dacian and Sarmatian raids ravaged Rome's weakened frontier. There was discontent in Mauretania and Egypt, and apart from Greece (which flourished under the Hellenophile Nero) hardly a portion of the empire was content.

The Roman aristocracy had become progressively more mutinous and violent oppression had encouraged greater resistance in a downward spiral of discontent, which culminated in the upheaval and bloodshed of AD 69. That year saw the devastation of much of north Italy, the near-complete destruction of Cremona and the burning of the Capitol in Rome. In AD 70 the revolt of Civilis and the Batavians rounded off a truly miserable decade.

Then came the pragmatic rule of Vespasian. By AD 74 – when Cerialis wrapped up the final matters outstanding from AD 69 – Vespasian ruled a flourishing empire. He was to do so for another five years before passing his imperium to each of his sons in turn.

Even before he arrived in Rome in AD 70, Vespasian's first challenge had been to make sure that Rome remained fed. Thanks to the blockade he himself had imposed, there were barely ten days' grain supplies left in the capital. Fortunately, Vespasian had the docks of Claudius and new warehouses constructed by Galba to speed the delivery of grain. He also had the profits of the Jewish War and the spoils from the sack of Jerusalem to pay for reconstruction.

Vespasian personally removed the first load of rubble from the Capitol as rebuilding began of a new and even larger temple of Jupiter. While he was at it, Vespasian ordered the reconstruction of the Tabularium, the record house of Rome that had been severely battered by the same fire that had destroyed the temple of Jupiter.

Reconciling the people and senate of Rome with imperial rule was something Nero had ignored altogether. Vespasian took it very seriously. Nero's folly, the exquisite Domus Aurea, was torn down or had parts converted to public use. The ornamental lake at the centrepiece of the Golden House was drained. There work began on the Flavian Amphitheatre, which, as the Colosseum, became a lasting symbol of the city and its empire.

Building programmes were instituted elsewhere in Italy. Perhaps the only benefit of the campaigns of AD 69 was that a number of senior Romans had become personally acquainted with the wretched state of the roads in northern Italy. A rebuilding project was launched to rectify this. Also, the penitent Flavians sponsored the rebuilding of Cremona.

In the provinces, Vespasian showed the same tendencies that he had with imperial rule in Britain – governors were preferably men with local experience. If these governors taxed their subjects heavily, they at least knew how to do so with the minimum of unrest. (Vespasian was in the habit of later recalling these governors to Rome and fining them heavily. Such men were nicknamed Vespasian's 'sponges', as he allowed them to soak up money and then squeezed them dry.) One reason that some provinces remained peaceful was because Vespasian settled large numbers of former soldiers outside Italy. He concentrated particularly on Mauretania and Moesia. The latter province saw settlements of veterans of the civil war from VII Claudia, VIII Augusta and XIV Gemina Martia Victrix.

Judea was peaceful, not least because it had been extensively depopulated. Nevertheless, rather as Cerialis had done at Eboracum, Vespasian made a permanent settlement and legionary fort out of his former camp at Caesarea, which became Colonia Prima Flavia Augusta.

Overall, the archaeological evidence across the empire points to a stimulated economy driven by reconstruction work. Money flowed into the imperial treasury and immediately flowed out into building work and other projects. In the process, private enterprise and trade flourished.

There seems little reason to believe that Petellius Cerialis did not also flourish. In AD 83, as Agricola was wrapping up his final conquest of Britain, the consuls for the year were Domitian (now emperor) and 'Q Petellius Rufus'. Whoever this Petellius Rufus was, his appointment as co-consul with the emperor was a great honour – and all the more so as Titus had died in September of the previous year. Therefore this Petellius was the first man whom Domitian could have so honoured. Who was Petellius Rufus? His existence is known only through an inscription found in the eastern city of Smyrna and by a summary of the Fasti, the list of Roman magistrates, where he is called only 'Rufus'.

It may have been Petellius Cerialis himself – his full name was Q Petellius Cerialis Caesius Rufus. If so, then the former general was celebrating his third consulship, for Vespasian had honoured Cerialis with a second almost as soon as he returned from Britain in AD 74. Another possibility is that this was a son of Petellius Cerialis. However, even if the holder of this consulship is hard to identify, the name shows that the family and probably the person of Cerialis was held in high regard by the emperor.

In his selection of consul, Domitian may have wanted to highlight his own, entirely spurious, direction of Cerialis' campaign against the Batavians in AD 70 (which is another indication that this campaign finished with highly satisfactory results all round).

The brief plaudits of the historian Josephus indicate the spin the later Flavians put on Domitian's intervention in Germany. Josephus praises the prompt intervention of Cerialis, who forced the Batavians

> to cease their madness and see sense. Indeed had Cerialis not so suddenly attacked them, retribution would have soon arrived ... for as soon as he heard of the revolt Caesar Domitian set out immediately against the barbarians. When they heard that he was coming their courage failed them, and they surrendered immediately.[10]

It may be that Cerialis' last consulship was his reward for acquiescing to this pack of codswallop becoming the official record. Domitian and Cerialis were still on friendly terms. When Domitian went to war with the Germans, both Frontinus and Cerialis came along as advisors. Again, the brief treatment of this episode by contemporary historians (who generally loathed Domitian) suggests that this campaign was competently conducted and yielded satisfactory results. Had this not been the case, writers such as Suetonius would certainly have highlighted Domitian's shortfalls as a general in loving detail.

These last vague traces aside, we have no further record of what became of Petellius Cerialis. While one might wish that he enjoyed a long and fruitful old age, it is unlikely that he did. In the reign of Domitian, Cerialis could have been not much more than in his fifties. The general's talents would have been called on again in later years, had he been around to exercise them. Yet Cerialis, like so many of those he fought, now simply bows out of the historical record. Rome was always an unhealthy city. The probability is that illness or infection succeeded where Boudicca, Nero and the Batavians had not and put an end to the career of one of the most intriguing characters ever to command the Roman legions.

Notes

Chapter 1
1. The Roman army's adoption of superior enemy equipment, e.g. Spanish swords, Gallic helmets and Greek cavalry equipment, bears eloquent testimony to this.
2. The via Saleria, the ancient road that carried salt from the pans of Ostia to the Italian interior. Modern diets are so laden with salt that we forget that even in neolithic times it was essential for health and was an early incentive for trade. So important was it that soldiers were sometimes paid in salt (*sale* in Latin), from which we get the modern 'salary'.
3. This was only ever achieved afterward by two other generals – Cornelius Cossus, who defeated an Etruscan king, and Claudius Marcellus, who killed his Gallic counterpart. A son of the Triumvir Crassus also qualified, but Augustus, then emperor, jealously denied him the privilege.
4. Plutarch, *Life of Romulus* 25.
5. The closing of the doors of the temple of Janus officially signified that Rome was at peace. This happened in the time of the consul Manlius Torquatus in 235 BC.
6. The birth dates even of famous republican Romans are seldom more than approximations and this is true also of the year in which the first three generals died.
7. That Sulla saw his own interests as being identical with the proper interests of the Roman state is not relevant here. This is not how a democracy works.
8. When Sulla tried to replace him, Pompey's father absented himself from his army for the short period it took for his troops to lynch his successor.
9. The Romans did not distinguish between generals and admirals. A land commander was expected to be equally good at war by sea.
10. According to Goldsworthy, this was one of the primary reasons for the fall of the western empire. *The Fall of the West* (Wiedenfeld & Nicolson, 2009).

Chapter 2
1. Velleius Paterculus, *Roman History*, 2.119.3.
2. P Atius Varus – the cognomen was not unique to the Quinctilius clan.
3. Velleius Paterculus, *Roman History*, 2.117.2.
4. There is no record of whether the Vipsania whom Varus married was divorced or died.
5. R Syme, *The Augustan Aristocracy* (Oxford University Press, 1989), table XXVI.
6. Josephus, *Jewish Antiquities*, 17.6ff.
7. The same king who caused the family of baby Jesus to flee into exile.
8. Velleius Paterculus, *Roman History*, 2.117.2.
9. Suetonius *Life of Augustus*, 23.

10. The Jewish triumph of Titus in AD 71 was jointly celebrated with Vespasian, who was emperor.
11. One of these tablets has been recently discovered and basically substantiates Tacitus' account of the affair, albeit without Tacitus' addition of rumour and innuendo.

Chapter 3

1. Mauri: from whence we get the modern name of the Moors.
2. For the difficulties in determining exactly what happened in Mauretania in the 40s AD, see D Fishwick, 'The Annexation of Mauretania', *Historia: Zeitschrift für Alte Geschichte* 20, 4 (3rd Qtr, 1971), pp. 467–487.
3. Pliny, *Natural History* 5.1.
4. Namely XXI Rapax, I Germanica, V Alaudae, XVI Gallica and VIII Augusta.
5. M Halsall, 'Batavians and the Roman Conquest of Britain', *Britannia* 1 (1970).
6. Suetonius, *Life of Claudius* 17.
7. Cunobelinus: Shakespeare's Cymbeline in the eponymous play.
8. This is based on one interpretation of the ambiguous Greek of Dio. It is also possible that Togodumnus and Caractacus were rivals, and that Togodumnus favoured the Romans.
9. Plautius never again held a military command. This is possibly because his wife came under suspicion of 'practicing a foreign superstition' (probably Judaism or Christianity), but more probably because Claudius felt his stature was already high enough. Geta's family allied with that of the Severi, and Geta is thus an ancestor of the later tragic emperor Geta killed by Caracalla in 211.
10. Caractacus was spared by Claudius and peacefully lived out his final years as an imperial pensioner in Rome.
11. Though he was a direct descendant of Augustus through the maternal line.
12. 'It was considered their scared duty to soak their altars with the blood of captives, and to find messages from their gods in human entrails.' Tacitus, *Annals* 14.30.
13. Ibid.
14. If we accept Tacitus, everything happened in AD 61, but this leads to an impossibly compressed time span for events.
15. Cassius Dio, *Roman History* 62.3. In this section Dio says explicitly that the Britons 'did not want' these loans. Note also that 'Dio' here refers to his epitome by Xiphilinus.
16. Ibid., 62.12.
17. The site is today appropriately surrounded by bunkers, albeit those of a Peterborough golf course.
18. Tacitus, *Annals* 14.33.
19. Cassius Dio, *Roman History* 62.7.
20. Ibid., 62.11.
21. Tacitus, *Annals* 14.35. Though it is improbable that the daughters were bare-breasted, as shown by the sculptor, and the scythes on the chariot wheels are a far-fetched flight of fancy.
22. Cassius Dio, *Roman History* 62.4–5.
23. In 2011 the body of a teenage girl killed by a Roman sword thrust to the back of the head was discovered in this area.

Chapter 4
1. Cassius Dio, *Roman History* 62.15.
2. For example, when St Perpetua was thrown into the arena to be killed by the beasts, the crowd protested bitterly – not about the killing, but the immodesty of her clothing. *Martyrdom of St Perpetua* 20.
3. The only survivor was a lady called Junia Calvina, who sensibly decided that the way to survive was to keep a low profile and refrain from having any offspring, as this might be seen as a threat.
4. Agrippina is alleged to have ordered the centurion sent to kill her to strike the first blow at her womb.
5. Suetonius, *Life of Vespasian* 4
6. Cassius Dio, *Epitome* 63.22.
7. Suetonius, *Life of Domitian* 1
8. Said Tacitus – literally – 'Omnium consensu capax imperii nisi imperasset.' *Histories* 1.49.
9. Ibid. 1.4.
10. 'They were indignant over the execution of Capito, even if they knew he had deserved it.' Ibid 1.9.
11. Augustus' successor Tiberius famously described the job as 'like holding a wolf by the ears'.
12. Not co-incidentally these were often the same people, for those who had been favoured by Nero were most vulnerable to Otho's persuasion.
13. Says Tacitus *Histories* 1.29
14. Suetonius, *Life of Galba* 20
15. cf CIL 16.22.
16. Ibid. 23.
17. Tacitus, *Histories* 2.21. This is the gist of the insults the two threw at each other in the preliminaries to the siege of Placentia later that year.
18. Agricola will become a significant character later, but it is also important to note that Julia Procilla was related by marriage to Tacitus, so her killing may have prejudiced the great historian's attitude to the combatants.
19. And as the Alamanni were to do in AD 271 when they defeated an army led by the emperor Marcus Aurelius.
20. Nor did Vitellius do so. When he saw the tomb he merely remarked that Otho well merited such a modest memorial. Suetonius, *Life of Vitellius* 10.
21. The Fourteenth were in the process of being transferred from Britain to Dalmatia when they were drawn into the troubles in Italy.
22. Tacitus, *Histories* 2.56.

Chapter 5
1. Suetonius, *Life of Vespasian* 6.
2. Tacitus, *Histories* 2.80.
3. A pass was required for Romans moving between provinces, and customs officers checked boats for contraband, so travel was not merely a matter of booking passage on the first available ship.

4. Tacitus, *Histories* 3.22. Roman senators took a keen interest in military affairs because in his time they were still expected to be capable of leading legions at a moment's notice.
5. Ibid. 3.25 claims this account was given by Vipstanus Messala, legionary legate at the battle.
6. Cassius Dio, *Roman History* 64.12.
7. An alternative reading might be *paegniarii*, the mock-gladiator clowns who performed at the arena in Rome, or again '*pagani*' in this context might simply mean 'civilians'.
8. Tacitus, *Histories* 3.53.
9. Ibid., 3.84
10. Martial, *Epigrams* 10.23.

Chapter 6
1. Note that in this text 'the Batavians' refers to the tribe as a whole and 'the Batavi' refers to the Batavian cohorts.
2. They also rioted on hearing of the death of Galba.
3. Tacitus, *Histories* 4.14.
4. And certainly inscriptions in later years refer to *I cohors millaria Batavi*.
5. That is, the eight infantry cohorts and the ala of cavalry that had just deserted to him.
6. Not to be confused with the other Fifteenth Legion, XV Apollinaris, who were with Titus in Judea.
7. In fact, reports of his death were exaggerated. Sabinus remained alive but hidden for almost a decade thanks to his faithful wife.
8. To the extent that the current war, which involved Romanized leaders and Roman-trained soldiery, was not in any case a civil war.
9. Tacitus, *Histories* 4.72.
10. Frontinus, *Stratagems* 4.3.14.
11. Tacitus, *Histories* 4.74ff.
12. Tacitus, *Histories* 4.77.
13. Probably to have them ready for return to Britain at short notice, as there were problems developing with the Brigante.
14. Famous today for the 1944 battle named after the modern town – Arnhem.

Chapter 7
1. For example IA Richmond, 'Queen Cartimandua', *The Journal of Roman Studies* 44 (1954), pp. 43–52.
2. See C Haselgrove, L Fitts and P Turnbull, 'Excavations in Tofts Field, Stanwick, North Yorkshire, 1989', *University of Durham and University of Newcastle upon Tyne Archaeological Reports for 1989*, pp. 40–45.
3. Tacitus, *Histories* 3.45
4. It is probable that another of Cerialis' tasks was to wrap up the kingdom of Cogidubnus, a client king who had been a faithful servant of Rome since the time of the conquest.
5. JB Ward Perkins, 'The Career of Sex. Julius Frontinus', *The Classical Quarterly* 31, 2 (April 1937), pp. 102–105.

6. Tacitus takes every opportunity to subtly (and sometimes not so subtly) denigrate Cerialis in order to magnify the achievements of Agricola: cf. AR Birley, 'Petillius Cerialis and the Conquest of Brigantia', *Britannia* 4, 19 (1973), pp. 179–190 for his precise technique.
7. Tacitus, *Agricola* 12.
8. For example Frontinus sponsored the forum at Verulamium in AD 73/74.
9. Tacitus, *Agricola* 17.
10. Josephus, *The Jewish War* 7.4.2.

Bibliography

Birley, AR, 'Petillius Cerialis and the Conquest of Brigantia', *Britannia* 4, 19 (1973), pp. 179–190.

Carbone, ME, 'The First Relief of Castra Vetera in the Revolt of Civilis' (A Note on Tacitus 'Hist.' 4.26.3), *Phoenix* 21, 4 (Winter 1967), pp. 296–298.

Carradice, L and Buttrey, T, *Roman Imperial Coinage Volume 2, Part 1: From AD 69 to AD 96 – 'The Flavians'* (Spink & Son, 2007).

Chilver, GEF, 'The Army in Politics, AD 68–70', *The Journal of Roman Studies* 47, 1/2 (1957), pp. 29–35.

Fishwick, D, 'The Annexation of Mauretania', *Historia: Zeitschrift für Alte Geschichte* 20, 4 (3rd Qtr, 1971), pp. 467–487.

Goldsworthy, A, *The Fall of the West* (Wiedenfeld & Nicolson, 2009).

Griffin, M, *Nero: The End of a Dynasty* (Routledge, 2000).s

Halsall, M, 'Batavians and the Roman Conquest of Britain', *Britannia* 1 (1970).

Hanson, WS and Campbell, DB, 'The Brigantes: From Clientage to Conquest', *Britannia* 17 (1986), pp. 73–89.

Haselgrove, C, Fitts, L and Turnbull, P, 'Excavations in Tofts Field, Stanwick, North Yorkshire, 1989', *University of Durham and University of Newcastle upon Tyne Archaeological Reports for 1989*, pp. 40–45.

Morgan, G, *69 AD: The Year of Four Emperors* (Oxford University Press, 2007).

Nicolay, J, *Armed Batavians: Use and Significance of Weaponry and Horse Gear from Non-military Contexts in the Rhine Delta (50 BC to AD 450)* (Amsterdam University Press 2008).

Richmond, IA, 'Queen Cartimandua', *The Journal of Roman Studies* 44 (1954), pp. 43–52.

Salway, P, *The Oxford Illustrated History of Roman Britain* (Oxford University Press, 1993).

Sullivan, P, 'A Note on the Flavian Accession', *The Classical Journal* 49, 2 (November 1953), pp. 67–70.

Syme, R, *The Augustan Aristocracy* (Oxford University Press, 1989).

Townend, GB, 'The Consuls of AD 69/70', *The American Journal of Philology* 83, 2 (April 1962), pp. 113–129.

Wallace Gilmartin, K, 'The Flavii Sabini in Tacitus', *Historia: Zeitschrift für Alte Geschichte* 36, 3 (3rd Qtr, 1987), pp. 343–358.

Ward Perkins, JB, 'The Career of Sex. Julius Frontinus', *The Classical Quarterly* 31, 2 (April 1937), pp. 102–105.

Woodside, M St A, 'The Role of Eight Batavian Cohorts in the Events of 68–69 AD', *Transactions and Proceedings of the American Philological Association* 68 (1937), pp. 277–283.

Index

Achaea, 50
Actium, battle of, 17
Aemilius Paulus, 7
Africa, 7, 9, 14, 23–4, 31, 39, 42, 72, 78–9, 89, 100–1, 106, 125
Agricola, Gnaeus Julius, 57, 90, 106, 165, 168–70, 172, 174
Agrippa, Marcus Vipsanius, 16–18, 23, 27, 69
Agrippina, 17, 27, 31, 71–2, 172
Albania, 130
Alba Longa, 4
Albintemilium, 90
Alcmeon, 75
Alexander the Great, 157
Alexandria, 105
Alps, 16, 26, 89, 97, 104, 106, 109, 131, 142, 154, 160
Ampius, Flavianus T., 87, 108, 118
Andate tribe, 58
Anglesey, 51, 59
Antium, 71
Antonia Augusta, 78
Antonius, Marcus (Mark Antony), 14–17, 21, 41, 69, 97
Aquitania, 74, 79
Arenacum, 158
Argentorate (Strasbourg), 146
Armenia, 30, 34, 46, 50, 63, 105
Arminius, 25–6, 29
Artabanus, 30
Artaxata, 34
Artaxias, 30
Asia Minor, 7, 11–12, 17, 32, 47, 50
Atlas Mountains, 39
Atrebates tribe, 44
Atticus, 121

auctoritas, 11, 28, 97–8
Augusta Treverorum, xi, 142–3, 146–7, 151, 154, 160, 165
Augusta Taurinorum (Turin), 99, 144
Augustus, emperor, 14, 17–18, 20–8, 41, 43, 66, 69–70, 73–4, 78, 81, 84
Aventine Hill, 123

Batavian cohorts (Batavi), 42, 95, 98–9, 106, 117, 129–37, 133–42, 144, 147, 160–2, 164
Batavians, 125, 129, 131, 133, 138, 143, 150, 158–9, 161–4, 167, 169, 173, 175
Batavorum, 158
Bedriacum, 91, 95, 99, 102, 106, 109, 111, 114, 116–17, 131, 144, 146, 166, 168
see also Cremona
Berbers, 39
Beth-horon, 73
Betuwe, 129
Bithynia, 12
Black Sea, 105–6
Bolanus Vettius, 106, 117, 166, 168
Bonna (Bonn), 133, 136, 147, 160
Boudicca, 34, 52–64, 71, 77, 90, 143, 157, 164, 172–3, 175
Boudiga, 53
Boulogne, 41
Brexellum, 93
Brigante tribe, 45–6, 56–7, 117, 166–72
Brigantia, 166–8, 171
Brinno, 131–2
Britain (Britannia), 39–41, 43–7, 50–4, 58–61, 63–5, 72–3, 88, 90, 93, 97–8, 101–2, 106, 117, 130–2, 144, 149, 153, 156–8, 164–72, 174

Brutus, Lucius, 4
Brutus, Marcus, 17

Caecina, Aulus, 82–3, 89, 91–8, 103, 106–9, 111, 116, 140–1
Caenis, Antonia, 78
Caesar, Julius, 11–17, 20, 22–3, 28, 32, 40–1, 43–4, 61, 69, 79, 97, 135, 142
Caesarea (also Colonia Prima Flavia Augusta), 174
Caesariensis, 39
Caesi gens, 47–8
Caesius Nasica, 47–8
Caesonia, sister of Caligula, 33
Caledonia, 172
Caligula, Gaius, 17, 28–9, 32–3, 42–3, 73, 80
Calpurnius Piso *see* Piso
Cambridgeshire, 43
Camertines tribe, 4
Camillus, Marcus Furius, 6, 32
Campania, 105, 118–19
Campus Martius, 5, 123
Camulodunum, 43–5
Cannenfates tribe, 131–2, 144, 153, 157
Capitoline Hill, 120, 124
 see also Capitol
Capitol, 121–2, 125, 141, 173
Cappadocia, 30
Caractacus, 44–6, 167
Carlisle, 171
Carthage, 7, 24, 105
Cartimandua, queen of the Brigante, 45–6, 56, 58, 106, 166–71
Casiavellaunus, 40, 43–5
Cassius Longus, 109
Cassius Longinus, 32
Castor, 91
Castra Vetera (Xanten), 25, 135–41, 155–6, 158, 161
Cato Porcius the younger, 11
Catuvellauni tribe, 43–4
celeritas, 16
Celtiberians tribe, 7
Ceninensians tribe, 4
Cerialis Flavius, 169
Cestius Gallus, 73

Chatti tribe, 21, 129
Chauci tribe, 33, 158
Cherusci tribe, 25
Cicero Tullius, 15
Cincinnatus, 6
Circus Maximus, 134
Civilis, Julius, 42, 97–8, 106, 130, 132–53, 155–9, 161–4, 171, 173
Classicus, 90, 141–3, 147, 150–2
Claudia Pulchra, 23
Claudia Sacrata, 161
Claudii, 27
Claudius, emperor, 18, 23, 32–3, 39, 41, 43–8, 54, 70–4;
 Docks of, 173
Claudius Marcellus, 7
Clodius Macer, 81
Cohors Tungri, 132
Colchester, 45, 53–5, 58–9, 65–6
Colline Gate, 122
Colonia Agrippinensis (Cologne), 135, 138, 143, 153
Comitia Centuriata, 5, 8, 18, 75
Commagene, 30
Commius, 44
Corbulo Domitius, 33–5, 39, 50–1, 63, 72–3, 100, 154
Corfinium, 23
Corinth, 79, 87
Crassus Marcus Licinius, 12–13, 69
Cremona, 91–2, 97–8, 102, 106–11, 114–19, 122, 124, 138, 144, 147, 173–4
 see also Bedriacum
Cumbria, 167
Cunobelinus, 44
Curio, 23

Dalmatia, 27, 165
Danube River, 41, 89, 92, 101, 103, 105–7, 118, 125, 173
Decianus Catus, 52–4, 58, 63–5
Decius Mus, father & son, 7
Didius Gallus, 46
Dio Cassius, 25, 61–2, 74
Domitian, son of Vespasian, 77–8, 102–4, 119–21, 124, 148, 154–5, 159, 165, 174–5
Domitilla, 78

Domitius Ahenobarbus, 9, 47
Domus Aurea, 173
Druids, 51–2, 59
Drusus, Nero Claudius, 20–2, 27, 29, 32, 134
Drusus Germanicus *see* Germanicus
Durotriges tribe, 42

Eboracum (York), 171–2, 174
Egypt, 14–15, 30, 32, 101–2, 104–5, 125, 173
Elbe River, 25
Emmaus, 24
England, 44, 172
    see also Britannia
Etruria, 117
Euphrates River, 39, 165
Exeter, 55

Fabii, 27
Fabius Fabullus, praefectus castrorum, 109
Fabius, Quintus Maximus, 7
Fidenae, 4
Flaccus, Aulus, 32
Flaccus, Hordonius, 80, 83, 106, 132–8, 140–2, 145, 150–1, 156, 164, 166
Flaminia Via, 122
Flaminius, Caius, 7
Flavians, 20, 77–8, 86–8, 101–4, 106, 112, 120, 123, 135, 137–8, 146, 163, 165, 168, 174–5
Flavian Amphitheatre (Colosseum), 173
Flavia Domitilla, 48
Flavius Sabinus, brother of Vespasian, 42, 72, 77–8, 88, 93, 96, 102–4, 108, 117, 119–22, 124
Flavius Sabinus, nephew of Vespasian, 77
Flavius Silva, 86
Favonius Facilis, Marcus, 55
Fonteius Capito, 80
Frisians, 132, 135
Frontinus, Julius, 148–9, 169, 172, 175
furor Teutonicus, 137

Gabinius, Aulus, 15
Gaetulicus, Lentulus, 31–2, 80
Gaius, grandson of Augustus 17, 27
Galba, Servius Sulpicius, 32–3, 75–6, 78–87, 90, 95, 97–8, 100, 107, 117, 130–1, 134, 144, 156, 173
Galba, Servius Sulpicius, consul 211 BC, 79
Galba, Servius Sulpicius, consul AD 22, 79
Galeria, wife of Vitellius, 97
Galilee, 24, 86–7
Gallia Narbonensis, 90
Gallia Transalpina, 16
Gallus Annius, 143
Gallus, Didius, 47
Gaul, 13, 15–17, 21, 26, 29, 40–1, 59, 74, 88, 91, 117, 119, 130–1, 133, 141–2, 146, 148–9, 151, 153–4, 161, 165, 169
Gemonian Steps, 124
Geneva, 21
Germanicus, Tiberius Julius Caesar, 27–32, 41–3, 134, 154, 158
Germany (Germania), 21–2, 24–6, 28–9, 31–3, 41, 44, 73, 75, 80, 82–3, 102, 106, 119, 125, 129, 133, 142–3, 146–7, 149–50, 153–4, 158, 164–6, 175
    see also Rhinelands
Gladiators, 70–1, 90–1, 93, 95, 122
Greece, 35, 72, 74, 78, 167, 173
Grinnes, 159

Hannibal, 7, 22, 47, 91, 137
Helvetii, 13
Helvidius Priscus, 104
Herod, 24
Hispania, 75, 79
    see also Spain
Hosidius Geta, 39, 41–2, 44
Humber River, 170
Humberside, 167

Iceni tribe, 44–5, 50, 52–3, 55–6, 58, 63–4, 166
Idistavistus, 29
Illyria, 102
imperium, 15, 27, 118, 173
imperium, proconsular, 10

imperium maius, 10, 30–1
Italy (Italia), 9, 16, 22, 27, 33, 48, 59, 71, 78, 88, 90–1, 96–7, 99, 101–8, 117–19, 130, 133, 136–7, 143–4, 160, 163, 166, 169, 173–4
Jerusalem, 32, 73, 87–8, 101, 173
Jesus, 24
Josephus, 24, 87, 175
Jotopata, 87
Judea, 15, 24–5, 72–4, 77–8, 86–7, 89, 101–5, 153, 167, 173–4
Jugurtha, 7
Julia Procilla, 90
Julii, 11
Julius Sabinus, 142–4
Jupiter, temple of, 173
Jupiter Optimus Maximus, 121

Kalkriese, 26
  see also Teutoberg
Kent, 42, 57

Legio
  I Adiutrix, 72, 89, 92, 94–5, 98, 117, 144, 169
  I Germanica, 83, 134–6, 141–3, 145–7, 151–2, 154, 165
  I Italica, 88, 91, 95, 109–10, 112, 114
  II Adiutrix, 89, 144, 146, 153, 156, 169
  II Augusta, 41–2, 57, 59, 63, 65, 90, 112, 117, 166, 168
  III Augusta, 39, 55
  III Gallica, 102–3, 106–7, 111–13, 115
  IV Flavia Firma, 165
  IV Macedonica, 82–3, 112, 133, 136, 143–4, 146, 165
    see also IV Flavia Firma
  V Alaudae ('The Larks'), 13, 83, 91, 95, 109, 133, 135–6, 141–3, 155, 162–4
  VI Victrix, 117, 144, 146, 152–3, 157
  VII Claudia, 40, 96, 102, 106, 107, 111, 115, 118, 174–5
  VII Galbiana, 79, 107–8, 111–13, 115
  VIII Augusta, 102, 106–7, 111, 144, 146, 174

VIII Gemina, 111
IX Hispana, 41–2, 46–8, 51, 55, 57–9, 63, 65, 77, 106, 112, 117, 166–7, 169–71, 173
X Gemina, 116–17, 144, 146, 152, 158
XI Claudia, 144, 146
XIII Gemina, 13, 89, 92, 95, 97, 99, 102, 106–7, 109, 111–12, 115–16, 124, 144, 146
XIV Gemina Martia Victrix, 41, 51, 57, 65, 89–90, 96–7, 99, 106, 117, 130–2, 146, 153, 155–6, 158, 166–9, 174
XV Primigenia, 112–13, 136, 141–3, 155, 162–4
XVI Flavia Firma, 165
  see also XVI Gallica
XVI Gallica, 112, 136, 138, 141–3, 145, 147, 165
Teutoberg legions (XVII, XVIII and XIX), 24–5, 27
XX Valeria Victrix, 41, 45–6, 48, 51, 55, 65, 106, 112, 117, 167–70
XXI Rapax, 83, 91, 94–5, 109–10, 112–14, 144–6, 152–3, 156, 165
XXII Primigenia, 22, 82, 133, 136, 138, 143, 145–6, 165
Lepidus, Marcus, 15, 17
Lincoln, 169
Lingones tribe, 130–1, 133, 142–3, 147–8, 151
Livia Drusilla, 20, 31
Locus Castrorum, 91–2
London (Londinium), 50, 55–9, 63, 66
Longthorpe, Peterborough, 56, 58
Lucan, 73
Lucius, grandson of Augustus, 17, 27
Lucullus, 11
Lugdunum, 75, 154
Lupercus, Minius, 133, 135–7, 139, 141, 161, 164
Lusitania, 82, 88–9

Macedon, 7
Mago, 22
Mainz *see* Moguntiacum
Mancetter, 59

Marcomanni tribe, 21
Marius, Caius, 7
Mars, god of war, 4–5
Mauretania, 39–42, 47, 173–4
Mauri tribe, 39
Medway River, 42, 44, 55
Miletos, 12
Misenum, 119
Moesia, 106, 108, 174
Moguntiacum (Mainz), 82, 132–3, 136, 140, 143, 146, 165, 169
Mona Island (Anglesey), 51
Mons Graupius, 172
Mosa River (Meuse), 33, 159, 161
Moselle River, 151
Mucianus, Licinius, 73, 89, 101–2, 105, 107, 114, 118, 125, 134, 142–3, 154
Mummius, Lucius, 79
Musulamii, 31

Narcissus, 48, 72
Nemesis, 86
Nero, emperor, 9, 17, 19, 28, 33–5, 46–7, 50–4, 58, 63–4, 69–75, 77–82, 84–6, 88–90, 96–7, 100, 125, 130, 149, 167, 172–3, 175
Nero Claudius Drusus Decimus, 20
Netherlands, 129
Nicomedes, 12
Noricum, 142
Noviomagus (Nimenjen), 158
Numisius Rufus, 136

Octavian, 15–17, 41, 69, 97
 see also Augustus
Oedipus, 75
Orestes, 75
Osnabruck, 26
 see also Kalkreise
Ostorius Scapula, 45–6
Otho Salvius, emperor, 79, 82–102, 106–7, 130–1, 166
Ouse, 171

Padova (Padua), 107
Palatine Hill, 71, 85–6, 124

Palestine, 105
Palmyra, 30
Pannonia, 17, 25–7, 32, 42, 87, 108, 165
Paphos, 88
Parisii, 171
Parthia, 30, 32, 34, 51, 105
Parthians, 16, 30, 32, 34–5, 63, 102, 113
Paullus Julius, 130
Pennines, 167, 170
Petellii, 47, 78, 101
Petellius Rufus, 174
Petellius Quintus Spurinus, 47
Petronius Turpilianus, 65
Pharsalus, Battle of, 14
Philippi, Battle of, 16, 23
Piso Calpurnius, governor of Syria, 30–1
Piso Calpurnius, imperial heir, 83–7
Placentia (Piacenza), 91
Plancina, 31
Plautius, Aulus, 41, 43–5, 55, 170
Pliny the Elder, 39
Plutarch, 4, 71, 95
Po River, 91, 93–4, 96, 108–9
Poenus Postumus, 57, 63, 65
Pollux, 91
Polyclitus, 64
Pompey, Gnaeus, 9–14, 17, 69, 97
Pompey, Sextus, 17
Poppea Sabina, 89
Portica Vipsania, 81
Postumia Via, 91, 109, 111
Praetorian Guard, 43, 76, 80–2, 84–6, 88–90, 92, 95, 97–9, 104, 106, 111–13, 117, 119
Prasutagus, 50, 52–3
Primus, Antonius, 107–16, 118–25, 132, 140, 142, 144, 147, 169
primus pilus, 48
Proculus, 73
Ptolemy XII, 15
Publius Petronius, 32
Pydna, Battle of, 7

Raetia, 146
Ravenna, 89, 108–9, 117, 119, 144, 169
Regulus, Marcus Atilius, 7

Remus, 4
Rhine River, 29–30, 33, 39, 41, 80–1, 83, 88–9, 95, 107, 109, 129, 132–6, 140, 142–3, 145–6, 153–5, 157–64
Rhineland legions, 28, 33, 80, 82–3, 86, 93–6, 104, 106, 112, 114, 118–19, 124, 134, 143, 146, 156, 159
Rhinelands xiv, 25, 27, 75, 79, 91–2, 98, 102, 138, 140–4,169
Richborough, Kent, 41
Rigodulum (Riol), 147
Rochester, 42
Romulus, 4
Roscius Coelius, 168
Rufus Petellius, 48

Sabinus Nymphidius, 80
Salaria Via, 120, 122
Sallust, gardens of, 122, 123
Salvius Titianus, 90
Samnites, 8
Sarmatians, 113, 165
Saturnalia, 122
Saturninus, Aponius, 24, 101–3, 107–8, 118
Scipiones, 27
Scipio, Aemilianus, 7
Scipio, Cornelius Africanus, 7, 32, 47
Segestes, 26
Sejanus, 78
Seneca, 53–4, 71, 73
seniores, 5
Sepphoris, 24
Sequani tribe, 142–3, 146–7
Sertorius, Quintus, 10, 69, 137
Severn River, 45
Sicily, 9, 17
Silures tribe, 45–6, 172
Smyrna, 174
Sol Invictus, 114
Somerset, 64
Spain 7, 10, 12, 14, 17, 41, 79–80, 82, 88–9, 97–8, 106, 116–17, 144, 152–3, 158
  see also Hispania
spolia optima, 4
Sporus, 74

Stainmore, 171
Stanwick, 168, 170–1
St Albans, 43, 59
Suetonius, the biographer, 43, 74, 77, 95, 99, 175
Suetonius Laetus, 95
Suetonius Paulinus, 33–4, 39–41, 47, 49–51, 53, 55, 57–65, 90, 92–3, 96–8, 143, 157, 164, 172
Sulla, Lucius Cornelius, 7–10, 12–13, 28, 122, 134
Sulpicia gens, 79
Sulpicius Tertullus Sextus, 79
  see also Galba
Switzerland, 21
Syria, 23–4, 30–4, 73, 89, 101–2, 113–14

Tabularium, 173
Tacfarinas, 31
Tacitus, 33, 40, 47, 51, 56–8, 61–2, 71, 77–8, 84–5, 88, 111, 116, 120, 130, 132, 135, 138, 149–51, 155, 159, 164, 167–8, 170,172
Tarquin, 4
Tarraconensis, 75, 79
Tencteri tribe, 151
Terracina, 119, 125, 134
Teutoberg forest, 26, 29, 44, 142
  see also Kalkreise
Thames River, 42, 61
Thetford, 52
Thrasea Paetus, 72
Thusnelda, 29
Thyestes, 75
Tiber River, 122
Tiberius, emperor, 20–3, 25, 27–33, 39, 43, 73, 78
Tiberius Claudius Nero, 20
Tiberius Julius Alexander, 101–2, 105
Tigellinus, 69, 81, 89
Tigranocerta, 34
Tilbury, 42
Tiridates, 34
Titianus, brother of Otho, 97
Titus, son of Vespasian, 64, 77, 86–8, 101, 105, 124, 174

Togodumnus, 44
Towcester, 59
Trajan, 169
Treveri tribe, 141–3, 147–8
tribunus laticlavus, 48
Trier *see* Augusta Treverorum
Trinovantes tribe, 43–4, 53, 56
Tullianum, 124
Turin *see* Augusta Taurinorum
Tuscus Sextus Caelius, 157

Ubii tribe, 151, 161

Valens Fabius, 83, 91–3, 97–8, 103, 108, 117, 119
Vale of York, 171
Valerius Corvus, 7
Valerius Flaccus, 28
Varus, Publius Quinctilius, 22–6, 44, 49, 63, 66, 142
Varus, Quinctilius, consul in 453 BC, 22
Varus Quinctilius, dictator in 331 BC, 22
Varus Quinctilius, in Punic wars, 22
Varus, Sextus Quinctilius, 22–3
Varus, Atilius, centurion, 113
Veientes tribe, 4
Veleda, 161, 163–4
Velleius Paterculus, 22–4
Vellocatus, 167
Venutius, 46, 167–8, 170–1
Veranius Quintus, 47
Verginius Rufus Lucius, 73, 75, 80, 90, 96, 101
Verulamium, 43, 59
Vesontio, 75

Vespasian, emperor, 42–3, 45, 48, 64, 72, 74, 77–9, 86–9, 93, 99, 101–9, 112–13, 117–22, 124–5, 130, 132–3, 140–4, 147, 150, 152–4, 163, 165–6, 168, 170, 173–4
Vestal Virgins, 122
Vesta, Shrine of, 86
Vettulanus Cerialis, 86
Viminal, 123
Vindex, Julius Gaius, 74–5, 90, 130
Vindonissa, 146
Vipsanian portico, 85
vir militaris, 79, 97
Vitellius, Aulus, emperor AD 69, 80–3, 86, 88, 90–1, 95–107, 109, 112, 117, 119–20, 122–4, 130–4, 140, 143–4, 150, 154, 163, 166
Vitellius, Lucius, consul in AD 34, 32
Vitellius, Lucius (brother of Aulus), 89–90, 119, 125, 134
Vocula, Gaius, 138–41, 145, 150–1, 156, 164–5

Waal River, 129, 159
Wales, 45, 172
Watling Street, 59
Weymouth, 43
Wight, Isle of, 43
Windisch, 146

Xanten *see* Castra Vetera

York *see* Eboracum
Yorkshire, 170